PSYCHOANALYSIS

Peter Zagermann

PSYCHOANALYSIS

A General Theory
of Psychical Structure
Formation and Pathogenesis

IPBOOKS.net
International Psychoanalytic Books

Published by IPBooks, Queens, NY 2019
Online at: www.IPBooks.net

Copyright © 2019 Peter Zagermann

Translated by Eva Ristl

Cover Design by Blackthorn Studio
Typesetting and formatting services by Self-Publishing Lab

ISBN: 978-1-949093-35-3 (pbk)

Take care of all of your memories at night
For you cannot relive them.
And remember when you are out there
Trying to heal the sick
That you must always first forgive them.

Bob Dylan

For the guardians and protectors
of the mind

Contents

1

The formulation of a general psychoanalytic theory of psychical structure formation on the basis of a new formulation of the concept of the drives

This book presents a theoretical model. Its aim is to furnish proof that a general metapsychological theory of the genesis and structure of the psychic apparatus based on today's empirical knowledge of psychoanalysis and on the partial theoretical formulations derived from this knowledge is possible. As with any scientific theory that takes itself seriously, this does not come with an absolutist truth claim, although theories, the more general they are, may give that impression. Theory is always approximation, and a model is the attempt to depict the workings of reality in their functional context, in order to explain that context.

It is, however, within the psychoanalytic field at large, one of the characteristics of group identification and of the resulting sense of group identity, to reject the concept of truth as such, right up to accepting the absolute relativism of a normative subjectivity. To this I wish to object with this work. I think there are, also in our field, fundamental interrelationships and criteria of such high degree of clinical and theoretical plausibility, coherence, and convergence that they come close to the notion of truth with the same earthly possible approximation as in, let us say, the frontier areas of theoretical physics, which in a similar manner deal with the development of—in this instance—mathematically controlled-conceptual models. Their truth criterion is, on the one hand, agreement with empirical data, and on the other, their ability to predict as yet not collected data and to make their collection conceivable at all.

It appears to me that the future of our science is highly dependent on how far it accepts the challenges of the so-called empirical sciences, and dares to formulate, based on a claim of scientific equality, fundamental psychic laws, a binding fundamental structure of the psyche.

In her 1997 essay "Psychic structure and psychic change—changing models of the mind", Hanna Segal writes: "Almost from the beginning, when formulating a theory of mind, Freud saw the mind as having a structure. I think it is not often appreciated or emphasized how revolutionary this way of looking at the mind was. Until Freud, the mind was a rather vague concept. Seeing it as a structure implied that the psychic world, like the physical world, can be studied in terms of elements, or parts, combining into a structure." (in Segal H. 2007, p. 83).

In the history of the development of psychoanalysis and in psychoanalytic theory formation it has been pointed out time and again that this structure of the psyche is an open system. This openness was considered a kind of trade mark, in as much as it was seen as necessarily linked with the notion of the unconscious as the essential discovery of Freud, with its unknowability, by nature and by definition, and thus with its infiniteness.

I am convinced that this conclusion is an error which does not do justice to Freud's thought by failing to think it through to the end. I

2

am of the opinion that the basic structure of the psyche, by all means, has a definite, delimited and describable form which arises out of very specific, existentially unavoidable demands for work and exigencies and which, by its very own nature, is completed when a solution to these demands and exigencies is found. I am further convinced and will attempt to outline that this structure has such great capacity and flexibility that all existing cases of sane and pathological mental life can be carried by it.

The considerations and thoughts I want to discuss in this sense essentially consist in the attempt of a theoretical integration of the classical Freudian structural theory with the findings of Melanie Klein and her school about early psychic development, while also taking up the criticism leveled at Freud's last theory of the drives and including the object relations approach.

This book does not present and discuss new clinical material. The data I refer to are, in a way, the massifs central of our clinical findings, be that with respect to the Oedipus complex and general psychosexual development, be it with respect to Melanie Klein's paranoid-schizoid and depressive position. As Daniel Widlöcher stated in one of his presidential columns: "Our clinical work always requires a theoretical model and our theories of the treatment necessarily have technical implications. We have both explicit and implicit theories (Sandler, 1983)" (2002, p. 3). In the following, I will attempt to make my implicit theoretical ideas as explicit as possible.

The aim of this book is the formulation of a general psychoanalytic theory of psychic structure formation, with the assumption that it is built upon logical principles such as pertain to the nature of structure, of the structural. The touchstone for a conceptualization like this is, besides internal consistency, one, to what degree it is capable of absorbing the clinically secured theory elements and putting them into a logical context, and two, in how far it is possible to make correct clinical predictions based on it. To the extent to which the formation of a general theory like that should be possible, psychoanalysis would open itself and invite access to scientific understanding from the outside, without having to reserve essential elements of its central evidence context for the insight of the practicing analyst only. This also means an explicit opening up of psychoanalysis for falsification and verification.

I especially would like to propose a new formulation of the concept of the drives. The drive concept and the metapsychological formulations connected with it have been under fire the last couple of years, or better, decades, be that through the criticism of the propagation of a one-person psychology and a mechanistic-hydraulic conceptualization, or be that—especially as concerns Freud's death drive—by faulting those formulations for their biologistic and materialistic approach. I cannot give an exhaustive overview of the respective literature here, but pars pro toto refer the reader to the exemplary work of Holt (1976) on that topic.

2

The origin of the psychical drives out of the polarity of perception The problem of representational object constancy

I n this sense I proceed from the basic assumption or axiom of an ontogenetic initial situation, in which based on a certain neuronal stage of maturity of the cortical and subcortical CNS, perception sets in and with it an experiencing which is still directly identical to perception to begin with, and thus, as I would argue, the ego is also immediately given, in as far as agreement can be reached that the ego must be centrally and fundamentally regarded as the instance, as the subjective agent of perception and the formation of experience which derives from it. By perception I here understand the ability to create a central representation of an afferent stimulus. With this moment— and this now is the axiom—the object as an archaic representation is also given, for perception is logically impossible without that which is perceived, and this exactly is the first, the primary object.

Presupposition for this axiom is solely the system properties of the human brain, the fact that neuronal activity patterns are expressed as perception and as experiencing tied to perception.

This opens the dimension of the psychical, and what follows next from this train of thought is that it is not the id which must be regarded as the first instance of the psychic apparatus, but the ego. A conclusion of this kind has been brought up in the history of psychoanalytic theory formation time and again, and as a rule has been linked with the idea that the formulation of an id only makes sense as from the point in time when defense by countercathexis has been established.

In the same way Fairbairn (cf. 1963, p. 224) and Melanie Klein (cf. 1959) proceeded from the assumption of a primordial ego which from the very first beginnings is involved in object relations and is taking on defensive tasks. This corresponds with the findings of modern infant research. Melanie Klein writes: "My work has led me to assume that the ego exists and operates from birth onwards and that (...) it has the important task of defending itself against anxiety stirred up by the struggle within and by influences from without. Furthermore it initiates a number of processes from which I shall first of all select *introjections* and *projection*. To the no less important process of *splitting*, that is to say dividing, impulses and objects (I shall turn later)". (Writings p. 249-250, italics M.K.)

For the following it is important to note that the primary object, which is perceived by the primary ego, must be thought of as the sum of those sensory data mediated by the senses which hit the central nervous system at a certain point in time and by this contiguity of time are experienced as a uniform representation. From a descriptive point of view, most variously generated data enter into this representation: external world stimuli, proprioception, stimulation from human contact, etc. mingle completely undifferentiated, as the respective categorizations cannot be made yet, that is to say, a differentiation between an inside and an outside cannot be made yet, and a concept of reality does not exist. What we are dealing with here is the level of the very first objectal representations in the sense of the precipitate of sensory stimuli, organized, that is to say bound together, only by their simultaneity within a primordial constitution, which, apart from the sensory stimulation, does not know differentiated psychic content like phantasies, thoughts, or symbols, as the necessary mental space for it has not yet been built.

We are, therefore, far before the level of part-objects, which represent a far more highly developed objectal formulation. The prototypical part-object of the breast, for instance, with the associated functional opposites and images of nipple and enclosing and sucking mouth space unfolds its importance as an organizer of experience and experiencing only post-partally when the experience of alternation between need and satisfaction begins to arise. At this point in time the experience of satisfaction organizes the regular and repeating sensory patterns associated with it into a certain image and progressively keeps it up over time, directed by what Bion describes as pre-conceptions.

The primary object on its pertaining level of the structurally most basic organisation of the mental state is the only thing that exists at all. An outside of the primary object cannot yet be conceptualized as such an outside would, as I will demonstrate below, presuppose the experience of time as the correlate of a beginning object constancy. I define object constancy differently however than the common use of the term as coined by ego psychology, and thus it is necessary here to discuss this term first.

As mentioned above, with this paper I pursue the goal, amongst other things, to deduce the fundamental findings of psychoanalysis epistemologically step by step, in a way that psychoanalysis will become accessible in its claim as a scientific theory to a virtual non-specialist reader. At this point, though, I have to interject a short intradisciplinary

7

conceptual clarification referring to theoretical concepts which are only later being explained.

In the classical terminology as represented by Anna Freud, Hartmann and Hoffer (cf. A. Freud 1952), Edith Jacobson (1964), and the ego psychological school, object constancy is seen as the expression and result of the constant direction of both drives to the same object, independent of the actual need-tension, the consequence of which is deemed to be the fusion of the drives.

Obviously, this definition cannot be made to match my above formulations on the nature of the primary object. For if it is true that the primary object in the structurally most simple organization of the mental constitution is the only thing that exists at all, and an outside of the primary object is not yet conceivable, the situation is rather the opposite, namely that both drives are directed to the same object from the beginning. And this simultaneous focus is independent, a priori, from the need-tension because there is no alternative and, by definition, drives must cathect the object. If the so-called fusion of the drives would only lie in this one point of their direction to the same object, it would have to exist from the start.

This essentially results in two questions of fundamental importance: If the psyche in its constitution proceeds from a uniform imago of the primary object which ab initio knows no alternative and no outside, where does the splitting of the object, later on, come from? And is it true that this splitting purportedly directly reflects a drive polarity thought of as the opposite between love and hate, love and aggression, whereby hate is understood as the pragmatic form of Freud's concept of the death drive?

In my opinion the ego psychological terms of object constancy and fusion of the drives in a disguised way refer to the whole range of problems in early development, which Melanie Klein described in the concept of the paranoid-schizoid and the depressive position. The concept of the fusion of the drives presupposes a duality of love and aggression as a drive model, whereby both these drives are thought of as independent from each other originally, and thus each engender and cathect separate object representations, meaning a factual splitting of the object.

This refers, in a very condensed way, to the problems associated with early object splitting and the overcoming of it which ego psychology, in the fusion of the drives in a quasi-mechanistic sense, associates with the constant direction of the drives onto a common object. In this way ego psychology does not take into consideration the existence of the early splitting mechanisms resulting from the conflict between the drives and which cause the very separation of the drive representations for as long as these splitting mechanisms are active. The ego psychological fusion of the drives is no linear maturation process as ego psychology assumes, but is not possible without first resolving the conflict of the infantile depressive position, as only through this resolution the splitting is overcome, that is to say, the unification of the object imago is established.

The situation is therefore in its temporal and causal sequence exactly opposite as thought of by ego psychology: ego psychology sees the fusion of the drives as a consequence of object constancy, that is to say, as the cathexis of a joint object through both drives which is independent of the need-tension. Such joint cathexis, however, is only possible if the splitting of the object has been overcome beforehand, and thus the fusion of the drives has already happened, for the splitting of the object is carried by the polarity of the drives.

As I would contend, the concept of object constancy in its above ego psychological definition has a merely descriptive meaning. In this respect it differs from the Piagetian object permanence which is defined as the awareness of the continued existence of an absent material object—i.e. an object in the sense of a thing—only in that psychoanalysis, unlike Piaget, does not focus on cognitive, perception and awareness oriented psychological criteria and the development of intelligence connected with it, but on the foundations of the development of a relationship with human objects. Where Piaget examines the physical absence, ego psychology takes the missing need-tension as a criterion: object constancy is given if, also in case of absent need-tension, both drives remain directed to the same object and thus the relationship with it remains intact. To be exact, this is referring to object relations constancy.

From the point of view of the early object splitting and its psycho-dynamics, however, this relationship constancy comes about based on the formation of a phantasmatic space of symbolization, the elaboration of which is the result of dealing with the conflicts that stem from the splitting of the object. Thus it is not about a simple maturation of psychological functions, even if aspects of maturation contribute to the process.

If this criticism of descriptiveness is to be regarded as substantiated, the ego psychological object constancy would strictly speaking not be a genuine psychoanalytic term, that is to say referring exclusively to the inner psychic world and its dynamics, the world of representations and their vicissitudes.

In contrast to this, for the purposes of my present investigation in which I first want to clarify the basic conditions in the relationship with the imago of the primary object, I use the term object constancy as the mental maintenance—that is to say, the keeping constant—of a representation that goes beyond the time frame of the immediate stimulus situation which the representation depicts. The descriptive aspect, observable from the outside, shall remain unconsidered in this definition. As the term object constancy is the one that does best justice to the content of this definition and as the classical use of the term leads to the problems mentioned, I draw from this the legitimization to rephrase this definition.

In order to continue after this important conceptual clarification, I would now like to explain in more detail my above argumentation with respect to the interrelation between representational object constancy, development of the time concept, and the concept of an outside of the primary object: The mental concept of time, of a temporal progression, develops from the only gradually forming overview over a certain series of momentary stimulus situations, that is to say, from the first rudiments of experience formation. As these momentary stimulus conditions are the respective evocations of the primary object, this formation of experience is identical with the beginning of object constancy. Only the developing object constancy—that is to say the maintaining of a representation of the primary object over time—allows the comparison of an object representation with one that follows or went before, that is to say the comparison of experiences, which initially can only be a comparison in time, because the respective current stimulus constellation is depicted as a uniform representation filling the totality of the given time moment and representing the respective activated primary object. Only from this comparison in time does the concept of an outside of the object arise, simultaneously with that of the boundary, the limitation of the object and thus its relativity.

In the beginning, the primary object of the time moment A, because of the not yet developed rudimentary constancy, cannot be compared yet with the primary object of the time moment B. Consequently, object A and object B, firstly, cannot modify each other; and secondly, there is no outside of the primary object, as this mental concept presupposes time and the comparison between the object conceptions in time.

11

For the primary ego therefore, the primary object in this primordial condition, before representational object constancy is reached, is, so to speak, the universe, the all-that-is, outside of which nothing exists.

The psychic dimension thus constitutes itself in the perception of the primary object and outside of the perception of this primary object there is nothing. There is no outside as yet, and also pertaining to this primary level of functioning is the quality of timelessness. Conversely this line of argumentation means that this primary condition of the psyche ends as soon as object constancy and thus the concept of time is being established.

Besides, the same lines of thought would have to be applied to the ego itself. An objection may be raised which points out the supposed primary incoherence of the ego, that is to say, that initially there are, in a descriptive sense, several egos or ego nuclei; let us say in one moment of time there is an experiencing of the ego primarily localized in hearing as the predominant sense modality, in the next moment, for instance, it identifies itself with the olfactory sense. In the words of Melanie Klein: "I would (...) say that the early ego largely lacks cohesion, and a tendency towards integration alternates with a tendency towards disintegration, a falling into bits." (1946, *Envy and Gratitude*, Writings p. 4).

I think that from the point of view of subjective experiencing this is not a principal argument, for the same reasons which I have just formulated for the relationship to the primary object: under the condition of the as yet undeveloped time perception in a primary ego constitution making no structural presuppositions as yet, the ego is also unable to perceive its possible factual disintegration into various ego nuclei. The experience of an incoherence of the ego paradoxically presupposes a rudimentary ego constancy, that is to say, the possibility to compare an ego state A with an ego state B within the time axis. In other words, an ego which experiences itself as split and disintegrated into bits and thus weakened, presupposes a beginning ego coherence or ego constancy.

This means that the indication that there is a probable primary disintegration of the ego into various ego nuclei—important as this may be under the developmental-descriptive aspect—plays no role, psychoanalytically, that is to say, with reference to subjective experiencing, in the same sense as the indication that the primary object, under the point of view of reality, has a completely illusory character.

It follows from these considerations that the ego as the subject of perception, precisely on the conceivably simplest level of its functioning, from a perspective of subjective experiencing, acts in every single time moment in its full potential identity and energetic wholeness and completeness, even if, seen from the outside, it may appear ever so deficient and fragmented. The primary ego does not yet have a reflexive distance to itself. There is no relativization of the ego by comparing its states, just as there is no concept of an outside of the object as yet and thus no relativization of the object.

This, in my view, is that early psychic condition which Freud had in mind when he says in "On Narcissism: An Introduction" (1914c) with reference to the lost omnipotence of the infantile narcissism: "What he (man) projects before him as his ideal is the substitute for the lost narcissism of his childhood in which he was his own ideal" (p. 94). In any case, this stage, in my opinion, cannot be understood however—as in Freud's concept of primary narcissism—in the sense of a psycho-economic state, where the total available cathectic mass collects in the ego. What is important to me is to show that this hypothesis of a solipsistic energetic maximum cathexis of the ego is not at all necessary in order to explain the phenomenon designated in Freud's above quote, which is meant by the term primary narcissism.

This primary ego which is not yet relativizing itself is confronted, rather, in the primary object, with the full implication which we psychoanalytically connect with the term of the object—well, one could say, in a more comprehensive sense than at any later time, for the relationship with this primary object, after what has been said, knows neither an alternative nor an outside. This defines the power of the object and allows a glimpse, gives an idea of the elementary dynamics of the emotional conditions which are involved here. Perhaps it is due to this circumstance that this basic experience seems to have such formative power to determine the fundamental conditions in the psyche, which I will try to describe in the following.

In any case, if ego and object constitute themselves in the same moment ex nihilo and if their relationship with each other is that of perceiving subject and the perceived, this means on the energetic plane that the cathexis of the object by the ego is primary and spontaneous, the event with which the psychic life begins, the immediate given. There is therefore no primary cathexis of the ego alone—Freud's pseudopodia model—and the object is not being invested only by the withdrawal of cathexes from the ego. The narcissistic withdrawal of the cathexes from the object to the ego is therefore already pathology and presupposes a complex phantasmatic process. I point this out specifically under the aspect of the truly absolute significance of the primary object.

3

The aim of the death drive and the traumatic nature of the ego

Following these considerations, the next step on the way to psychic structure formation can only consist in the ego which experiences the first physiological tensions as unpleasure, interpreting this unpleasure as the result of a lack, that is to say something missing from itself, a deficiency. Because psychically, apart from the ego there only exists the primary object, the ego cannot localize the capacity to do away with what is lacking anywhere else but in this object.

The ego must, therefore, pressured by unpleasure and supported by the mode of orality, necessarily and unavoidably arrive at the first phantasy, the first wish, to incorporate the primary object into itself and to become one with it, in order to achieve a state of freedom from tension. As at this early point in time, as we have to assume, no mental concept whatsoever of ego boundaries or of an identity of the ego has been developed, such incorporation of the primary object can only have the form of a global fusional movement.

Insofar as outside of the primary object nothing exists for the primary ego, and the object therefore, as I said further above, is the all-that-is, the universe for this ego, this wish for the fusional union is the phantasma of the ego-cosmic ego which insofar—that is to say precisely

15

as a striving for the merging of object representation and ego—has been identified as the motor of the narcissistic striving. Narcissism therefore is not an imaginary primary state—Freud's pseudopodia model—but the precipitate of a fundamentally defensive movement, consisting in the attempt to suspend the separation of ego and object. (This by the way corresponds exactly to Rosenfeld's formulation which is based on the clinic, and which he proposed in his work "On the psychopathology of narcissism" of 1964. Furthermore, these fundamental conditions harbor the cause for Melanie Klein (1957) to be able to describe the primary, primitive envy as the earliest destructive force as such, insofar as the ego then attacks the object to the degree that the latter evades the fusional union).

This defensive narcissistic movement that comes about under pressure of deficiency must be differentiated from the primary narcissistic state described above, in which the general feeling, from the point of view of the primary ego and of the primary object, is limitlessness.

At the same time it should be noted that the express objectality of the object—that is to say its quality as non-ego—only constitutes itself in the experience of lack, which thus produces <u>the experience of separation</u>, of the separateness of the ego from its perception, from the primary object. Now this formulation might be understood in a way suggesting that after all, I proceed from a primary undifferentiated state of ego and non-ego. This is not what is meant here. One has to realize that the experience of lack, the experience of physiological tension is something so immediately given, physically, that one cannot really speak about a period before the first appearance of unpleasure. Rather, my argument has a strictly logical meaning, namely to point out that it is unpleasure which brings forth the awareness—better: the existential experience—with reference to the quality of the primary object as non-ego and thus constitutes the dimension of the outside of the ego.

The onset of representational object constancy as the ability to compare an earlier present with an existing present, that is to say a past representation of the primary object with a present one, implies the beginning of the acknowledgement of separation from the object via the theme of the past, or time, for the past object is an object with which the ego can no longer spontaneously attempt to become one. The struggle against the acknowledgement of this separation consequently always implies a struggle against the acknowledgement of time. That time and the confrontation with its inevitability could be called one of the "facts of life" by Money-Kyrle (1971) has its root here, in my view. The acknowledgement of its inevitability is identical with the acknowledgement of the fact of the separation from the object.

The above described phantasmatic step in which the ego attempts to suspend the experience of lack by establishing fusional union with the object, harbors an unforeseen danger; however, from the perspective of the ego, insofar as by this act the effected suspension of the differentiation between ego and object would bring the whole dimension of the psychical down again, when it has hardly unfolded through the separation of ego and object, perception and the perceived. It would be a self-suspension of the psychical, so to speak, and this is the basic danger, in my opinion, which threatens the psyche and which I equate with the death drive, which in this definition is purely psychically captured, and is no longer, as with Freud, a drive with biological origin. The respective formulations are well known. In 1924, in "The Economic Problem of Masochism" he says for instance: "In (multicellular) organisms the libido meets the instinct of death, or destruction, which is dominant in them and which seeks to disintegrate the cellular organism and to conduct each separate unicellular organism into a state of inorganic stability (...)" (p. 163).

17

In my opinion the death drive, by comparison, is not to be understood as the striving for the suspension of biological life in consequence of the aim to "undo connections and so to destroy things" (1938 in "An Outline of Psychoanalysis", p. 148). That which is deadly in the psychical sense derives only from the unforeseen consequence of the self-suspension of the ego in the fusional movement. The movement itself, however, is an absolutely understandable and compelling consequence of the first concern of life about itself, on the psychic plane. The death drive, in this definition, is therefore not—as, in the succession of Freud, especially Melanie Klein and her school have done—per se, that is to say because of its very nature, to be equated with aggression.

Then again I am of the same opinion as Freud as far as concerns the reason for having the concept of the death drive. For Freud it lies in the Nirvana principle—"The Nirvana principle expresses the trend of the death instinct (...)"—and he defines this as an "(...) effort to reduce, to keep constant or to remove internal tensions due to stimuli (...)". These quotes are taken from "The Economic Problem of Masochism" (1924, p. 160) and "Beyond the Pleasure Principle" (1920, p. 55).

I think, however, that it was a theoretical mistake in the sense of a categorical transgression to assume behind this effort and as its motor a psychic drive to bring about biological death, and more, the inorganic state. The psychoanalytically important question is not in how far a biological motive affects the psyche, but how the psyche deals with this—that is to say with the tension due to stimuli. And here, I think, one cannot but conclude that the psyche, the ego, can only search for the removal of the tension due to stimuli in the primary object—where else, if there is no outside of the object?—and that, if the means to achieve this removal lies in the object, the removal can only take the form of the phantasy of the inclusion of the object into the ego,

18

made possible by the fact that on this primary but nonetheless basic level there is no insight into reality whatsoever. Whereby, as said, the reigning oral mode is backing the process.

This of course formulates a dependence on the object that has both a ruthless and unconditional quality—the ego is inconceivable without the object, in the same way as perception without the perceived cannot be thought either.

In any case, in a contemplation of the dimension of the psychical, it is not important to ask where the wish for the removal of tension comes from. It is in fact just as natural as, on the bodily plane, the wish for pain to stop. What is important is how the psyche, how the ego, reacts within the scope of its own ambit.

It is by all means conceivable—as Freud formulated as his starting point—that tension, or unpleasure, basically result from the work demand, seen from a physical perspective, to maintain a multicellular organism. But it is, in my view, a categorical mistake that disregards the fundamental difference, the leap from the biological to the psychical, to assume immediately also for the psychic life that it contains the aim of dissolution of this organism. The biological tendency which we refer to briefly as 'tension', instead encounters the psychical with its own phantasmatic laws and has a totally different effect there than a phantasy of bringing about death in the sense of disintegration. Even though the death drive, which I conceptualize in a psychical sense, if it was fulfilled, would again effect the resuspension of the dimension of the psychical in the fusional coinciding of ego and object representation, it would do so taking a very specific detour, this detour containing the total psychical fate, the psychical constitution of the human being, and which does not consist, by any means, in the search for death.

In this sense, I consider the further structural development of the psychic apparatus as a consequence of the necessity to neutralize these inevitable dynamics of the death drive and to shape them so that their potential which threatens the dimension of the psychical is bound up. This is, as I will be attempting to show, the task of the Oedipus complex.

In any case, insofar as the ego, with the beginning of its existence, pursuing its very own legitimate goals, namely, to suspend tension due to unpleasure, runs into a situation of an inevitable, elementary thread of annihilation, one must describe the nature of the ego as <u>primarily traumatic</u>. The push from this traumatic quality and dimension is the motor for all further, directly resulting structural development.

4

The life drive as the drive of the safety of the ego and of the object
The pre-schizoid phase as the primary narcissistic world

First of all, from the above-described basic situation of the wish of the ego for union with the primary object, the question results how and with what means this fusional phantasmatization could be countered in order to prevent a self-suspension of the psyche. This happens in principle through a complementary string of phantasmatization, which has its core in the imago of the devouring object—in the images of the later infantile ego the crocodile, the witch, the dragon, etc. On the mythological-religious plane, it is Satan as the devourer of souls who surfaces here and has his place: "(...) diabolus tamquam leo rugiens circuit quaerens quem devoret" – "The devil prances around like a roaring lion looking for whom to devour" (1st Letter of Peter, Ch. 5, Vers 7).

Through this imago of the devouring object the self-preservation effort of mental life expresses the danger of self-annihilation inherent in the fusional tendency. This counterreaction, in my understanding, is the core of the psychic life drive, and we basically end up here in the split world of Melanie Klein's paranoid-schizoid position, whereby quite remarkably, the apparently bad, devouring object as a countervailing force to the idealized fusional union, is in reality the imagination of the life drive. It should be stressed, however, that this danger of self-suspension is an objective, actually existing danger and not a production of the life drive. The life drive only stands in for this danger; in other words, this danger is the cause, the raison d´être of the life drive.

As it is the interest of the life drive to preserve the objectal character of the object with respect to the fusional tendency of the death drive, the life drive is the <u>objectalizing tendency</u> and force in the psyche. In this sense, it is precisely the objectalizing and thus image creating character of the life drive which captures the danger of ego dissolution into an image, into an imaginative phantasmatization.

This interpretation thus sees the origin of the bad object of the early paranoid splitting dimension in the dynamic of the drives, more exactly in the counterreaction of the Eros to the death drive's vision of fulfillment, and specifies the bad as the devouring object. The devouring quality is hereby the psychic representation of the annihilation of the ego in the fusional self-suspension, and simultaneously the projection onto the object of the devouring tendency of the ego suffering an experience of lack.

Thus, in my opinion, the <u>primary</u> and fundamental good-bad split of the object is therefore no defense mechanism of the ego as it is for Melanie Klein (see above 1959), but an effect of the immediate drive antagonism. Secondarily, this situation is intensified and exacerbated, however, by further active splittings of the object which retroactively lead to respective splitting of the ego, and also by projections and introjections, which stem from the actual frustration experiences during the time of the infantile paranoid-schizoid position. These now are actually active defense processes of the ego in the struggle with the bad object, which produce the full clinical picture of the paranoid-schizoid position.

These now are actually active defense processes of the ego in the struggle with the bad object, which produce the full clinical picture of the paranoid-schizoid position.

It will also be true that the imago of the devouring object when it passes through the paranoid-schizoid and depressive positions is progressively taking in sensory moments arising out of the actual frustration situations. This does not change the fact that the basic phantasmatization in the described sense is of a purely psychogenic nature. The imagination of the devouring object sets the scene within which the aversive stimulation organizes itself.

One could argue against the above train of thought by asking whether the bad object should not be thought of, in a much more direct and simpler way, as the representation of the frustrating, unpleasure producing moment. I am of the opinion that a response to this objection will lead to fundamental considerations and conclusions which cast a light on the genesis of the dynamic forces in the mind.

Further up in this text I start with the assumption of a very primary, primitive condition of the psyche where, according to the law that every organization proceeds from its most basic elements and builds itself up by progressively connecting these most basic elements, in the realm of the psyche one must assume sensory stimulation, held together by temporal contiguity, as this most basic element. This is the first object of perception and thus of experience, the primary object.

In this primary constitution of the psyche there is no cognitive object constancy as yet. That means, experience is always experience of the present to begin with, there is no maintaining of representations over time yet, and therefore they also cannot be compared with each other. There is no experience of time, of temporal continuity.

If these claims about the primary functional level of the mental apparatus and thus of the psyche are true, then it follows in logical consequence that there cannot be, in this primary constitution, a direct objectally bound representation of a bad present, of a frustration experience as a, in this sense, bad, that is to say, frustrating object. For if an experience of unpleasure would translate so directly into a representation of a bad object, then the ego, on this level of functioning in which, as said, the primary object is the all-that-is outside of which nothing exists, would be confronted with a bad cosmos. This is not imaginable as the ego then would have to negate the only object available to it, which would equal the ego denying itself the fundamental basis of life. This also means, in principle, that the splitting of the object—that is to say the parallel representation of a good and bad split object—is only conceivable once representational object constancy is reached, insofar as then, in the background, the life-sustaining memory of the good object enables the manifestation of the bad object.

A further still more fundamental argumentation which leads to the same result is the following: According to our primary hypothesis the initial situation out of which the dynamics of psychical life unfold, tends to be one where the primary ego, confronted with the cosmos of the primary object in its globality and totality, can only deal with the experience of need-press—in other words an experience of lack—by locating the means to suspend this lack in the primary object, and it could not do otherwise. For outside of the primary object there is nothing, and the lack, by definition, cannot be remedied out of the ego itself, or it would be no lack. Before this backdrop the ego attempts, by creating the egocosmic, primary narcissistic fusion with the primary object, to incorporate the source that can suspend the lack, and thus to compensate the lack.

But if this is so—then the primary object can only be the representation of abundance. A primary object as the representation of lack is not conceivable. The object, therefore, in both lines of argument, is always to be assumed on the primary and thus fundamental level as that which is positively given and the connection of the experience of lack with the mental representation of a sensory stimulation is already a complicated operation with many requirements, which therefore belongs to a later stage of development of the ego.

One could define this primary conditionality of the object as that which is positively given as the fundamental affirmation of life in its psychic dimension.

This means that the lack, the disturbance of the physiological homoeostasis and thus the psychical experience of unpleasure on the level of the most basic mental units, that is to say before object constancy, cannot have an objectal or object-related representation, but is only present as an energetic phenomenon in the sense of an inescapable pressure to change the existing overall situation in psychic space. It is evident that this refers to the basic energetic quality of drive, to that which is related to the drives.

And as a reminder, this level of functioning before representational object constancy is reached is tied to an ego experience and an experiencing of the primary object which is unconditional, all-comprehensive, and in this sense absolute, and it takes place in timelessness. In my opinion, it is the complete package of these characteristics which gives a continuing, dynamic, radiating potential to this earliest layer of the ontogenesis of mental life, for mental life preserves all ontogenetic layers of its functioning and keeps them simultaneously active. More exactly stated, however, one would have to say that here we are dealing with the drive momentum of the life drive, for the imagination of the bad (split) object, which is not possible

25

yet in the phase before object constancy is reached and which is being substituted by the pressure to change the existing overall situation, only in the paranoid-schizoid organization becomes the means of expression and deterrence of the life drive. We can therefore say that the bad, devouring split object of the paranoid-schizoid position, as the, then, manifestation of the life drive, would have to be, paradoxically, energetically carried by this pressure stemming from the phase before object constancy is acquired, i.e. from the energetic source of the life drive within the pre-schizoid constitution of the mind that, as ontogenetic layer of the psyche, continues to exist and proliferate throughout life. The drive moment of the death drive, in contrast, always consists of the unconditional and direct wish to establish egocosmic, fusional union with the object, which is seen as the condition where lack is annulled.

Thus the drive concept as I posit it defines itself in the sense of a general theme running through the total unconscious constitution of man, and is the basis as well as the cause, the impetus, for psychic structure formation. This definition of drive is thus fundamentally different from, for example, Kernberg's (cf. 1990 a,b; 1991; 1992) pragmatic definition as a hierarchical organization of connections of self—and object representations through an affect which links them and which is open to the physical-instinctual end, if though this description is valid, as an operative definition so to speak, also in my view of the drive, for each single manifestation of the drive. But the underlying drives to which the affects refer are not libido and aggression for me, as they are for Kernberg. From the quality of the affect that does the linking one cannot deduce the pertaining drive directly. There are libidinous affects in the context of a death-drive motivation, and aggressive affects which serve the assertion of the life drive.

A consequence from the above considerations is that they would suggest the existence of a phase before the paranoid-schizoid object splitting—that is to say a pre-schizoid phase—for object splitting, for the above reasons, is tied to representational object constancy. In other words, the good-bad split of the object would not be regarded as the primary form of mental functioning. Conversely this means that the beginning of the infantile paranoid-schizoid position has to be set at the point in time when object constancy is reached. Thus a psychic organization built on the good-bad split of the object is only possible with object constancy.

The above-named characteristics of this pre-schizoid constitution—comprehensive, absolute, timeless—are those that were traditionally linked to primary narcissism and deduced from the supposed absence of an object in this constitution. The train of thought I propose is in reference to showing that the object, based on the ego's infantile omnipotence, is included in this constitution without it leading to a limitation of the ego and that this object of the pre-schizoid phase cannot be negated yet—in the sense of a good/bad split—as there is nothing outside this primary object, and the primary ego cannot negate the only object it has. It is therefore the pre-ambivalent object. The negative is as yet unrepresentable. The constitution of the pre-schizoid phase thus posits a powerful experience of wholeness, completeness, and omnipotence, which, as is easily conceivable, may become the basis and reference point of a mystical yearning back to the past, and, on the psychopathological plane, the fixation point and point of attraction of a correspondingly powerful regressive tendency. In any case, primary narcissism thus conceived could not be regarded as an objectless phase.

The fundamental course of things is thus as follows: the experience of lack leads to the phantasy of fusional inclusion of the primary object into the ego, which, in its turn, after object constancy is reached, produces the threat of the manifestation of the devouring imago; whereby the latter is the representation of the danger of self-suspension of the ego and uses for its formulation the projection of oral aggression. This means that the bad object of the paranoid-schizoid splitting is always the devouring object, as the result of a specific phantasmatic processing. A bad object in the sense of a direct precipitate of the experience of a denial situation does not exist on this level. This is an adultomorphism or an idea, respectively, derived from later acquisitions like the suspension of the primary good-bad split and the thus acquired reality concept. My view at this point is contrary to Bion's when he states in *Learning from Experience*: "This needed object is a bad object. All objects that are needed are bad objects because they tantalize" (1962, p. 84).

When Freud, in 1915, in "Instincts and their Vicissitudes" states that "hate, as a relation to objects, is older than love" and when he sees this hate deriving from the "narcissistic ego's primordial repudiation of the external world with its outpouring of stimuli" (p.139), this statement has to do with the above-discussed problem area. In the light of my study of the relationship of the ego to the first representations, however, I would have to argue with this and contend that the ego, at this "primordial" point in time, is not yet able to perceive the outside world as outside world, and therefore cannot repudiate it, either. The repudiation of a purely bad representation that would be experienced as denying appears not possible given the reasons stated above, because then the ego would have to repudiate its only existing object.

But what if it could? If, in spite of the above considerations, the global and total repudiation of the primary object was reconcilable with life after all? One could ask if this is not the constitution of early infantile psychogenic autism psychoanalytically described by Frances

Tustin (1972, 1981), in particular, as Tustin had distinguished between two forms, the confusional or entangled and the encapsulated or shell-type, in the genetically primary encapsulated form, that is to say, the earliest and most serious form of a mental illness. Tustin sees the beginning of both forms of psychogenic autism in the first four months of life and, in relation to the encapsulated type, speaks of the fact that these children are "as a rule reported to have withdrawn into themselves from birth on or shortly thereafter." (1981, p. 37).

Traumatization in these encapsulated children takes place, according to Tustin, before the primary attachment sets in, that is to say, before the beginning of the experience of being fed by the breast, possibly inter-partally, or even pre-partally. The clinical picture of the encapsulated autism is such that these children do not initiate relations neither with their parents nor with other people, avoid eye contact, do not speak and are not clean, their behaviour being characterized by incomprehensible and persevering psychotic idiosyncracies and rituals.

Tustin traces the basic problems of infantile psychogenic autism back to a premature and traumatic experience of separation from the primary object, more exactly to a traumatic experience of the not-me character of the primary object. In this not-me experience the child is experiencing in a traumatic manner the failure of the project to suspend the lack through fusion with the object. This failure, however, is not experienced in a way that the primary object as such turns into a representation of lack, but into an object that resists the fusional claim of the ego-cosmic primary ego and in this specific sense becomes a frustrating object. The frustration thus is not an expression of lack but of the rejection of fusion. Hence this traumatic primary object becomes a not-me-object and leads to a traumatic experience of separation, to which the ego of the autistic child reacts by rejecting the not-me object.

29

In this way the primary narcissistic illusion of omnipotent control over the object necessary for healthy development is being traumatically broken. This leads, according to Tustin, as far as concerns the encapsulated type, to a complete withdrawal from the primary object, the ego encapsulates itself and the object separated from the ego is being excluded from mental perception, an attachment is not being formed.

The place of the thus rejected primary object is taken, in a delusional manner, by the autistic object, that is to say, by one of those hard objects which the autistic child carries with him everywhere and on which it depends unconditionally as delusional protection against those panic fears arising from the respective actualization of the traumatic not-me experience. In particular, the autistic object is designed to close the 'autistic hole' in its self-representation, which has come about in the experiencing of the child as the result of the foreclosure of the primary not-me-object. The result is a termination of the relation with the human object and in its consequence a complete standstill of development.

Such foreclosure of the primary object can only be conceived as a global and total one. But this also means that such a global and total foreclosure is only possible in a phase prior to the beginning of object splitting. After splitting of the object begins, there would always be an aspect of the object that would remain outside of the foreclosure. We must, therefore, in fact be dealing with a foreclosure before object constancy is reached, that is to say, in the pre-schizoid phase. It is for this reason that the encapsulated form of infantile autism, in my opinion, can be regarded as clinical evidence for the existence of a pre-schizoid phase. In as far as Tustin, as already stated, postulates the point in time of the traumatic fixation of the encapsulation autism to be within the first days and first few weeks—two, three?—of mental life before primal attachment is formed, this would very likely then also narrow down the time period of the pre-schizoid phase in its pure form.

In any case, psychic survival with a cut-off relationship to the object representation seems possible, after all, if though for the price of the most severe form of mental pathology. Further below I shall discuss the syndrome of infantile psychogenic autism more closely under the aspects that this work puts forth.

5

The position of the ego outside the drive phantasma and the father imago

To return from this discussion of how to conceptualize the bad object in the early paranoid splitting constitution or, respectively, the bad object's inability to be conceptualized in the pre-schizoid phase, to the description of my model of the further course of structure formation, we can say that the transition to the depressive infantile position happens in the classic way described by Melanie Klein, by the child, before the background of its ongoing cortical maturation und its ongoing formation of experience, beginning to question its paranoid splitting reality and traumatically experiencing that its aggression directed against the bad object also damages the good object. Cortical maturation and the formation of experience contribute to the constellation of this depressive conflict to the degree that the child, in a balanced mental constitution, begins to experience and acknowledge the perceptual unity of the object, while under the pressure of deprivation it must resort to object splitting as the only available mode of defense.

The child then escapes from this dilemma not only through his reparative effort, but also, before the background of the dualistic drive dynamics, through a specific developmental leap: what develops under the pressure of repeated depressive crises, and more or less suddenly at that, is the ability of the ego to stand beside itself as an observer and to calm itself down in the actual crisis. This ability comes about out of the growing trust in his own reparative powers, as well as from the experience of the indestructibility of the good object resulting from all previous depressive crises which the child survived.

I call this the 'position of the ego outside the drive phantasma'. It is the position of the third which adds to the juxtaposition of ego and primary object. From it develops subsequently, in my view, the father imago in its meaning as the exemplary not-mother-object, that is to say, the imago of an experience, or better of a dynamic effect that is not in the direct genealogy of the primary object. Its meaning in view of the antagonism of the drives is that now the splitting of the object is not the only means any more to protect the ego from the danger of fusion. Rather, this protection is warranted in the future by the splitting of the ego within itself, out of which the ego, as long as it confronts itself in an observing position, cannot be lost any more in a fusional movement, because the observing part always remains outside of the fusion which, by its own logic, obeys the law of 'all-or-nothing'. The splitting of the object as the way of defense against the death drive is therefore being replaced by a splitting of the ego and thus becomes obsolete.

This is, and I wish to emphasize this, a psychologically simple procedure with, however, far-reaching dynamic and structural consequences. It is about the formation of experience, that is, about the growing overview of the ego over its states across time, from which results the ability of the ego, given a certain degree of saturation— and, as said, under pressure from the crisis of the depressive infantile position—to extract itself from whatever current state it is in, in the sense and to the degree that it is able to put itself beside itself and simultaneously observe and comment itself. This simple act implies a splitting of the ego within itself and consists of this split.

I therefore propose to consider this split in the ego as the actual central gain, as the structural result of the depressive position, in as far as it is linked with the suspension, with the overcoming of object splitting.

This split contains the other criteria of a resolved depressive position, like insight, tolerance of psychic pain, acknowledgement of the separateness from the object (Steiner 1993). Especially the acknowledgement of the separateness from the object is the central constitutive, intrinsic, essential characteristic of the position of the ego outside of the drive phantasma, in as far as through it the striving for fusional union with the object becomes suspended, i.e. made impossible. In this way the split within the ego also contains the mourning, the depressive working through of separation and is not possible without this work of mourning which is part of overcoming of the depressive position. Said the other way around, the fight against acknowledging separateness—which in its essence is narcissistic (see Rosenfeld 1964)—and which expresses the intention of the death drive, will always imply the fight against the self-reflexive position of the ego.

In any case, with this developmental leap to the position outside of the drive phantasma, and due to the suspension of object splitting, the demarcation line of the psychotic organization of the psyche is crossed, and in this context it is important to note again that the core of the father imago, in this view, is a split of the ego within itself, by which the ego is protecting itself.

As one of the findings of their investigations on affect regulation and mentalisation Fonagy, Gergely, Target and Jurist (2001) have described that this ability to take up a reflective distance to oneself is being prepared and made possible by the subtle shifts and transformations of meaning which the mother carries out in the process of mirroring the child's affect states, which for the child express and precipitate a becoming aware simultaneously of itself as well as of the other. Fonagy emphasizes in this context that the triangulation does not begin with triadic object relations; rather, that the father imago and thus the Oedipal configuration build on the beginning reflective distance, in the sense conceptualized by me above, in the mother-child relationship.

With the suspension of object splitting through the self-reflective split within itself, the ego acquires access to reality, as the latter presupposes not a split but a unified object conception. Therefore access to reality under a constitution of mental functioning based on the good-bad split of the object representation as the mode of drive regulation was structurally not possible as yet. I have pointed out further above that the crisis of the depressive position is brought about precisely by the fact that the unity of the object is already being recognized in states of emotional calm because of the cortical maturation and the formation of experience. However, in states of need-tension an activation of splitting as the only given mode of defense unavoidably occurs, and the antagonism of the drives can be seen to express and manifest itself in it. This leads to a situation when under need-tension with the splitting constitution then becoming activated, the bad split object must be fought against, although at the same time the ego already knows that good and bad object concur and are identical, so that the phantasmatic crisis of the damaging of the good object in fight with the bad object results; that is to say, the depressive crisis of being guilty of having damaged or allegedly destroyed the good object. Strictly speaking one would have to say that the depressive position is about gaining access to reality in a structurally guaranteed manner and in a way that it will remain stable and upheld even under states of need-tension and the pressure of gaining satisfaction. We are thus dealing with an alternative to the splitting constitution as a mode of defense, and this exactly is the position of the ego outside the drive phantasma, i.e. the self-reflective splitting of the ego within itself.

Subsequently it is then the massive impact of reality—in the sense of the enormous importance that access to reality has for the ego concerning the reliable option of access to the world—which secures the transition to the position of the ego outside the drive phantasma. This means that the father imago and access to reality are intimately related as to their psychic background.

I consider it important to stress that, in my opinion, with this new developmental leap of the ego to the position outside the drive phantasma the mental concept of an outside reality, that is to say, of the differentiation between inside and outside, is only ever just being introduced into the psychic realm. Before this point in time the object exists only as a subjective object which has its genetic core in the central nervous system's representational registration of a temporally contiguous sensory stimulation—without distinguishing whether the source of this stimulation lies outside or inside the body, that is to say, in the outside object or in the self.

Hence all psychoanalytic or descriptive formulations which for the time period before this developmental step proceed from a reaction to an external object—or which deny such a reaction—miss the nature of primary experiencing, in my opinion. Even a descriptive and apparently clear reaction to an external object does not mean just yet that the mental concept of an external real object, as distinguished from a subjective internal space, already exists. This distinction only comes about as a consequence of the position of the ego outside the drive phantasma, that is to say, through the suspension of primary object splitting, and in a psychosis it is exactly this distinction which gets lost again.

These difficulties, in the course of psychoanalytic theory formation, have led to the assumption of a primary lack of boundaries between

37

subject and object. This view is not correct in my opinion. There is not a lack of boundaries, but the boundaries that exist by all means, mentally, between the ego and the primary object—that is to say the object imago, the representation of the object—have not yet been brought into an agreement with the reality boundaries. Thus, in the borderline constitution, the pathognomical identity diffusion is a symptom of the beginning return to object splitting and with it to a subjective definition of the object, triggered on the practical-pragmatic plane through the massive use of the mechanism of projective identification which undermines the reality boundary between the ego and the object, while in the psychic background the negation of the position outside the drive phantasma—in other words the negation of the position of the third—plays the decisive role. It was Rosenfeld (1964, 1971) who had pointed out the importance of projective identification for the establishment of a narcissistic kind of object relation. In his early work on the psychopathology of narcissism (1964) he describes projective identification as the central mechanism with the help of which the separation from the object is being denied by the insertion of parts of the subject into the object.

The gain of access to reality through the position of the ego outside the drive phantasma is the point in development where Winnicott's concepts of the transitional object and transitional space (1953, 1971) come into play. In my view, it is the transitional space which enables the child, after access to reality has generally been established, to gradually extend its relationship with the primary object to encompass the whole world of real objects. However, my above argument also implies that, unlike Winnicott, I am not of the opinion that it is the transitional experience which brings about the separation of self and object in the first place. What descriptively looks like this is, as mentioned, the emerging of the child out of the cocoon of the early world of splitting of the object by solving the conflict of the depressive position, which only enables the ego to relate to the world of real objects.

I have consistently throughout the preceding discussion talked about good and bad split objects, but of course their representation has meanwhile long become organized as partial objects in the imagos of the good and bad breast. In the formation of this part object the imagination of the primary object attaches itself to the oral mode of a biologically determined psychosexuality. Put differently, the general lust and satisfaction quality which comes with orality as well as its specific orgasmic quality leads to the organization of the representation of the primary object around the central nucleus of the imago of the breast as the subjective experience of something hard (nipple/tongue) enclosed by something soft. This central sensory experience of orality is highly pre-conceptionally preformed and is largely independent of the fact of whether the child is being breastfed or bottle fed.

In this sense, therefore, the formation of the partial object of the breast follows Freud's (1905) description of object choice according to the anaclitic type. With this step, the primary object's early representation, which consisted in the mere temporal contiguity of a complex sensory stimulation co-occurring at the same time moment in the central nervous system, has thus bound itself to the manifestation of bodily sexuality. With this event, the central force which will carry forward the development of the psyche is locking into place. In particular this means that the imago of the primary object, in fusion with which the primary ego wanted to merge with the source of the suspension of all unpleasure, is now being equated and identified with the object of experience of sexual pleasure.

This is the metapsychological formulation of primary attachment. Only in the most severe form of psychopathology, namely in the encapsulated form of childhood autism, does this equation and attachment which is constitutive for the human situation, not occur; then again, and I will try to demonstrate this further below, the annihilatory aggression directed at the destruction of the real object has the dissolution of this same attachment to sexuality as its aim.

By acquiring the position outside of the drive phantasma and with it access to reality, this central partial object of the good, and consequently, the bad breast undergoes a suspension of its internal splitting and is clearly identified as existing in objective reality. I assume that it is this process which is behind the "recognition of the breast as a supremely good object", which Money-Kyrle names as one of the three "facts of life"—in addition to the "recognition of the parents' intercourse as a supremely creative act and the recognition of the inevitability of time and ultimately death" (1971, p. 443).

Hence, behind this interpretation of the breast "as a supremely good object," one would already have to assume the suspension of splitting through the position outside of the drive phantasma, that is to say through the position of the third, and thus a prefiguration of oedipality. Its precondition is the working through and the overcoming of the conflict of the depressive position. I think that it is this meaning as the encoding of this central task of early development which lends the phantasma of the breast as the supremely good object the position that causes Roger Money-Kyrle to name it one of the three facts of life.

The good breast in this meaning—perhaps one should say: the good reality breast—thus is not identical with the unilaterally idealized good breast of the splitting constitution. It still is a part-object but no longer a split object. Its quality as the "supremely good object" is defined by it containing and expressing the solution of the conflict of the depressive position, and by this it becomes the life-sustaining source of the good existing in reality. If Gérard Mendel (1968) states that the father is the one who makes the mother good, one could understand this in this sense of the overcoming of the good-bad splitting of the mother imago.

The "recognition of the breast as a supremely good object" thus refers to the 'reality breast', that is to say, to that concept of the breast which is being suspended in its original good-bad dichotomy by the self-reflexive splitting of the ego. The position of the ego outside the drive phantasma—that is to say, the self-reflexive splitting of the ego—constitutively implies the recognition of the separation from the object, by the very fact that the triangulation that comes with this splitting excludes the fusional merging with the object. The splitting of the object, as the early form of the defense against the danger originating from the attack on the separateness of the object, is then no longer necessary. Through this the breast becomes the object existing in reality and thus the supremely good object in the sense of Roger Money-Kyrle's "fact of life". John Steiner formulates this interconnection with the recognition of the separation from the object as follows: "The first fact, 'the recognition of the breast as the supremely good object', is a poetic way of expressing the fundamental truth that the chief source of goodness required for the infant's survival resides outside him in the external world." (1993, p. 95)

6

The structural unconscious and the two parallel worlds of psychical functioning

As the earlier splitting constitution of the object conceptualization is not compatible with the new time-space identity of the object, this earlier mode of mental functioning, and the concomitant way of experiencing that is tied to the identity of the ego with the drive phantasma, is now becoming unconscious. With this process, the dimension of the psychogenic unconscious of the mind is being created, in contrast to the so to speak morphological unconsciousness of those areas of the brain which display an essentially unconscious functioning as part of their structural characteristics. To my suggestion this is the primal repression that leads to the structurally unconscious as the core of the id. In so far as the crisis of the conflict of the depressive position is postulated to happen in the second quarter of the first year of life, this would more or less coincide with the moment of birth of the id as an agency of the mental apparatus. It is worth pointing out that this is the same time moment and the same process in which through the position of the ego outside the drive phantasma the birth of the father imago—in any case its structural root, the position of the third—is given.

Conversely one could also formulate that this is where the quality and the dimension of the explicit conscious comes into being. Such formulation is more in line with neurobiological research which shows that the majority of processes in the central nervous system proceed unconsciously. According to this, when considering the leap to the position outside the drive phantasma, we would be dealing not with a primal repression, but, one might say, with a primal becoming conscious, so this is not about a repression but about a step forward, a categorical new creation which retroactively stands out against the former, after all basal mode of functioning, and excludes it.

In this context it is important to note that the early functioning of the psyche which is tied to the identity of the ego with the drive phantasma and, following from it, to early object splitting, is not relinquished with the leap to the position of the ego outside the drive phantasma. The genetically earlier form of perception and experiencing continues to exist, namely in that mode of functioning of the ego in which the latter is not distanced from itself. This area of identity of the ego function, however, is no longer accessible to the self-reflecting ego outside of the drive phantasma, because we are dealing with—with reference, on the one hand, to object splitting, and to the identity of the ego with the drive phantasma on the other—a categorically different way of experiencing, and this is precisely why that area of identity functioning is unconscious in the structural sense.

Conversely, consciousness, the state of being conscious, can be defined as the self-reflexive mode of functioning of the ego outside of the drive phantasma.

We must therefore proceed from the assumption that the ego at all times perceives in two different and mutually incompatible modalities, of which only one is capable of being immediately conscious. It is obvious that these two mutually exclusive modalities or ways of functioning, respectively, of the mind are linked to the distinction between primary and secondary processes, but also to the dichotomies of word and thing presentation, perceptual identity and thought identity of. On the neurobiological plane it can be assumed that the difference of function and the tension between the limbic system and the prefrontal cortex play a role here.

In any case, I am of the opinion that this view of two forms of functioning of mental life and of the activity of the brain, operating permanently simultaneous and in parallel, offers a fruitful approach for the psychoanalytic understanding of a wide field of phenomena, for instance in the domain of the arts, but also with reference to understanding dreams and the dream process.

From this incompatibility of the two modes of functioning of the ego results a further consideration concerning the genetic priority of the agencies. Earlier in the text I have deduced the priority in time of the ego before the id, proceeding from the axiom that the dimension of the psychical arises out of the unfolding of the poles of perceiving and that which is perceived, by equating the perceiving agency with the primitive, primal ego.

Before the background of the above consideration, as a consequence of which this primal ego of the identity with the drive phantasma becomes the core of the id and, due to the incompatibility with the new mode of functioning, becomes structurally unconscious, this formulation must be specified: there are two fundamentally divergent modes of functioning of the ego, both existing simultaneously with each other, but the genetically earlier mode is linked to the splitting of the object, and thus does not meet the criteria of correspondence to reality and is ignorant of the ability of self reflection. This mode is therefore unconscious with relation to the new, henceforward dominant ego constitution, and what is more, constitutes the quality of psychogenic unconsciousness.

The structurally unconscious core of the id is therefore, according to this hypothesis, the early ego of the identity with the drive phantasma. This is also the reason why in the psychoses the classical separation of agencies is being lost, for a psychosis fundamentally consists in the very regression to the identity of the ego with the drive phantasma, which is linked to object splitting, and thus loss of access to reality and of the father imago. Hence, this regressive loss of the secondary-process position of the ego outside the drive phantasma implies the loss of differentiation of the agency of the id from that of the ego, and also, through the collapse of the father imago, the super ego of the structurally neurotic, oedipal plane, is lost.

When, in the introduction to this work, I had highlighted the requirement that a general theory of psychic structure building must allow the correct prediction and deduction of fundamental clinical phenomena, then the above paragraph on the structural regression in the psychoses is an example of the fact that the theory formulation as it is presented is able to do that.

In order to simplify things somewhat at least at the level of language, I shall in the following abbreviate the formulation 'position of the ego outside the drive phantasma' and instead use 'position outside'.

7

Incest with the mother as the oedipal formulation of the aim of the death drive

Regarding the description of the general course of structure formation, we are currently still at the point of the crisis of the depressive infantile conflict which leads to the reflective distancing of the ego from itself. Before the background of biological priming and from there on, the gender difference becomes the criterion of choice for the 'personal outfitting' of the position outside, the function of the third, and thus the father imago develops as an image of a categorically different object from the mother. Mentally figuring out the sexual-genital relationship of the parents is the task of the phases of development which follow after this, whereby anality, under the aspect of the themes dealt with here, fundamentally consists in the struggle with the moment of control over the object, especially via the development of the concept of the means—that is to say of the tool that is linked with voluntary motor functions—which then lays the foundation for the imagination of the phallus.

Even though Melanie Klein (cf. 1945) assumes the activity of the internal image of the phallus already in the first months of life, this early phallus in her opinion is initially still very orally defined and derives directly from the experience of the breast as something hard—the nipple—which is enclosed by something soft, thus lacks the specific

47

quality as the tool and the means with the help of which the father enters into contact with the mother in the primal scene.

In the oedipal stage then, before the background of the development that has occurred so far, the incest with the mother becomes the imagination corresponding to this level for the fusion with the object. Among contemporary authors, it was especially Janine Chasseguet-Smirgel (passim; cf. 1975) who emphasized this unconscious meaning of the incest, notably in both sexes. I am aware that it is a big leap to move from the consideration of the primordial constitution of the psyche and the conditions in the context with resolving the conflict of the depressive position to the fully-fledged oedipal conflict constellation, and to consider the latter as the expression of the same basal drive dynamics as a consequence of which the ego, dominated by the death drive, attempts to gain omnipotent control over the object and in fact merge with it. For the moment, I ask the reader for patience, as the justification of this approach only becomes evident from the analysis of the oedipal conflict themes and especially from the analysis of the relationship of the ego with the father imago. This analysis shows that here the exact same themes are active which I have described previously in this text regarding the relationship of the primary ego to the primary object and which have led to the construction of the defensive organization of the good-bad split of the object imago. The evidence for the justification to equate the conflict dynamics of the crisis of the depressive position with that of the oedipal constellation thus results from both their structural uniformity, and this at the same time is proof of the fact of an underlying consistent drive theme.

The psychic development described so far, on the one hand, as depicted, consisted in the attachment of the representation of the primary object to psychosexuality, which during orality led to the development of the part-object of the breast; on the other hand, in the overcoming of the split conceptualization of the object in the depressive position and the breakthrough to the position outside. Following this, the relationship with the part-object was expanded in the involvement with reality to encompass the relationship with the whole, time-space identical object of the mother, and psychosexuality developed through negotiating the psychosexual phases, the gender difference was recognized and sexually cathected.

However, at the basis of this whole development, to stress this again, is the attachment of the primary object, which initially had only consisted in the representation of a temporally contingent sensory stimulation, to psychosexuality during the breast-feeding experience. I understand the experience of breast-feeding which as such may not always be a factual experience, in the sense of a symbolic pre-conceptional proxy for all pleasurable contacts with the real mother, or the caregiver, respectively, whereby the latter on its part and depending on circumstances, does not have to be the real mother. The internal image, the imago of the mother is, in this sense, the condensation of all objectal experiences which are connected with the original representation of the primary object, develop from it, and more closely determine and differentiate this representation. The direct descent of the mother imago from this primal attachment makes it the centrally important mental object; makes it the imago from which, after access to reality is gained, the relationship to all other real objects is originating, thus, so to speak, the sum imago of the world.

The imago of the oedipal mother, before this background, must therefore be thought of as the central successor representation of the primary object, which in the confrontation with reality as well as with the biologically determined pre-conceptions, has taken on the form of the mother as the giver of birth. What is symbolized in her, in the world of real objects, most fittingly is the relationship to the primary object, in reference to which no outside is conceivable as yet, and which in this sense also contains the primary ego itself.

In this context it should be pointed out again that projective identification which, for the purpose of controlling the object, but also for the purpose of an archaic form of mental communication (Bion), consists in injecting parts of the self into the object, must be regarded, in its pathological sense, as the operative mechanism for the production of a fusional state insofar as through it the boundary between the self and the object is dissolved, which is its central intention. It is, therefore, the principal mechanism of the death drive, and its structural closeness to incestuous phantasy, namely via the insertion of parts of the self into the object, must not be overlooked. Earlier, I had already pointed out that Rosenfeld (1964) has described it in this sense as the mechanism of denial of the separation and separateness from the object. Beyond this, in 1983, he depicted a global kind of projective identification in which the self as a whole, in the context of a symbiotic kind of object relation, is projected into the object and seems to live like it was inside the object. Betty Joseph (1987, p. 178) formulates the issue poignantly: "At the very primitive end of projective identification is the attempt to get back into an object—to become, as it were, undifferentiated and mindless and thus avoid all pain." At the level of the not per-se pathological meaning in the framework of primal mental communication processes, Bion (1962) places projective identification within the context of his container-contained model, in as far as the child here with the help of projective identification injects content or sensory qualities, respectively, which are indigestible, incomprehensible for it, into the mental organism of the mother and which it obtains back from the mother on the same path in a mentally representable form (alpha process). In any case, it is here where we find the prefigurations which turn the incest with the mother into an unconscious representation of the fusional phantasma at the level of whole objects and genitality.

In his book on *Psychic Retreats* John Steiner writes: "Today, (...) we recognize the central role of projective identification in the creation of pathological object relations (...)" (1993, p. 61). If projective identification in the above sense is the direct operative mechanism of the death drive in the meaning I suggested, namely by striving to suspend the separation of ego and object, then Steiner's formulation implies immediately the acknowledgement of the death drive as the motor of psychopathology.

In this context belong also Hanna Segal's reflections (1957, 1978) on symbolic equation, that is to say, the collapse of symbol formation by equating symbol and symbolized object. In her opinion the symbolic equation is the cause of the concretistic thinking in the psychoses. She, too, considers the pathological projective identification as the motor of this regressive process and writes: "Parts of the ego and internal objects are projected into an object and identified with it. The differentiation between the self and the object is obscured. Then, since a part of the ego is confused with the object, the symbol—which is a creation and a function of the ego—becomes, in turn, confused with the object which is symbolized." (1957 p. 392)

In 1978 she adds: "The symbolic equation is used to deny the separateness between the subject and the object. The symbol is used to overcome an accepted loss" (in: Segal 1995, p. 316). And Hinshelwood defines: "The defensive (pathological) use of projective identification is carried on to such an extent that the self and object fuse, with the subsequent equation of symbol and object symbolized (symbolic equation)" (1989/91 p. 454).

As a basic principle it must be noted that the position of the ego outside of the drive phantasma, that is to say, the reflective distance

51

of the ego to itself, which eventually gets codified in the father imago, is the precondition for the ability of symbol formation as well as language development, insofar as this reflective distance in its turn is the precondition for the indexical designation. It appears to me that under this aspect the process of symbolic equation can be grasped theoretically more precisely still: pathological use of projective identification leads to the collapse, to the suspension of the position outside and thus of the father imago, and this is its central intention under the point of view of the death drive. With the collapse of the position outside, the symbolic function also collapses and is replaced by the symbolic equation.

I consider this an important additional assumption, for Hanna Segal's formulations are inherently problematic in that they say nothing about what leads to the equation of the symbol and the symbolized object at the strictly metapsychological level, that is to say at the level of internal structure formation processes concerning the attitude of the ego towards itself and also towards the object imago. Her argumentation is that the psychotic fusional identification of the ego and the object imago leads to a parallel identification of the symbol and the symbolized object, for the simple reason that the symbol is a function of the ego. Identification, with reference to ego and object, is a metapsychologically precise notion, however not with reference to the process taking place between symbol and symbolized object. The argument of parallelity here has the status of a phenomenological description and is no real explanation of the way in which the fusional process between ego and object leads to the falling together of the symbol and that which is symbolized. This explanation is furnished by the concept of the position outside and its collapse in the face of imminent fusion, that is to say, its collapse under the impact of the death drive.

This also includes a more exact understanding to the effect that the psychotic phenomena are not the result of an actual fusion, for the fusion as a factual realization is psychically not possible as in it the juxtaposition of ego and object, perception and that which is perceived would be abolished, out of which the mental space, the dimension of the psychical originates in the first place and which constitutes it. Fusion therefore would annul the dimension of the psychical. The process geared towards it which is carried by the death drive leads, however, to the collapse of the position of the ego outside the drive phantasma, thus to the collapse of access to reality, and brings back the good-bad split of the object imago, and this in turn gives rise to the phenomenology of the psychotic constitution. When Hanna Segal speaks of the fusional identification of ego and object in the psychoses, this is more precisely about an identification which works towards fusion under the influence of the death drive, but which can never actually bring it about.

8

The oedipal conflict and the imago of the phallus

Before the background of these considerations, anyway, the primal scene now is bestowed its central significance for the psyche inasmuch as, from the concretistic perspective of the death drive, it represents the seeming opportunity presented by the example of the father, to carry out fusion with the mother without the danger of ego dissolution. From the point of view of the life drive—which contains the symbolic function—that same image of the primal scene represents the suspension of the fusional danger and thus in fact of the death drive, in so far as the core of the father imago is the distancing of the ego from itself which impedes the fusion.

In this latter sense, the image of the primal scene, as seen before the psychical background of the meaning of the father imago, already implicitly contains the motive of the renunciation of the ego with regard to the fusional wish, and the incestuous misinterpretation and corruption by the death drive contain a purposeful denial with reference to the significance of the father imago, which of course is not unfamiliar to endopsychic perception.

Under both perspectives, however, the power of the father condenses in the imago of the phallus as the means that links the father in the primal scene to the mother. Thus the phallus, by definition, is the penis of the father.

According to Freud, in the phallic phase, which in his opinion lasts from the third to the fifth year of life and temporally coincides with the Oedipus complex, "...only <u>one genital</u>, namely the male one, comes into account. What is present, therefore, is not a primacy of the genitals but a primacy of the phallus" (1923e, p. 142; emphasis S.F.). Melanie Klein in turn writes: "In my view, infants of both sexes experience genital desires directed towards their mother and father, and they have an unconscious knowledge of the vagina as well as of the penis. For these reasons Freud's earlier term 'genital phase' seems to me more adequate than his later concept of the 'phallic phase'" (1945, Writings p. 414).

In my opinion, the above depicted genealogy of the meaning of the imago of the phallus can create the theoretical connection between these two positions by furnishing a reason for the "primacy" of the imagination of the phallus, but without containing an, as it were, genital monism, in the sense of the thesis about the representational accessibility of only one genital organ. The contrary is true, as the background phantasy is that of the fusional incest with the mother.

The classical threat of castration is put in force under these considerations in as far as the phantasmatic acquisition of the fatherly phallus by the death drive as a means to carry out the incest, leads to the collapse of its efficacy which is seen to consist in the banishment of the danger connected with the fusion. For the father imago, which stands behind the imago of the phallus, draws its dynamic meaning and effect and thus its existence, as we know, from the distancing of the ego from itself in the position outside, that is to say, from the separation of ego and father imago which would be revoked again in the concretistic appropriation of the phallus. This revocation would therefore be equivalent to the collapse of the father imago, and it is the threat of this event which is behind the threat of castration and which makes out its core, its significance.

When the conflict of the depressive position is resolved by taking the position outside, that is to say, through the 'invention' of the position of the third, and thus, subsequently, of the father, the threat of castration then contains the threat of the return of the conflict of the depressive position. The loss of the father imago brings back the old good-bad split of the object and thus the paranoid attack on the object which is hereby experienced as damaged and jeopardized in its existence. The subject therefore experiences the castration both on himself and on the object. The breakdown of the father imago is the real major catastrophe of mental life.

Because of both its dynamic and its structural importance, the threat of castration and behind it the threat of loss of the father imago becomes the agent of repression and in this way the agent of the creation of the dynamic unconscious part of the id. Repression here uses the dimension of the structurally unconscious which arises in the transition from the splitting conceptualization to a realistic identity conceptualization of the object by using the quality that comes with it, namely the categorially unconscious quality of contents that are psychically active nevertheless, in order to achieve a structurally secured non-identity of the repressed contents with respect to the ego of the position outside.

Incidentally, this point of view also serves to clarify an old contentious question, namely who or what is to be considered the agent of the dynamically unconscious, that is to say repressed parts of the ego. This agent is the life drive itself, inasmuch as it, via the quality of unconsciousness, establishes the non-identity of the ego with respect to those contents which are contaminated so to speak, by their much too close contact with those contents that express the aims of the death drive and that were repressed into the id. The dynamic means of the life drive, also in this case, is the threat of castration, that is to say, the threat of the disintegration of the father imago and thus of the phantasma of the phallus each time an attempt is made to create an identity between ego and object. If, on the other hand, I have described further up that the dimension of the psychogenic unconscious results from the incompatibility of the splitting conceptualization of the object with the suspension of this split through the position outside, the functional mechanism of repression can also be formulated differently: that in the case of an interpretation of the relationship to the object that stands under the reign of the death drive, the good-bad split of the representation of this object reappears in the background, and that therefore, this representation falls into the catchment area of that dimension of the psyche that is incompatible with regard to the position outside and that insofar is unconscious, or plainly: repressed.

In this manner, in any case, the primal scene becomes the central imago of the psyche, in as far as in it both drives simultaneously find their imaginative realization: the life drive in the sense of the ego's self-imposed abstinence with respect to the fusional implication of the incest, whereby this self-imposed abstinence—because of and via the anti-fusional meaning of the father imago—is referenced and expressed under the aspect of the Eros in the coupling of the father with the mother. In this sense the imago of the primal scene is <u>the phantasmatic definition of the life drive</u>. The death drive perverts this meaning of the primal scene concretistically, in the sense of the seeming possibility of the realization of the fusional incest, insofar as the father, in the sexual union with the mother, seems to be protected by the power of the phallus from the danger of annihilation contained in the fusion.

As the appropriation of this apotropaic phallus, however, is being thwarted by the threat of castration, or rather and more exactly, by the event of castration which consists in the catastrophic loss of the protective effect and power of the phallus in the incestuous approach towards fusion, the Oedipus complex in this way becomes the complex which bonds and neutralizes the death drive. This, in my opinion, is its psychobiological meaning, which not only makes it the "the central core of all neuroses" (Freud, 1931), but also the central core of the psyche in general.

In any case, in this consideration it becomes clear that genital sexuality is the field within which both drives articulate themselves. It cannot, therefore, be attributed unilaterally to one of the two drives only.

If the father imago is lost in the castration experience as the result of the transgression of the Oedipal prohibition, the mother imago—and in it the relationship with the whole world of real objects of which the Oedipal mother is the sum-total imago—suffers the loss of reality of the psychotic plane, with the time-space reality of this imago falling apart, regressing.

In this sense the primal scene imago represents, so to speak, a time shaft which, with respect to the psychological meaning of the parental images, refers directly to the earliest structural constellations and problems. I therefore regard the primal scene as that psychical imagination in which the natural law conditions are expressed which constitute and maintain the dimension of the psychical. This affirms also under this aspect the central meaning of the Oedipal constellation.

That the father imago prevents the ego loss resulting from being devoured by the regressive mother imago in the incestuous fusion, was incidentally, to my knowledge, formulated for the first time by Loewald (1951). But also Lacan's work is permeated by similar considerations on

59

the meaning of the father, the phallus, and its dialectic complementarity with the mother imago. Pars pro toto I quote in the following from notes taken in his seminaries: "Her [the mother's] desire is not something you can bear easily, as if it were a matter of indifference to you. It always leads to problems. The mother is a big crocodile and you find yourself in her mouth. You never know what may set her off suddenly, making those jaws clamp down. That is the mother's desire. So I tried to explain that there was something reassuring. There is a roller, made of stone, of course, which is potentially there at the level of the trap, and that holds and jams it open. That is what we call the phallus. It is a roller which protects you, should the jaw suddenly close" (2003, p. 129).

Bion describes in "Attacks on Linking" (1959) that the infant, even though it may be connected with the mother in a positive emotional experience, simultaneously remains identified with the excluded part, the excluded position, and insofar feels pain, envy, and jealousy. The infant's reaction, so Bion, consists in attacking the lustful connection between mouth and nipple, later the sexual union of the parents. Feldman (1989, p.126) in his discussion of this work concluded: "Thus, following Mrs. Klein, he postulates a very early form of Oedipus complex."

It is obvious that what Bion here describes as identification with the excluded part, from the angle of the death drive, is identical with my definition of the position outside, as a consequence of which a fusional realization is no longer possible. For in as far as the position outside comprises the exclusion from the pleasurable connection, the death drive must turn against this fact of being excluded, against the position outside and finally against the lustful connection itself, vis-à-vis which the experience of exclusion is to be seen. Bion therefore posits the beginning of the Oedipal constellation to start at the same time as I think it does.

Furthermore it is necessary to bear in mind a fundamental complication in the relationship with the parental images. To 'be a mother' and 'be a father' belongs to the everyday topics of our lives which are the reference points also for us psychoanalysts and therefore we easily fail to see that from the point of view of the inner perspective of our Oedipal constitution we are all egos, and that within ourselves we find ourselves opposite our motherly and fatherly imagos. Each flesh-and-blood man and each flesh-and-blood woman can take up the position of the father or mother only within the inner world of his or her children, but can never be it in his or her psychic reality. As concerns oneself, one is always the ego which finds itself opposite its own father and mother imagos, and which, as it were, declares itself ready and willing to play this role for the child, to take it on, to represent it.

Looked at it this way one could say that 'mother' and 'father' are the most monumental abstractions we have to deal with in our lives. And that at the same time the apparently unequivocal biological founding of our sociological family structure in this sense is an error. That there are only ever father and mother places so to speak, but that no one single living individual can ever be identical with these places.

One could, from this perspective, point out that also within the specific phantasmatization of humankind which is laid down in the Christian religion mythologem, the god that became man—Christ—is designated as son and thus as ego. The Father himself is extramundane—in the sense of the impossible identity of ego and father place-, he does not exist on this earth. For while the ego is being defined by the father imago, as I have attempted to show, it cannot, however, become identical with it, as the father imago arises from the position outside and as the latter would be annulled again by establishing an identity between ego and father imago. This would lead to a psychoanalytic understanding of that central tenet of belief according to which Christ

61

is one with the Father and then again not. I am going to revert to these themes further on in this work.

In the same vein, the mother in her ontogenetic background is the imago of the primary object, from which in the course of the individual developmental history—via the entry of the father imago, which is truly generative in this psychic sense—the whole world of real objects differentiates out, so that the oedipal mother in the unconscious background is the sum-total imago of the world. Ego and mother, therefore, cannot be identical either: the mother is the object, the perceived, which is opposite the ego as the subject of perception. The ego can only take up the mother place for its own child.

9

The structural identity of the oedipal conflict for both sexes

Further on, a consequence of these lines of thought which examine the basic structural conditions of the psyche, is then that the striving for fusion with the primary object—oedipally formulated for the fusional incest with the mother—would have to be deemed the fundamental unconscious motive for both sexes. This of course contradicts the dominant heterosexual expression of the manifest female sexuality.

I think that this contradiction can be resolved via the specific detour that would include the psychical fate of the child, which Freud in the "New Introductory Lectures on Psychoanalysis" formulated as follows: "The wish with which the girl turns to her father is no doubt originally the wish for the penis (..). The feminine situation is only established, however, if the wish for a penis is replaced by one for a baby, if, that is, a baby takes the place of a penis in accordance with an ancient symbolic equivalence" (1933, p. 128).

With the help of the child, which, on the unconscious transference plane represents the penis of the father, that is to say the phallus, the girl, the woman, then desires to carry out the actual fusional incest with the mother at the unconscious-phantasmatic level, by equating her body with the mother of the primal scene, and by identifying her ego with the phallus-child. Insofar as this identification with the phallus in fact signifies that with the father of the primal scene, we are dealing with an enactment of the oedipal situation within one's own person.

The always existing background attachment of the woman to her own mother as the primary love object is really not a new theme. I think what is important here is a more exact deduction within the framework of theory formation as presented in this work and thus the formulation of the hypothesis that this background attachment, even without any trace of pathological derailment, represents, in no way, only an inactive latency, a kind of genetic eggshell that has not been shed, but far more importantly, is the hidden prime mover also of the heterosexual female sexual interest. It is true also for female sexuality that the wish for the fusion of the ego with the primary object which satisfies all needs is the governing basic phantasy.

The specific threat of castration of the female death drive then would be that the child which cannot carry this attribution and use of itself as the phallus of the father, because of its own prohibition of fusion which in turn is interlocked with that of the mother, collapses under the weight of this attribution, or would collapse, respectively, if this attribution was realized.

So, biologically speaking, in justification of the purpose of this detour via the child, one could adduce that the relationship to the child is, in any case, part of the fundamental structural demands of the female psyche. One could further conclude that the woman as a mother through her own sublimative renunciation with respect to the child—that is to say, with respect to the use of the phallus-child within a phantasmatization of the realization of the fusional incest—is at the same time protecting the child itself from its own incestuous striving by not seductively inviting such striving and in this way opening the path to the basic work demand for the ego of the child, namely to renounce the fusional incest.

In this sense one must say, therefore, that the birth of the father imago and the stabilization of its function, on the plane of the psychic reality of the child, depends on the state of the Oedipal working through by the mother. The mother allows and enables the child to construct the phantasmatization concerning the father, or she prohibits it.

As I was able to show in another place (1988) in the framework of a clinical study, the idea of the child in the psyche of the woman arises from the unconscious phantasy of a regression of the partner in the orgasmic sexual contact; a regression, that is, in which the man through the orgasm becomes the child with which the woman is impregnated. With this phantasy the woman reacts to the transference effected by the death drive of the man, that is to say, to the transference of the Oedipal incest with the mother, behind which genetically we find the primary narcissistic phantasy of the fusion of primary ego and primary object, i.e. the complete line of regression down to the beginnings of mental life. Hence the idea of the child as the expression of this regression.

From this genealogy it becomes evident that the woman, by resisting her own longing for a death-drive motivated seduction of her child, in her unconscious experience also rescues the partner who has regressed to a child, from fusion which is the aim of the death drive. And, for the woman, the male sexual partner stands under her own Oedipal transference, in the context of which the woman, in the sexual act and under the impact of the death drive, via the transference incest with the father desires to beget the phallus of the father in the form of the child, in order to use it to realize the fusional incest with the mother, carried out within her own person. As concerns the equation of her own body with that of the mother, the woman avails herself of the Oedipal transference of her male partner. Insofar as the woman in

65

her sexuality unconsciously identifies her own body with that of her mother, we here have another way of understanding the strong bond between mother and daughter.

The basis for this identification, by the way, is that the representation of the primary object was formed by undifferentiated sensory stimulation from proprioception, as well as stimulation by contact with the outside world, and here especially from contact with the mother's body, all of which are only being sorted out when the concept of reality is acquired, that is to say with the break-through to the position outside. This therefore represents the umbilical cord, through which one's own body and the body of the mother at this primary level of functioning are connected, and regressively always remain connected. Note that this also applies to the man, if though this connection within the framework of heterosexuality does not acquire the same constitutive meaning as it does for the woman. One could ask, however, whether certain auto-stimulative forms of the search for lust and satisfaction— like the addictions—have their root cause here.

The negative Oedipus complex in the boy and the psychogenic homosexuality in the man, by the way, share similar, equivalent content in relation to the above in that both must be seen within the framework of the fight for the inner constitution of the imago of the phallus and its possession, that is to say both contain, as a prerequisite, a problematic struggle with the father imago or with its basis, respectively, which is the ability or readiness of the ego to distance itself from the drive phantasma. The variance here is considerable, between Oedipal forms of struggle which have the central theme of fight against the threat of castration, and where in consequence aggression plays a large role, and seemingly constitutional forms where the old equation of breast and penis gains in importance and the struggle with the problems of the depressive position is in the foreground, out of which the imago of the phallus constitutes itself.

The female homosexual position would then analogously consist in a shortcut which suspends and overrides the above-described detour via the child and which contains a direct bodily identification with the phallus, as described by, for instance, Joyce McDougall (1978).

In summary it can be said that the Oedipus complex, in my perspective, is a primarily intrapsychic, that is to say, interstructural matter and necessity, which inevitably results from the activity of the death drive. In this view the motive of the Oedipus complex in both sexes basically consists in the effort to circumvent the father imago, to lever it off and lastly to annul it, inasfar as the core of the father imago consists of the position of the third, i.e. the position outside the drive phantasma which opposes the fusional merging with the mother, with the primary object. The father imago comes into being as a bastion against the death drive, and the death drive therefore, for its realisation must strive for the reannulment of the father imago.

This theme concerning the internal structure of the psyche, of mental life, becomes secondarily transposed, projected to, and identified with the persons of the Oedipal triangle. It is for this reason that oedipality as a structural principle of organization is ubiquitous, that it can be shown to exist in forms of society the basal unit of which is not the generative family.

The basic model of the male Oedipus complex, therefore, consists in the phantasy sustained by passion to go behind the back of the father and by eliminating and overthrowing him, coalesce and connect with the mother in pleasure. In analogy, the female version would consist in the attempt to seduce the father, whereby from the perspective of the death drive the theme of seduction attacks the father principle in its very core, insofar as this principle derives from the ability of the ego to distance oneself from the drive dynamics.

Projected to the level of dramatic action, the male model of the Oedipal attack on the father imago is thus treason and murder, the female model is corruption. In the negative Oedipus complex of both sexes the roles are reversed. In addition to this there are then further complications in the next generational line, so to speak, when the man is confronted with the powerful female schemer, or the woman with the drive-driven usurper, and so on. The reader may feel free, at his or her own leisure, to browse the personae and actions of the great plays, from Lady Macbeth to Wagner's Kundry.

10

An outline of psychopathology

The pathology now defines itself within this dynamic scenario of the drives via the different degrees of opposition of the ego against the threat of castration, which I will attempt to sketch out briefly in the following:

At the neurotic level of structure the ego bows to the threat of castration, albeit under pressure, but it does not recognize its content. This leads to a continuous loss of wide areas of the personality by repression, insofar as everything that is connected with the fusional context becomes unconscious, in order to secure the non-identity of the ego with the themes around the danger of fusion. This is the dynamic unconscious.

In the borderline personality organization the denial of the separateness from the object and the active rebellion of the ego against the threat of castration lead to such far-reaching corruption of the father imago and thus of the position outside, that the old splitting of the imago of the object resurfaces anew. This leads to the further complications of the borderline constitution, namely the attack on the symbolization function, the ambivalence of the object relation, and affect instability, as well as the replacement of the perspective of 'not only but also' by 'either/or' in consequence of the loss of reflective distance, and further still the replacement of the defense modes of the countercathexis by those of the split. In particular, the imago of the primal scene turns into the frightening image of the combined parent-figure (cf. Klein 1952), that is to say, the combination of the bad split-aspect of the mother imago with the bad, sadistic split-aspect of the disintegrating father imago (whereby, as Steiner describes in 1993, perverse moments of excitation occur which have to do with the simultaneous recognition and non-recognition of reality, and which heighten the horror of this image).

In differentiation to Kernberg's position on that matter, I am of the opinion, therefore, that the borderline personality organization is in principle not based on a developmental arrest but on a structural regression, for the basic access to reality which borderline personalities do possess, demonstrates that the principal step of overcoming object splitting in the position outside had been taken, but could not be maintained.

At the level of the neurobiological parallel process, this structural regression in the borderline personality disorder seems to correspond to an insufficient 'top-down' control through the prefrontal cortex leading to hyperactivity of the amygdala, as suggested, for example, in studies on the neurofunctional correlates of disturbed affect regulation in the borderline personality with functional magnetic resonance imaging by Sabine Herpertz et al. (2001). She further found evidence for an increased activity in the gyrus fusiformis which in its turn is subject to a feedback-mechanism on the part of the amygdala. The task of the gyrus fusiformis is the upkeep of physiognomic memory and the physiognomic analysis of affects—that is to say, for functions which are directly related to triggering affective responses.

The work of Herpertz is based on findings from functional neuroimaging studies which in normal populations have shown "the critical role of the amygdala in the processing of negative emotions" (Herpertz et al. 2001; transl. P.Z). She concludes that "the findings from functional imaging studies [support] neurobiological models of BPD preferring a limbic hypersensitivity" (2006), whereby she traces the hypersensitivity back to the impaired 'top-down' control.

I mention this study to highlight in an exemplary way a convergence between psychotherapy research which emphasizes the insufficient affect and fear control and the ambivalence in the borderline personality disorder, neurobiological findings, and a metapsychological understanding which traces insufficient affect control and ambivalence back to the structural regression on object splitting along the lines of the good-bad dichotomy. This is therefore an example of that particular triangulation of neurobiological functional interactions, psychological phenomenology, and psychoanalytic metapsychology, where metapsychology proves itself as a *tertium explicationis*. Carlo Strenger (1991), in this context, speaks of the relationship of "external coherence" between neurobiological findings and metapsychological concepts.

In the psychogenesis of psychotic pathology, eventually, the father imago, and in it the position outside and thus the ability to form symbols, have been lost. Connected to this is the breakdown of access to reality characteristic for psychosis, as a consequence of returning to the splitting of the object imago, whereby the latter then would have to be seen in the genealogy of the imago of the primary object as the only type of representation which then—that is to say after the breakdown of the father imago and the representations derived from it—still exists in the psychic space.

Inasmuch as the levering out of the Oedipal triangulation in the attempt to establish fusion with the mother appears as the causal momentum of the pathological dynamics, we have an explanation of why the separation from the object is such a central motive in borderline states and in the psychoses—but not only there. If the striving of the death drive consists in the omnipotent control over the object, and lastly, in the fusional union with it, which unconsciously is regarded as the suspension of need-tension and unpleasure, the psychic struggle of course must be about the theme of separation. The other way round this explains why psychoanalytic findings and reflections on the process of healing are so closely linked to the recognition of separation from the object and with the necessary mourning that leads to this recognition. This mourning is the work of the life drive, so to speak. If, on the other hand, one regards the struggle against separation, the separateness from the object, as the underlying motive force for all pathological manifestations, then this simultaneously means that one must identify this motive with the narcissistic striving (cf. Rosenfeld 1964) which thus becomes the pervasive motive in all forms of psychic pathology. I will reflect on this further below from a fundamental perspective.

In the perverse personality organization, which also before the background of the thoughts presented in this work I consider a separate nosological category, the pathognomic splitting off of the phallus from the father imago described by Joyce McDougall (1972) leads to a situation in which this latter—that is to say the father imago—is being devalued and rejected on the one hand, but where on the other hand and in contrast, the phallic imago remains overly idealized and the phallic threat of castration, in the sense of the prohibition to create an identity between ego and phallus, continues to be active. The attempt to infringe this prohibition leads to the severe psychoses-like panic attacks typical for the perverse organization. As far as in the perverse structure the non-identity of ego and phallus continues to exist despite the devaluation of the father imago, in other words, the position outside is attacked only as it relates to the father imago, but not in relation to the phallus, the perversions represent a structurally relatively stable intermediary stage on the path of structural regression which engenders psychic pathology.

Maintaining the non-identity of ego and phallus implies that a regression to the level of object splitting does not occur, that access to reality is, in principle, not questioned as such, if though reality itself is simultaneously denied and acknowledged (cf. Steiner 1993). What arises in this way is side-by-side denial and acknowledgement of the separateness from the object in the midst of reality, which is typical for the perverse structure and which Steiner (1993)—to distinguish it from the concept of sexual perversion—called narcissistic perversion, by taking up and further elaborating on Freud's (1927) description of the simultaneous acknowledgement and non-acknowledgement of the gender difference in fetishism.

The paradox that constitutes the perverse structure and which I wish to point out, in this instance consists in the fact that the negation of the separation from the object, and thus the struggle against the father imago and the law of the father does not lead to the collapse of reality access in the splitting of the object, due to the splitting off of the phallus from the father imago; therefore the denial of the threat of castration—source of the most severe pathology—coexists together with its acknowledgement, without any recognition of this contradiction. This comes with a split in the reality concept which has an enormously destructive, corrupting implication in all contexts that are related to object-contact, and thus in social life. Steiner (1993), in the framework of his description of the 'pathological organizations of the personality' (cf. Rosenfeld 1971), presented these problematic issues and described this perverse splitting of simultaneous acknowledgement and non-acknowledgement of reality as the fundamental characteristic of 'psychic retreats', the internal places where the psyche withdraws to, which he considers as elaborated defensive formations against the recognition of the separation from the object.

Provided that those various forms of struggle against the incest prohibition and the threat of castration are the characteristic common feature of the neurotic, the perverse, and the borderline pathology, a special mechanism is particularly important in this context, from a social-pathological perspective, as a consequence of which threat and prohibition to which the subject, in his or her immediate experiencing, is mercilessly and irrationally exposed, in a turn from passivity to activity, are being enacted in social relationships. In my view this is the most important source of irrational authoritarian violence amongst all forms in which power is exercised in society. The driving moment lies in the triumph to actively inflict the coercion which one is intrapsychically subjected to in a passive way upon others, in the context of one's object relationships and in this way to deny one's own subjugation. The pleasure lies in the conversion of resentment into triumph.

The suffering at the bottom of one's own blind subjugation under a not understood and apparently incomprehensible law is being defended against through the pleasure in the despotic exercise of power against those who under the given structural conditions are in a dependent, subjugated position. This defense is very effective, in particular because on the unconscious plane it implies as a premium the usurpation of the place of the father in the Oedipal triangle. If one bears in mind to what extent processes in social life are determined by irrational exercise of power, the only apparent motive of which is the blind thwarting of things, then it becomes clear that this is a central destructive factor in how human beings coexist with each other, at least as long as it is not about the complete aggressive negation of the Other, of the object.

The pathology of the individual is here directly converted to social pathology, the driving force behind which, just as in the individual pathology, is the Oedipus complex. Specific motives like envy, jealousy, rivalry and competition; anal, sado-masochistic, narcissistic complications only get added to this central motive of the turnaround of the Oedipal prohibition from a passive suffering to active infliction. They are specific forms of the reaction to this Oedipal prohibition.

11

Hysteria

It is still hysteria which ranks as the highest-developed form of pathology of the mind, as here the elaboration of the parental imagos has reached the stage of their genital sexual definition concurring with reality, and not even in the process of pathology do these imagos lose their oedipally organized sexual significance, also not in the psychotic decompensation.

In my opinion, it is the central problem of hysteria that the confrontation with reality, which became available by overcoming the primary good-bad split of the object in the position outside, led to the insight into the difference between the sexes. All disease manifestations of hysteria only serve one single purpose: to suspend this insight, to cancel, deny, repress it.

In the psychoanalytic literature the disposition to hysteria is linked with a specific deformation of the mother-child contact in the sense of a switch between overexcitement and rejection through the mother (Bollas 2000, Fairbairn 1954). Also Khan (1988) with his concept of the hysterical grudge argues in this direction. Bollas specifies this view in the sense of a general overstimulation and overidealization of the child whereby a rejection and coldness referring specifically to the genitals is present, a withdrawal of cathexis. Christa Rohde-Dachser (2008) critically discusses this position in her excellent meta-analysis on hysteria, by, above all, referring to Fonagy (2008) who pointed out that sexual stimulation and arousal are quite normally those areas of infantile expression which are not mirrored by the mother and which therefore become a foreign area in how the child experiences itself. Lastly, however, Rohde-Dachser leaves the question undecided.

In my view this deduction is a piece of a conventional psychoanalysis orientating itself by following allegedly observable or reconstructable behavior and causally correlating this behavior with the pathological phenomenon in the sense of an "if-then" relationship. What remains unconsidered here is the intercurrent level of structure formation by the unconscious phantasmas which I am attempting to describe in this work. Out of these phantasmas, conflicts and complications may arise which to a great extent stem from the individual's unconscious and autonomous phantasmatic activity.

Although the specific form of and the specific solution of these conflicts can be influenced by outside factors, the situation is by far not as unequivocal as one would want to assume. Indeed I am of the opinion that this level of structure-forming phantasmas is the actual core area of psychoanalysis, and that it is in fact this level which is to be brought to the fore by the high-frequency analysis in order to work on it. The one-sided orientation on determining factors in the parental behavior is thus in my view a defensive attitude before the background of a fear of the autonomous dynamic force and the controlling power that these phantasmas have.

Speaking for the concrete case of hysteria, I think that the sexualization that constitutes the conception of the illness is not caused by an over or understimulation of the genitals, but results from the fact that the unconscious elaboration of the structure-forming phantasmas has progressed up to the point where the difference between the sexes, the doubleness of the sexes is not only grasped, but has been psychically recognized and conceptualized as that imagination which summarizes

78

the fundamental conditions of the psyche, as the final imagination of the goal and purpose of psychic development and as the driving motive for the turning to reality.

With the recognition of the differentiation between the sexes the theme of separation and separateness from the mother as the successor representation of the primary object is receiving a newly intensified and explosive power for both sexes. The fact of the existence of two sexes does indeed include the fact of separation, the impossibility of establishing the all-comprehensive fusional unity with the (primary) object as this now is no longer the only given object, regardless of one's own sex.

What we see again here on the level of the concrete sexual difference is the resurfacing of that dynamically effective logical moment, the appearance of the '2' preventing the creation of fusional oneness with the '1' which up to that point was considered all-comprehensive, because then the fusion no longer contains the all-that-exists, and no longer includes the remedy for every possible kind of lack. The '2', the Other, always remains outside of the fusion which thus is no longer sustainable as a totally comprehensive concept that expresses the aims of the death drive. This is what creates the experience of being excluded, and thus of despair. The phantasy of exclusion from the primal scene then is only the ongoing dramatizing elaboration of this problem, based on the idea that the father now establishes the gratifying fusion with the mother. In principle this is the same logical complication which already led to the overcoming of the primary object splitting with and in the appearance of the position outside.

On this newly reached level of the psychic elaboration of the difference between the sexes, the above complication immediately leads into the Oedipus complex in the sense of the confrontation with the Oedipal prohibition, that is to say, the confrontation with the experience of castration when an attempt is made to appropriate the phallus of the father, whereby the mechanism, both of the appropriation itself and of its being carried out by actively entering the primal scene, is that of projective identification, with both sides of the primal scene couple, a mechanism described by Britton (1999) as "the hysterical solution":

"The hysteric, I suggest, 'gets in on the act', mounts the stage and takes one of the parental parts. By an omnipotent phantasy of projective identification, they believe they are one of the primal couple performing whatever they imagine takes place in the phantasised primal scene. This I think constitutes hysterical enactment; that is, phantasy in action such as that so vividly described in the case of Anna O. The 'private theatre' of her day-dreaming became incarnate in a bodily based psychic drama enacted by herself, and in which she subsequently involved her family and her doctor in a total transference scene" (op. cit., p. 9).

With this projective identificatory entering into the primal scene, the war of the hysteric against the threat of castration breaks out, against the sexual difference and all that has led to this process, especially against the position outside and the reflexive consciousness that is connected with it; we are in the middle of the hysteria war. In the light of the complication of triangulation that I have been discussing above, and that, with the perception of the difference between the sexes as a reality, cannot be refused any more, the point could be made that the alternating projective identification of the hysteric with both sides of the primal couple—of the 'beast with two backs' as Shakespeare makes Iago say—contains of course the implication to dissolve the primal scene in this way, within the projective identification, into a dyadic organization. In this sense, Bollas (2000), too, speaks of the pseudo-triangulation of the hysteric as the attempt to cling to the mother as the primary object.

I think the hysteric uses these alternating projective identifications with both parents of the primal scene to combat not only exclusion from the primal scene and thus the threat of castration, but at the same time he uses them to psychically push through the constitutive denial of the sexual difference, not only on the level of the parents with whom he alternately identifies and thus, so to speak, dissolves the sexual difference, evaporates it, but also on the level of his own sexual identity. It must be seen before this background when Christa Rohde-Dachser states: "In Kohon's (1999) view female hysterics avoid a final definition of their sexual identity and remain on the level of bi-sexuality" (op. cit. p. 332). And: "The female hysteric alternates in her identification with male and female sexual designs, without ultimately tieing herself down by deciding on one of them." (op. cit. 341; transl. P.Z.).

The phenomenon of hysteria is that of the dissolution of concrete sexuality based on sexual difference in a sexualized cosmos carried by bi-sexual individuals with undefined sexual identity, and which is about the search for the possession of the phallic attribute that is detached from the concrete person of the father. The denial and destruction of the sexual difference then leads to the known regressive prevalence of pre—and paragenital interests and activities.

In my view this denial of the sexual difference by alternating projective identification within the primal scene, enforced on the psychic level while simultaneously maintaining reality consciousness about the fact of the difference between the sexes, is the cause for the hysteric tendency towards dissociation. At the same time, however, the alternating excessive projective identifications not only dissolve the differentiation between the sexual genders, but as a side-effect, so to speak, also the boundaries of identity itself, one's own and that of the Other. Hence the theme of the hysteric's proneness towards identification and projection, and his or her suggestibility.

81

The phallic capacity, over which the battle of hysteria is waged, as we know comes into being through the position outside, out of which the father imago constitutes itself. The two central effects of the position outside are reflexive awareness and access to reality as the result of the suspension of primary object splitting. The ability to access reality in turn culminates in the recognition and acknowledgement of the sexual difference which is constitutive for the Oedipal formulation of the parental relationship in the formation of the imago of the primal scene.

The growing awareness of the sexual difference is the sign and symbol of the ability to perceive reality; it is what this newly acquired ability brings about in the first place, and how it provides evidence for its truth. The difference between the sexes and reality are therefore psychically speaking synonymical factors. The attack against one is always also directed against the other.

If then it proves impossible to gain possession of the phallic capacity of the father in the primal scene, the hysteric ego turns against the process which led to this experience of castration, consequently turns against reality, the gender difference and sexuality that manifests through it, turns against reflexive awareness. It is evident that this addresses the main symptom areas of hysteria. Wolfgang Loch, in his work on hysteria, described the hysteric defense as such: "Not seeing, not hearing, not feeling, saying nothing, and—this in particular—not knowing (1985, p. 136; transl. P.Z.).

Christa Rohde-Dachser, in reference to the notion "to have to concede the mother to the father and to be excluded from the primal scene oneself" (op. cit. p. 337; transl. P.Z.) speaks of a suspension of thinking and points to Bion's (1959) "attacks on linking" and to André Green who, in this context, speaks of a "phobic position" (2000b, p. 429) which concerns thinking. If, in the introduction to her work, she understands the "hysterical defense (...) as a double negation with which both the symbolic castration and one's own sexuality is being denied" (op. cit. p. 331; transl. P.Z.), I am going to extend this definition to a triad: denial of the threat of castration, of the gender difference, and of reflexive awareness.

Amongst these three I consider the denial of reflexive awareness the central moment, from the point of view of the genetics of structure formation, for it contains the reference back to that developmental step which constitutes entry into the symbolic order in the first place, namely taking up of the position of the ego outside the drive phantasma. I assume that hysteria in fact turns against and opposes the whole process which has been triggered with this crucially important developmental step. And I think that this—that is to say independent of any possible additional traumatisation or fixation which often enough is not really there or at least cannot be proven to exist—represents the early core disturbance of hysteria, that is to say the regular connection to orality. For the developmental step of the position outside lies in the middle of the oral phase, approximately at the turn of the first six months of life.

It is furthermore enlightening how Freud in his work of 1909 "General Remarks on Hysterical Attacks" deducts the origin of the hysterical blurring of consciousness: "The loss of consciousness, the 'absence' in a hysterical attack is derived from the fleeting but unmistakable lapse of consciousness which is observable at the climax of every intense sexual satisfaction, including auto-erotic ones. (...) The so-called 'hypnoid states'—absences during day-dreaming-, which are so common in hysterical subjects, show the same origin. The mechanism of these absences is comparatively simple. All the subject's attention is concentrated, to begin with, on the course of the process of satisfaction; with the occurrence of the satisfaction, the whole of this cathexis of attention is suddenly removed, so that there ensues a momentary void in consciousness. This gap in consciousness, which might be termed a physiological one, is then widened in the service of repression, till it can swallow up everything that the repressing agency rejects" (Freud 1909, pp. 233).

According to Freud the hysterical hypnoid state—the "widened gap in consciousness" brought about by the denial of reflexive awareness—comes about in an explicitly sexual manner and derives from the function of orgasm. Insofar as the latter, the sexual satisfaction, never takes place without accompanying phantasy, one can assume that in the hysteric a denial of the threat of castration lies at the bottom of this phantasy. In this way, therefore, both events of denial are combined, and the path on which the suspension of the reflexive awareness of the position outside is sought, is precisely the transgression of that prohibition—that is to say the threat of castration—that results from the position outside and underlines its importance: namely the necessary non-identity of the ego with itself, which is the condition for the suspension of the early object splitting and which has been psychically expressed in the form of the commandment of non-identity with the father; the so-to-speak operative manifestation of which is the threat of castration.

From the denial of the reflexive awareness in the hypnoid states of the hysterical blurring of consciousness results, in Christa Rohde-Dachser's formulation, "a constant to and fro between the poles of the imaginary and the symbolic order, or, to use a term created by Bollas (2000, pp. 71), *the order in the name of the mother* (in French: du nom de la mère) and *the order in the name of the father* (in French: du nom du père). The motherly order is the one of the imaginary, recruiting itself from inner images and phantasies; the fatherly order represents difference, language, reality, and law" (op. cit. p. 342, italics R.-D.; transl. P.Z.).

84

In this manner the typical situation for hysteria comes about, namely that the crude sexual themes and symptoms in the hypnoid area of the personality may be juxtaposed with an aseptic or even ascetic asexuality and anhedonia in the area of the conscious identity. Anna O. is the model case for this. Breuer reports that in 1880, at the beginning of her treatment, she was after all a 21-year-old attractive and intelligent young woman who had never even shown an inkling of erotic involvement and, equally so, had consciously not entertained any sexual thoughts at all.

This is not to do with the special rigidity of a repressional defense but with the fact that—as Bollas (2000) also pointed out—the lived sexuality would presuppose an acknowledgement of the difference between the sexes and thus an acknowledgement of the separation of the union with the mother. (For Bollas, though, this is about a real experience of unity, while I consider the phantasy of the fusional unity the leading phantasma of the death drive.)

I would go one step further, however, and want to point out that sexuality in the area of conscious experience and thus of clear perception of reality must be strictly circumvented because otherwise, the denial of the perception of the sexual difference as such—that is to say as perception of a piece of reality—could not be maintained. This is therefore, so my argument goes, not a repression, but a dissociation.

To sum up, the "internal theatre" (Rohde-Dachser) of hysteria therefore arises from the hysteric's denial reaction to the phallic castration, and to the act of exclusion and the state of being excluded from the primal scene, which the phallic castration expresses. It arises above all from the ensuing forceful intrusion of the hysteric into the primal scene via projective identification with both sides of the primal couple, as well as, further, from the phantasies which he or she comes up with about what happens in the primal scene, and which come to play in his or her phantasmatic enactments. It arises from the envy and the jealousy, from the projection of one's own aggression and from the feelings of annihilation resulting from both this projected aggression in the sense of an attack by a hostile primal scene imagination and from the subject's own rage attack onto the primal scene and its phantasized destruction; it arises from guilt and shame, and finally from the attack on the foundations and consequences of the primal scene imagination, that is to say, the position outside, reflexive thinking, the difference between the sexes, the thought links (attacks on linking), procreativity and creativity in general.

It seems to me that a word on the theme of seduction is in place here, a theme which had troubled Freud at his early original reflections on hysteria, insofar as he initially took the frequent reports of his female patients about actual abuse seriously. A theme that, as it were, persecutes him beyond the grave when today he is accused of having relabeled these facts out of "conventional horror" into phantasies of his abused female patients, and thus of having built psychoanalysis on a lie, not to mention the betrayal of his patients.

The problem in my opinion lies in the fact that the denial activity of the hysteric against the threat of castration, the sexual difference, and the reflexive awareness leads him or her onto a structural path of regression where he or she, at the level of the hypnoid state of awareness, actually does take back the position outside and thus loses the basic access to reality, so that the differentiation between inside and outside cannot apply any more; key word here being the early core of the disturbance in hysteria. The functional states of the hysteric, which are close to psychosis, are well known.

This differentiation between inside and outside which is lost implies that, in the experience of the subject, a phantasy can assume the full and complete appearance of an outer event. The theoretical mistake which often makes an assessment impossible here is that of assuming a confusion of self and object differentiation for the earliest phases of development. The actual confusion, however, does not lie in the differentiation of the ego and the object or the object imago, which is there from the beginning, but in the confusion of what belongs to the reality aspect of the ego, on the one hand, and of the object, on the other. For reality as an independent variable has gone missing due to the attack of denial with regard to the position outside. This is the specific hallucinatory quality of hysteria, that makes for its phenomenological closeness to psychosis.

Hence the danger arises to take a subjective memory, which has all characteristics of clearly delineated ego and object experiencing, for probable reality because of these very characteristics, and to overlook the fact that the decisive point lies elsewhere. This, in my view, is one of the prime examples for the extent to which a wrong theoretical basic assumption relative to the early development may lead to a complete misjudgement of a clinical fact and this misjudgement is such that it cannot be remedied out of itself.

Finally I would like to point out an elucidating differentiation by Britton on the differential diagnostic delineation of hysteria from the borderline states: "Like André Green (1997 pp. 39-42) I see hysteria as a distinct psychoanalytic state that though it has features in common with the borderline syndrome is not the same. If I were to generalise about the difference between the essential thrust of the two syndromes it would be to say that in hysteria priority is given to the claim to possess the object in the realm of love whereas in the borderline syndrome the claim is to possess it in the realm of knowledge. Thus in hysteria the insistence is on possessing exclusively the analyst's love, leading to a transference 'illusion' that ignores the importance of any other reality than love and annihilates the analyst's erotic bonds with anyone else. In the borderline transference the insistence is on complete intersubjective understanding with the annihilation of anything that might hint at the analyst having derived knowledge from or shared significant knowledge with anyone else.

As a consequence of the different use of projective identification in hysteria and the borderline syndrome, a major diagnostic difference is in the analyst's experience of the transference and the countertransference. (...) The characteristic countertransference in the analysis of the borderline patient (...) is one of feeling constrained or tyrannised. In contrast, until the hysterical defensive organisation breaks down the analyst's feeling is of being especially important, and the risk is of an unconscious collusive partnership of mutual admiration" (1999, pp. 11).

In my opinion, this difference that Britton highlights has to do with the fact that in hysteria, the elaboration of the parental imagos has reached the level of an unavoidably sexual interpretation, carried by the full power of sensual reality perception, while the theme of the borderline constitution has to do more directly with the principally cognitive changes and problematical issues resulting from taking up the position of the ego outside the drive phantasma; that is to say, with that leap that leads to the suspension of the primary splitting world with its paranoia and depression and which introduces a principle into the psychic cosmos the experiencing of which can only be called magical and which sexually, later on, will be captured in the imago of the phallus.

When the borderline patient is after the analyst's knowledge, and wants this knowledge not to be conditioned by anything else, that is to say wants it to be absolute, and wants to enter with this knowledge into a mystical communion, it is about the hunt for the phallus on the structural level of the borderline constitution. The borderline patient wants to own the means which has brought about that magical change, and, once he possesses it, so the calculation goes, he can suspend the unwelcome consequences which come with this change: namely, to make the realization of the death drive impossible.

Before this psychodynamic background presented so far, in hysteria the typical sexualization of the delay of gratification, of "not now, later" is the result of the constitutive denial both of the difference between the sexes and the threat of castration, for the realization of sexual union would confront the hysteric, female but also male, not only with the denied difference between the sexes but also with the very impossibility to "create access for oneself to the mother's body after all in the identification with the penis of the father who enters into the mother" (Rohde Dachser, op. cit. p. 351; transl. P.Z.). This is the phallic threat of castration, or experience thereof, or—as Christa Rohde-Dachser names it quoting Lacan—the symbolic castration.

The hysteric idealization of the specifically absent or unreachable man (or woman) has, by the way, the same purpose as the delay of gratification itself, namely that of avoiding the realization of the threat of castration which is being denied. Bollas (2000, p. 26), in the same context, has pointed out that the theme of unrequited love is a specifically hysterical pattern. In the same sense of this denial "even the idealization of the father, which, from the point of view of the female hysteric must be upheld at all cost (Israël 1976), upon closer inspection proves to be an erotization of something unattainable, while sexual fulfillment is being moved to the unreachable beyond" (Rohde-Dachser, p. 346; transl. P.Z.).

Similarly, the hysteric games of confusion, according to which the male or female hysteric, as a rule, can never be found where someone is looking for him or her, are equally an expression of that same denial of the difference between the sexes and the threat of castration, for one must not be found, as this would confront one with the untenability of denial and furthermore affirm reality which is being negated by the hysteric in the same movement of withdrawing one's presence. The simultaneous hysterical sexualization, in so far as it serves the theme of erotic manipulation of the Other in the sense of exercising power over him, thereby serves to maintain the phantasy of, in reality, possessing and controlling the fatherly phallus.

The hysteric struggle against the physical body and the physical sexual lust, which is being waged based on the connotation with the sexual difference, can further lead to the ascetic and anorectic forms of expression of hysteria on the one hand, and on the other to the transformation of sexual excitement into suffering and pain, in the conversion symptoms and equally in the hysterical functional disorders and the hysteric pain syndromes.

The critical train of thought for understanding the importance of the primal scene imagination in the inner theatre of hysteria, in any case, is that the position outside is based on the ability of the child to maintain the memory of the good object also in its factual absence, that is to say, to endure the fear of its destruction, implying the child's belief, acquired during the conflict of the depressive position, in its own reparation ability. This leads to the establishment of what Britton (1995, p. 120-127) calls "the other room", that of the imagination. "I suggested (...) that the 'other room' of the imagination comes into existence developmentally when the primary object is believed to continue existing in its perceptual absence. It is the place where the object spends its invisible existence. I think it is conceived inevitably as in relationship with another object that is a condition of existence. The 'other room' is, in other words, the location of the invisible *primal scene*" (1999, pp. 7, italics R.B.).

This other room, the room of the imagination, thus becomes the room of the primal scene, whereby Britton's formulation remains somewhat vague as to how the father comes into play here. The understanding that I propose, however, makes this totally clear, for the father is the very personalization of the dynamic effect of the position outside, namely to overcome the splitting of the object. And the core of the 'position of the ego outside the drive phantasma' consists in the ability, suddenly available at a certain moment in time, of the child to place itself next to its direct experiencing of the immediate present, and, with a reflexive distance towards its depressive fears, to maintain the inner representation of the good object also in the object's absence.

It is important to note that in this view the primal scene is first of all the mental version and imaginative formulation of two immensely positive events, namely one, of the child's ability to maintain the idea of the good split-object also in its absence, and two, of the effect which arises from the related ability of the child to step outside its own experiencing and take a reflexive position, namely of the effect of the suspension of the primary object splitting, and thus of access to reality. The primal scene captures this dynamic development into a picture, in which the effect on the imago of the primary object, namely to achieve the suspension of its splitting, is being ascribed to a personalized force, step by step with the identification of this imago and this force with the real persons—mother and father—and their investiture with the insignia of sexuality.

That way the primal scene is and remains the most important image, the most important phantasma of the psyche, for in it lies the key to overcoming the terrors of splitting, and access to reality.

It is important for one thing to realize this, because, if considered in this way, it is incorrect to understand the primal scene primarily and basically as the cause and sign for the separation of the child from the mother, as it is being reflected for instance when Christa Rohde-Dachser speaks of the "phantasma of the invisible primal scene", "which from the viewpoint of the child is the cause for the absence of the mother" (op. cit. p. 333; transl. P.Z.). The primal scene is first of all the image of a colossal presence, namely of the ability to maintain a psychical presence of the absent object and to build up a reflexive frustration tolerance against the depressive anxieties connected with the absence. It is an adultomorphic misunderstanding to consider the primal scene as something primarily real, over which, as it were, the child must stumble in the outside world and which it must cope with. It is primarily a pure intrapsychical production which agrees with reality, a fact that is only gradually being discovered by the child, or also, which the child itself constructs and develops.

The moment of separation only comes into play when the child fails in the attempt to put itself in the place of the father in the primal scene, and to establish the unity with the primary object via the father, via his dynamic potential; in other words, when the child is being confronted with the phallic threat of castration. Only then does it experience the exclusion from the primal scene and experiences the primal scene as the separation from the object. When looked at in this way, this experience of separation is synonymous with the threat of castration, here we have the two sides of the same coin. However, the primal scene is principally never simply the sign for separation, this is a crass reduction and one-sided view of its meaning, it already is the reduction which is the effect of pathology.

As noted above in the discussion of the seduction theory of hysteria, I have already pointed out the occasional fatal consequences of incorrect theoretical assumptions. The theory is, in many instances, the microscope without which we could not grasp certain clinical states at all and assess their meaning. For this reason it is a question of life and death, in my opinion, for psychoanalysis as a science, to develop a theory of structural ontogenesis which can be taken as a binding basic concept and reference system. Without such basic theory, psychoanalysis as a scientific discipline will suffocate from its own theoretical outgrowths, its entropy.

As one example of such outgrowth I regard Bollas' (2000) theory of hysteria, where he proceeds from the assumption that the child, in normal development, through a combination of threat of castration and oedipal seduction must be enticed to give up the auto-erotic stimulation and enter into the stage of object love. He speaks of the necessity of the "parental seduction of the child's heterosexual desire (or homosexual desire, if the case so be) lest the child remain in the autistic universe of imagined objects and hand-held reliefs" (p. 35). "By seducing the child into intense love of the mother, the human race uses her body as the lure to drive the child out of the solipsistic world of auto-erotism" (p. 37).

With reference to the hysterical pathology, he writes: "Hysterical symptoms not only ensure the private continuation of auto-erotic life, they also constitute a rebellion against the claims of object love" (p. 36). Of course Bollas can invoke a whole host of Freud quotations which describe the interrelationship between hysterical symptoms and masturbation. The problem lies in constructing a theory out of this, in which Oedipal object love is set against an auto-erotic solipsism and the threat of castration is primarily seen as the means to prevent masturbation, only secondarily receiving its Oedipal meaning.

As a matter of fact, however, we find that the child, from the beginning, has an intense relationship with the primary object, and that the project of Oedipal development consists solely and exclusively in linking this representation of the internal object with reality, opening the path for it. Confronted with the threat of castration the hysteric pushes through to the 'other room' of the imagination, as described by Britton, where the primal scene happens, and attempts to

93

become a part of this primal scene through the violent act of projective identification. The hysteric masturbation is part of this process, insofar as it serves the attempt to give the incestuous phantasies a sensual reality and reason.

At the same time, however, masturbation is linked with the hysterical struggle against reality as the place of the confrontation both with the threat of castration and the difference between the sexes. Masturbation underpinned with incestuous phantasies is to dissolve the connection of satisfaction to reality—that is to say, override reality in its importance as the only place, where, in the words of Woody Allen, you can get good steaks—in order to, in this way, open the path for structural regression. There is of course an interrelationship with the events in the 'other room'. In no case, however, can one deduct from this clear process of disintegration and illness a reputedly normal autoerotic-autistic-solipsistic early constitution, the existence of which would be evidenced by the hysteric who, according to Bollas, allegedly has not relinquished this constitution.

In order to further break down the spectrum of the theoretical misunderstandings and confusions, I would like to more extensively quote Christa Rohde-Dachser, who in her very instructive and helpful paper on the psychodynamics of hysteria brilliantly presents and summarizes the respective psychoanalytic theoretical approaches. The critical examination of these theoretical approaches, cumbersome as it may be, has the great advantage that one can demonstrate here, by using an important theoretical detail, how easily theoretical formulations go astray. Although they grasp a clinical fact correctly, they do not place it in the field of tension of the drive antagonism, and insofar do not comprehend it as a manifestation of only one of the two drives. Consequently, in quite a few cases, genetic reconstructions are made back to a primordial constitution of the psyche purportedly resulting from the clinical fact—for instance by claiming an early fusional-symbiotic mother-child union and a corresponding fusion of the representations—which in reality only depict the leading phantasma of the death drive, which is the agency responsible for symptom production in the first place. I have, therefore, in the following excerpted those passages from the text of Christa Rohde-Dachser which illustrate these misunderstandings:

"By primal scene I understand, and I am following Freud here, the phantasies of the small child about the sexual union of the parents in which it has no share itself. The primal scene, therefore, symbolically also represents the separation of the mother-child union and the introduction of difference into the originally symbiotic universe. This includes the difference between inside and outside, between ego and Other, between man and woman as well as between the generations" (op. cit. p. 334; transl. P.Z.).

First of all, this is only a further elaboration of what was said before. The fact that the small child has no share in the sexual union of the parents is not part of the original, genuine meaning of the primal scene, which, as already mentioned, is primarily an intrapsychic production of the child, not simply the confrontation with an external fact. Rather, this not-having-a-share is already the formulation of the castration experience.

That the primal scene stands symbolically "for the separation of the mother-child-union and the introduction of difference into the originally symbiotic universe" (see above) I can only reject from my point of view. There is no mother-child-union and a symbiotic universe does not exist, these are erroneous conceptualizations which for one part result from the outside perspective, under conditions of human neoteny, onto the most intimate factual dependent relationship of the child with the mother and onto the deep vegetative and emotional

95

connection of mother and child; for the more important part perhaps they derive from the phantasmagoria of the sick on the nature of the mother-child relationship, of course also from our own death-drive related longings.

Psychic experiencing, from the beginning, spans the poles of ego and primary object which factually has not yet become an "Other" in the sense of conforming to reality; and that this difference was introduced only through the primal scene into the "originally symbiotic universe" runs counter to the whole clinical reality of what we know about early splitting processes.

When Christa Rohde-Dachser goes on to relate "the difference between inside and outside, between ego and 'Other', between man and woman, and between the generations" (see above) to the primal scene, this is summarily correct, but should we not ask why these things should be related? There is, in this list, a decisive hierarchy: the central moment is the differentiation between inside and outside, the other items depend on it, to be exact, they depend on access to reality. But why should the primal scene bring about this differentiation between inside and outside, access to reality? A simple answer would be because the primal scene, conceived as the sexual union of the parents, does take place in the outside and the child is confronted with this. With this argumentation we are, however, caught in a tautological trap. How should perception of the primal scene as an outside event come about, if perception of the outside—according to Rohde-Dachser—only becomes possible through the primal scene?

It is obvious that more exact information is necessary here. In my opinion, this information is to be found in the conceptualization of the primal scene as the phantasmatic definition of overcoming the early good-bad split of the object through the position outside which does open up access to reality. Only then can the external parents be perceived at all in their reality and be brought into congruence with the primal scene imago that is being formed, only then can the difference between the sexes be recognized and used for defining the parental relationship, and last but not least, only then can the "Other" in the perceptual external world be localized and purposefully entered into contact with, one's own body really be recognized as "ego" and cathected.

Christa Rohde-Dachser continues: "Up until that time the child could feel itself to be the center of maternal attention. Now it discovers that the mother also entertains a quite specific relationship with the father. 'It is NOT I *(but the phallus) who (what) she wants*' is the consequence drawn from this (Kohon, 1999 p. 8, italics and emphasis Kohon). With this insight the child enters into the symbolic order. In the symbolic order the law of the father applies, which puts a stop to the child's unlimited enjoyment of the mother. Lacan (1975) designates this step therefore also as 'symbolic castration' which is indispensable for the human subjectivization" (op. cit. p. 334; transl. P.Z.).

This "NOT I..." is no doubt the one formulation of the phallic castration experience in which the oedipal competition is most clearly expressed. It is, however, not the only one and surely not the fundamental one. The fundamental experience is that of the appropriated phallus of the father losing its power. In this way the task of the phallic castration expresses itself, namely to secure the non-identity of the place of the father with the place of the ego and thus to guarantee the functional principle of the position outside.

We must differentiate more clearly, therefore, that the child does not enter the symbolic order with the 'symbolic castration', but before this, with the step of taking up the position outside. This is the crucial step which suspends the primary splitting constitution. Insofar as the ego, with this step, enters into the reflexive distance to itself, this step is

97

correctly described as the entry into the symbolic order. It makes a big difference, however, whether one links this step with an achievement of the ego or with the experience of a prohibition. I remind the reader that the full formulation of the position outside is that of "taking up the position of the ego outside of the drive phantasma".

If, further, Christa Rohde-Dachser references Lacan, saying that the symbolic castration, or the law of the father, respectively, "puts a stop to the child´s unlimited enjoyment of the mother", we must then ask what unlimited enjoyment this might refer to? In my opinion this is also about a shared phantasy between analysts and patients, that such unlimited enjoyment might have taken place at all. This expresses a theoretical idealization of the earliest childhood which has its precipitate also in the typical formulations of 'mother-child-union' and the 'originally symbiotic universe'. From the beginning, and certainly also in utero, the child has to cope with the unavoidable physiological tensions of unpleasure, even if all further accidental causes of unpleasure were excluded by optimal mothering, which in this manner is not possible at all.

All this is, however, not really about the quantification of unpleasure. The problem is that already by a relative minimum of factual unpleasure the process of the drive dynamics is being triggered which consists in the early ego's development of the phantasy of fusional merging with the object representation, in order to absorb the source for the abolishment of unpleasure into one's own omnipotence. But this attracts the counterreaction of the life drive in the shape of the formation of the deterring split imago.

I have shown that from this dynamic interplay the ego development and the structuring of the psychic organism is generated, and one would do best to assume that already relatively minor amounts of unpleasure are sufficient to trigger this process, and that it builds itself up and escalates to its full impetus, simply and purely because this is necessary and intended by the course of development, that is to say in other words, results from the system properties of the dimension of the human psyche.

If it is important that mothers do not expose their babies to traumatic stress; if mothers are endowed with a special sensorium in order to feel the needs of their children, then this is not in order to afford them unlimited enjoyment, but rather to avoid inciting the, as it is, dramatic confrontation of the drives in the early splitting world to a degree which could not be dealt with by the instruments of the ego that are only about to take shape. The goal to basically spare suffering and enable unlimited enjoyment is an illusion, a precipitate of the objective of the death drive.

Christa Rohde-Dachser goes on: "Connected with this (with the symbolic castration) is the acknowledgement of one's own limitation and of the feeling of lack which has taken the place of the lost object and which accompanies human life from there on. The experience of lack is the inevitable other side of the coin of human desire which strives for the restitution of full satisfaction with the lost object, a satisfaction that lies outside of human possibilities and is thus unachievable.

The hysteric development refuses this acknowledgement and maintains the belief that an object of desire exists which promises full satisfaction. The step into the symbolic order therefore is only half taken" (op. cit. p. 334; transl. P.Z.).

Here we have a further theoretical mythologem of psychoanalysis, namely the idea of the lost object and the experience of lack as the inevitable other side of human desire, which strives for restitution of full satisfaction with the lost object. It is easy to see that behind this theoretical conception hides what I consider the vision of fulfillment of the death drive, namely the wish of the ego to bring the object under its total control and to merge with it in order to eliminate the cause of each and every lack in this way.

Therefore, this is not about a lost early state, or precisely the "lost object", but about the phantasma, the utopia of one of the two basic drives. This is why I consider it so dangerous to regard this phantasy, even only in theory, as a justified striving for a real condition that once existed, for by doing so, one involuntarily coalesces with that force which is responsible for all forms of psychic pathology. It would be easy to demonstrate and it is evident that this position, carried through to its conclusion, results in a specific category of serious technical mistakes which have occupied the psychoanalytic discourse from the beginning. This is, therefore, not about engaging in pointless argument. In any case, the theme of the necessary renunciation of the lost object is the counter piece to the illusion of the unlimited enjoyment.

It has to do with interrelationships like these that I sceptically look upon formulations like the one that symbolic castration is linked to the recognition of one's own limitation and recognition of the lack as the inevitable other side of human desire, as for me, this compares to the attempt to pull the teeth out of the death drive. It seems to me that the demand for such recognition carries strong traits of a countercathexis. The male or female hysteric, in any case, are not prepared and willing to give such recognition.

In my opinion, there is only one valid solution to the conflict of the drives, and this is the insight that the threat of castration in reality protects the ego from its annihilation, and, to spin this thought further yet, that the ego itself, in the threat of castration, formulates the principle of its own security and safety insofar as the threat of castration results from the position outside which, as we know, is taken up by the ego itself, and is an achievement of the early ego.

Christa Rohde-Dachser summarizes the results of her examination on the current status of the psychoanalytic considerations on the psychodynamics of hysteria in the following manner: "The renunciation of the illusion to be the idealized child—in the language of psychoanalysis: the phallus of the mother—is not carried through, the recognition of the symbolic castration is refused. In the hysteric phantasy there is no fertile parental couple from which a child springs forth. In the omnipotent universe of the female hysteric only dyadic relationships exist, where she alternately projectively identifies with the positions offered in the primal scene. Entry into the symbolic order is refused. Instead, the daughter attempts to get access to the womb of the mother after all by identifying with the penis of the father which enters into the mother.

Whether the act of hanging on to this stage of internal development is the inevitable consequence of deficient motherly care and mirroring in the first years of the child's life, or whether it is an active refusal to accept the symbolic castration and instead maintain the phantasy of an object that promises total fulfillment, cannot be finally decided here. The more the process of symbolization has progressed at this point in the development, the more the scales will probably tip towards an active refusal. It is my impression that hanging on to an inner omnipotent universe where phantasies are unlimited is not only exciting, but also holds out the prospect of finding the lost object again, and be that in an ever so far away future. Solely from this perspective it is not only owed to the safety principle, but contains an active, narcissistically triumphant 'no' to the limitations of the symbolic order" (op. cit. pp. 350; transl. P.Z.).

Christa Rohde-Dachser here has captured the theoretical problem of hysteria in an admirable way and thus also formulated the reason why, in my view, a new formulation of the dualistic drive concept as

I have suggested cannot be avoided: Only through an understanding of the drive confrontation in which its contents are argumentatively discussed—namely about the attempt, inherent in the human condition and existence, to establish unity with the need-satisfying object, and about reactions to the dangers which grow unrecognized from such an attempt—does it become understandable why the subject, for internal reasons, should oppose the symbolic order and thus should oppose the continuation of its own development.

Without such a theoretical turn which opens up a thorough dynamic formulation of the processes of pathology, what remains is only the theoretically crude and unsatisfying alternative to speak of an—in this stringent etiological causality so far unproven—"unavoidable consequence of deficient motherly care and mirroring in the first years of the child's life" (see above), which allegedly brings about the search for the lost object and for the unlimited enjoyment of the mother within a symbiotic universe; and further, to list the pathological symptoms and manifestations, without being able to put them into a more than fragmentary and systematizing context with only partial approaches for explanation, for instance, as the consequence of a conventionally and descriptively conceptualized Oedipus complex.

12

Psychogenic encapsulated autism

Earlier in this work I have already discussed the infantile psychogenic autism described by Frances Tustin (1972, 1981), asking the question of the representability of the bad object in the primary narcissistic phase before representational object constancy is reached. Under the aspect of general psychopathology I would like to take up this discussion again with a fundamental examination, for infantile psychogenic autism is, as we know, the first form of a mental illness. One should, therefore, be allowed to proceed from the assumption that the circumstances of the ego's relationship with the primary object and the complications arising from this, which this work has tried to hypothetically identify in a logical deduction and conclusion procedure, must still represent themselves directly in this genetically earliest illness. Let me first of all briefly present the conception of the illness and its psychogenesis and psychodynamic aspects as Tustin describes them.

Historically, the clinical picture of this illness as such was first described and named by Kanner in 1944 as 'Early Infantile Autism'. Tustin basically distinguishes two genetic causes of infantile autism: "I have come to realise that autism may arise in several different situations—for example, as a reaction to brain damage or to sensory defect, as well as to a traumatic situation which seems to threaten life and limb. The latter is the type of autism I have treated with a certain amount of success" (1991, p. 585).

This not primarily organically caused form of autism was labelled as psychogenic autism by Tustin. Within psychogenic autism she describes two forms of the illness, the encapsulation type and the confusional type, whereby she equates the encapsulated form with the (non-organic) Kannerian autism regarding it as the genetically earlier illness, the first signs and symptoms showing already at or shortly after birth.

Both forms of the illness, according to Tustin, have their cause in the fact that the newborn experiences the primary object in a premature and traumatic way as outside the reach of its own omnipotent control, as not-me object. This is the "traumatic situation which seems to threaten life and limb". The encapsulation type reacts to this trauma—or sequence of traumas—by breaking off all contact with the object, and he does that before the primary attachment is established, by excluding the object from psychic perception and withdrawing into a delusional state of encapsulation. The confusional type of autism does not break off connection with the primary object, but the child attempts to engulf the object and/or enter it, to become entangled with it, by using archaic-concretistic pre-forms of projective identification in order to, in this way, delusionally reverse the separation which was experienced as traumatic.

Firstly, I would like to point out that Tustin thus matter-of-factly assumes an ego-function as the carrier of perception and experiencing right from the beginning of mental life, which equally matter-of-factly interacts with an archaic object representation. This is congruent with the central postulates of my own work. Tustin comments how she could imagine that the encapsulation type might experience an already intra-uterine appearance of the traumatic not-me experience of the primary object. In both forms of the autistic illness, however, she postulates the decisive traumatizations within the first four months of life, which she describes as 'postnatal womb', as postnatal uterus. This is the stage, in my terminology, before the position outside is acquired, where the ego has no access to reality yet and struggles with the subjectively defined primary object. Tustin calls this the 'autosensual mother'.

The trauma of the premature not-me experience of the object signifies the loss of the primary narcissistic illusion of omnipotent control over the primary object, that is to say, the loss of the illusion, more precisely of the delusion, to be able to absorb the experience of lack psychically via control of the object as the source to remedy and suspend this lack. The ego would then be exposed to the physiological experience of this lack, without protection. The autistic pathology is the attempt of a counterreaction to this unbearable state.

For the purposes of my investigation I will concentrate in the following on the encapsulation type of infantile autism, as it represents the reaction to the genetically primary situation and therefore must illustrate it exactly.

These children do not establish contact with their parents or other people, they avoid eye contact, are mute as a rule and not clean. In Tustin's words: "Since his first traumatic experience of bodily separateness, the child has had virtually no sense of bodily separateness. (...). (.). For most of the time the child behaves as if fused with the outside world, and outside objects are experienced as a prolongation of his bodily sensations or movements. In his state of imitative fusion, everything is experienced as "me", (...).(..) the 'not-me' is quickly made into 'me', by feeling that it is part of his body and under his control" (1981, p. 29).

This state of imitative fusion might easily be misunderstood as evidence for a primary symbiotic undifferentiatedness of the ego and object representations, both with reference to the situation in autism and extrapolated to normal development, as the official doctrine had also propagated for a long time. Tustin however clarifies that we are dealing with a defensive formation against the traumatic not-me experience here. The core of the imitative fusion is the denial, more exactly the foreclosure of the objectality of the object, in the sense of its independence separate from the ego, which expresses itself traumatically in the not-me object. The crucial point here is that this is about the <u>simulation</u> of fusional merging via the path of imitation. The fusional symptomatology thus serves as defense against the traumatic perception about the separation from the object, is thus a pathological distortion in the sense of denial and reaction formation.

The imitative fusion, in this sense, naturally carries a special meaning and importance within the mother-child relationship: "Almost invariably, the *Encapsulated* child has an obviously good contact with the father, but seems to shut out the mother, although on a deeper level there is an underground connection going on between them, based on imitation and on fringe cues such as muscle 'sets' and tones of voice. However, their fusion is not obvious. (...) The Encapsulated child is in a state of imitative fusion with the mother, echopraxia and echolalia being striking examples of this" (pp. 60).

This imitative fusion is, according to Tustin, not the expression of a hidden but close relationship or attachment in the objectal sense, but much to the contrary, the manifestation of the rigid denial of any potential not-me quality of the mother. In this same sense she speaks of "(...) tricks such children use to get other people to do things for them, in order to maintain the delusion that the 'not-me' world is part of their body and under their control. Their passivity and lack of development of their capacities is also part of these 'tactics'" (p. 29).

Tustin describes the mechanisms which the autistic child uses to maintain the state of imitative fusion, whereby these mechanisms at the same time preserve the kind of perception of this earliest period in life when this primitive mode of defense of imitative fusion developed. Hence these mechanisms provide invaluable insight into the quality of perception within a psychical constitution which as yet does not know a differentiation between inside and outside, between animate and inanimate, between one's own body and the real object, and where perception is still directly identical with experiencing, as at this time neither object constancy and thus memory, nor the ability of symbol formation connected with the position outside, have been acquired:

"Such a child lives mostly in terms of the outlines of shapes and the sensations aroused by touching, or seeming to touch, surface contours. Touch seems to be the predominant mode of experience, and seeing, hearing and even smelling are felt to be tactile experiences. (...) 'Looking' and 'hearing' are felt to make things exist. 'Not-looking' and 'not-hearing' are felt to 'black out' their existence—to make them not exist.

Such a child makes no distinction between animate and inanimate. People are treated as things which are an extension of his own bodily 'things'. He does not draw on paper, but he makes shapes with his faeces in his anus or the tongue in his mouth. These shapes are felt to be made on surfaces. The child has no sense of their being inside, for he has only two-dimensional awareness. He has virtually no fantasies or thoughts. His experience is on a concrete, physical, tactile surface level.

In outward expression, such children are predominantly asymbolic, although not completely so. Their psychological functioning has been halted at a very rudimentary level by awareness of bodily separateness which they experienced as traumatic. It had been a catastrophe when they realised that the sensation-giving mother was not part of their body. (...) As a reaction to this unbearable disturbance, he cultivates the illusion that he is fused with hard objects. By his withdrawal he feels he turns his hard back to protect his soft front. The encapsulation mechanisms also protect his vulnerable softness.

This total encapsulation to form the delusion of a protective shell is characteristic of global, undifferentiated states and is a primary pathological autistic manoeuvre" (1981, pp. 29).

When Tustin speaks about the fact that seeing, hearing, and smelling are translated into tactile experiences by the autistic child, this must not be regarded as a mere, for instance, neurological idiosyncrasy. The sensory modalities of seeing, hearing, and smelling are rather the distance perception modalities. By suspending their proper character and coenesthetically incorporating them into the tactile register, the autist also here turns against perceiving the separation of the source of excitation from his own body, or the immediate ego and thus against the perceptual basis of the recognition of the separation from the object. As Tustin elaborates, this suspension of the perception of distance directly affects the experience of dimensionality—the third dimension, space, must not be experienced. Thus an inside and outside are not available, in the same way as the differentiation of the criteria of animate and inanimate would imply the recognition of an existence separate from the ego, and therefore is ruled out. Due to the undifferentiatedness and asymbolic quality of the mental functioning of these children it can be assumed that it is not the defense against the separation from the object which actively engenders these deficiencies of perception, but that the defense that expresses the aims of the death drive fixated the formal qualities of perception which it encounters on the organizational level existing at the time of the occurrence of the trauma and where, for instance, the perception of the third dimension, the differentiation between inside and outside, and of inanimateness and autonomous animateness, had not been given yet.

Tustin writes: "The Encapsulated child lives in a two-dimensional world. He is preoccupied with surfaces, textures and shapes. If he gets inside an object, for him it is not the getting *inside* which is significant—he is not aware of that as such—it is the sensation of being covered up, of being sheltered and protected which matters. He is forever seeking analogies and identities in terms of shapes. Things which seem dissimilar to us are equated by him on the basis of their sharing some characteristics which is important to the child" (1981, p. 42).

The artificial shapes that are created in this way Tustin (1984) calls 'autistic sensation shapes'. The above mentioned hard objects with which the children identify, are, in her terminology (1980), 'autistic sensation objects'. According to Tustin "these seem to swathe such children in a sensual protective 'shell' which Esther Bick (1968, 1986) has aptly called 'a second skin'" (1991, p. 588). Tustin understands the pathognomic compulsory and perseverative search leading to the autistic sensation shapes—a search for formal analogies and artificial identities that dissolve the real boundaries of things—as the expression of the striving to suspend the differentiation between the self and the object. This she also bases on her understanding that the suspension of the differentiation between things is a characteristic of the anti-objectal quality of the fusional tendency. In this sense, this is an expansion of the imitative fusion.

Tustin points out that because the psychic functioning of these children is tied to two-dimensionality, no concept of an internal psychic space, or mind, can develop, which might contain thoughts, feelings, phantasies and memories, but which is also the basis for psychic mechanisms like projection, introjection, or projective identification. As no concept of their own inner space exists, such space cannot be ascribed to the object through the process of primary identification either, and from there be reintrojected again, a situation that supports the lacking differentiation between an animate and an inanimate world. Imitative behaviour, echopraxia and echolalia, and the obsessive search of these children for formal analogies in their turn support the sensorial binding to tactile experience of a two-dimensional kind which ignores the boundaries between real things. They are the mechanisms of foreclosure, or of the exclusion of the perception of the not-me, respectively. By that they secondarily support the lack of the concept of an inner space, in the person itself and in the object.

"There is no discrimination of differences [in autistic children]. Similarly fantasies are not present; only things that can be touched and handled to produce sensations are meaningful to autistic children who have been found to have no capacity for empathy (Hobson, 1986), and to lack imagination (Frith et al, 1985)" (1991, p. 589).

Tustin pointedly notes that the motive of the fusional striving of autistic children is the maintenance, or restitution, respectively, of omnipotent control over the object: "Insulated by the autism, the unhealthy omnipotence becomes monstrous, so that when they began to talk, autistic children will say such things as 'I am God', or 'I am a King'. In an autistic state they are unaware of their actual weakness and neediness. Also, their fusion with the mother and, later, the autism, mean that the father's influence is absent. Thus, they do not experience the discipline of sharing the mother with the father. This means that wayward omnipotence is not checked. Underneath their passive exteriors, autistic children are extremely wilful and tyrannical" (1991, p. 586).

Therefore, when Tustin speaks of the "unhealthy" and "wayward" omnipotence of autistic children and further, that they "in an autistic state (...) are unaware of their actual weakness and neediness", these are not, in my opinion, pathological changes of an original state, no matter what that state may be like. In fact, Tustin describes the global and total experiencing in the pre-schizoid phase, in which, as I have formulated earlier, the primary object is the all-that-is, outside of which nothing exists, and where, equally so, the ego in complete contrast to its real neotenous helplessness and weakness, experiences itself as not limited and not conditioned, because it does not yet experience its real boundaries and is not identified with them yet. I have identified this as that state which Freud had in mind when he described the constitution of primary narcissism; only that in my opinion, as I have outlined, the primary object which takes up the total space of psychic experiencing would be included in this constitution. I am convinced that the encapsulation autism preserves this primary narcissistic constitution and conveys an impression of the tremendous psychic impact which results when neither object nor ego are subjected to any kind of condition or real limitation. As I will still discuss later, it is from this totality and globality that the formative power derives which this primordial constitution has for the further life of the psyche.

The decisive point in the formation of the autistic pathology, Tustin goes on to describe, is that these children experience the trauma of the not-me quality of the primary object as a hole, or wound, respectively, in their own bodies, as this is how the traumatic collapse of the primary narcissistic illusion of omnipotent control over the object expresses itself. As the encapsulated children experience themselves and the object as inanimate, they tend to experience this collapse as a hole, while the confusional children who, at the time of the traumatization have already progressed a little further in their development, experience it as a wound. In both forms of autism the delusional phantasy develops to close the hole, or wound, respectively, with a kind of ritual thing called the autistic or confusional object, which an autistic child always carries on him. Because of these two shared characteristics, that is to

111

say the genesis from a traumatic not-me experience and the filling up of the traumatic void through a compensatory object, Tustin groups these two otherwise phenomenologically very different forms of childhood psychogenic autism into one uniform clinical picture.

In the encapsulated autist, the theme of the autistic hole is not only expression of the traumatic not-me experience alone, but more importantly and in particular, it is the expression of the post-traumatic active exclusion of the primary object from the psychic space. This exclusion concerns that manifestation of the primary object where the latter has become the traumatic not-me object. The traumatic events of which we speak here take place before the point in time when representational object constancy is reached. Therefore there is no splitting of the object which would presuppose the ability to maintain the good representation as a memory, in other words, would presuppose object constancy, but we have a succession of, on the one hand, foreclosure, and on the other, imitative fusion, as the reaction to the trauma. The autistic encapsulation serves to protect from this not-me object and represents a definitive separation, a dividing wall towards it. In my opinion, even if Tustin is not using the term, this psychic event we are dealing with here is a foreclosure, a foreclosure of the primary object in its not-me quality.

This very succession or, later, side-by-side of the foreclosure of the traumatic not-me version of the primary object and the reactive imitative fusion with its non-traumatic form of manifestation is evidence of the encapsulated autism being in fact about preserving the conditions of the pre-schizoid phase, for such parallelity of contradictory relations with the object is only possible before the background of a not yet established object constancy, so that successive states of the relationship to the primary object cannot be compared yet with each other and thus be recognized as incompatible. This is a theoretical, metapsychological conclusion of prime importance. In terms of theory, it is the gain that we draw out of our understanding of this earliest form of psychic pathology. It proves that our inferences about mental functioning at the primordial level are correct.

The problem with autistic objects is, that they so-to-speak enshrine the foreclosure of the not-me object, the autistic child putting them in the place of lack caused by the traumatic loss of the primary object, so that the autistic hole is being filled and closed, thus providing the child with the delusional illusion of intactness. Simultaneously, the autistic object in the encapsulated form of autism also represents the encapsulation itself which is supposed to protect against the not-me object and the archaic fears it engenders. In order to safeguard against this, the autistic objects used here tend to be hard objects with which the child identifies on a purely sensory level.

Tustin emphasizes that no phantasy or meaning in the normal sense is connected with the autistic object, as the autistic psychotic child is yet unable to achieve a psychical feat like the formation of phantasies or symbolic meanings. The autistic object is selected on a purely sensory, sensual basis according to criteria of contour, surface texture, shape, etc. The task of this autistic object is to compensate and close the sensory deficit of the autistic hole by way of sensory analogies and formal similarities that are, for this reason, central to these children.

Anyone who has worked with autistic children or has had only fleeting contact with them, knows the unconditional dependency of these children on the autistic object as the only means which— by way of delusion—might protect against the archaic panic surfacing in the respective manifestation of the traumatic not-me experience of separation from the object. Other than the transitional objects which open up access to the world, the autistic object bars this path definitively and absolutely, and, without therapeutic help, once and for all: for the autistic object, as said, is put in place of the primary object in its meaning as the foreclosed traumatic not-me object, whereas in compensation an imitatory fusional relationship is being entered into with the non-traumatic manifestation of the primary object, which in its turn negates the ego-independent objectal character of the primary object. In doing so any human relationship, as an object relationship that is, is given up by the autistic child, or does not even come about, because the encapsulation of the autist takes place before the primal attachment even occurs.

Tustin stresses her point that this pathological meaning of the autistic object—and by the way, in the exact same sense, also of the hidden sensory autostimulation of these children (faeces in anus, tongue in mouth)—is the key to understanding the psychotic symptomatology of the autistic children and how it is maintained. The bodily sensations mediated through the autistic object and also through the autostimulation give the child the feeling "(...) he had a perfect mother always with him who gave him ecstatic and instant sensual satisfaction" (1981, pp. 103).

As a consequence, the encapsulated autistic child does not acquire the frustration tolerance which is the 'conditio sine qua non' for the reflexive distance of the ego in relation to its own states in the position outside, and thus for gradually acquiring the capacity for symbol formation, and for any higher functioning of the mind. But apart from this, the encapsulated autistic child does not even get as far as the splitting constitution of the paranoid-schizoid and depressive positions. The encapsulated autist remains tied to the concrete sensory stimulation which, as said, is predominantly tactile. Thinking only takes place in the form of sensual analogies.

The missing frustration tolerance also expresses itself in the equally pathognomonic tendency of encapsulated autistic children to display raging anger tantrums and panic attacks. In Tustin's words: "The constant use of Autistic Objects means that the psychotic child has little possibility of learning to tolerate frustration and to develop a more realistic evaluation of inner and outer stimuli which are felt to be life-threatening. When frustration impinges, tantrums pound through muscle and vein and cause the child to fear total annihilation. To counteract this deadly terror he clutches a hard Autistic Object. He never learns to deal with bodily and mental irritation in a considered, thinking way" (1981, p. 110).

The problem with autistic objects and likewise with the sensory autostimulations which serve the same function is, therefore, that they replace the foreclosed primary object in a delusional manner. With this, so Tustin, psychic development comes to a complete standstill at a very early stage. Equally, the autistic child has no inner concept of bodily growth, psychical development, or even healing. Tustin: "The *unintegrated* Encapsulated type of psychotic child experiences it (the body) as an inanimate thing; (...). (He) experiences bodily separateness from the outside world as a 'hole' (...). Since the psychotic child has no knowledge of growth and healing, the hole is a 'hole' and remains a 'hole' (.)" (1981 p. 179).

In other words, in these children the splitting dynamics of the paranoid-schizoid and depressive positions do not take place, the central results of which are the acquisition of psychical concepts like growth, development, and healing. That this splitting does not come about is simply the consequence of the circumstance that the pathogenic trauma takes place before the point in time when representational object constancy is acquired and therefore a split of the object representation cannot yet be performed.

Further up I have already pointed out that Tustin places the start of the traumatic not-me experience of the encapsulated autistic child very early, in the first few days of life, perhaps interpartally, perhaps even still in the womb. She states that the primal attachment in any case has not yet occurred. "The encapsulated child has experienced bodily separateness from the mother precociously. This may have been before he was put to the breast (or bottle experienced as breast)" (1981 p. 164). And in another location in this work I have already quoted Tustin stating that the encapsulated children are "usually reported as being withdrawn from birth or just after birth" (1981, p. 37).

Let me therefore summarize: If we may proceed on the basis of Tustin's clinical findings that the origin of the autistic encapsulation is to be set in the first few days of mental life, that is to say in the first few days of the juxtaposition of primary ego and primary object, independent of whether this point in time is thought of as pre—or postpartal, then this fixation point must lie within the primary phase before paranoid-schizoid splitting sets in, where object constancy is not yet developed, that is to say, in the pre-schizoid phase. I have, on the basis of theoretical considerations, postulated such a phase further up in the text.

To recapitulate, I have first pointed out that the splitting of the imago of the primary object is only conceivable as of the time when a rudimentary memory function—in other words a rudimentary representational object constancy—is present, where the ego simultaneously with calling up a negative, bad split image, can *in principle* maintain the memory of the good object. The splitting presupposes the parallel maintaining of the representation of the good and bad objects in time, and consists in it. Only when the condition of object constancy is met, is the splitting of the object representation possible. The breakthrough to the perception of time via the maintenance of a past experience of the object in memory constitutes the definitional content of representational object constancy.

116

Insofar as the primary object in the primordial constitution is to be considered as the totality of the stimulus situation activated in a given moment in time, I have further pointed out that, therefore, within a pre-schizoid constitution of experiencing where psychically nothing exists except the primary object, there is notably also no outside of the primary object, and where this primary object thus is the all-that-is, so to speak, the experience of a bad denying object would mean that the ego is confronted with a bad cosmos only, as no counteracting via splitting is possible. I have described this—that is, the confrontation with only a bad primary object—as incompatible with the maintenance of psychic life in principle, but had to find out that this case in some way arises indeed in the genetically primary encapsulation form of the two variants of early infantile autism and explains this most severe of mental disturbances where a global foreclosure of the relationship to the primary object within the framework of a traumatic not-me experience occurs. Such global and total foreclosure of the primary object is only possible in the phase before splitting sets in, as otherwise the complementary part of the split object would remain outside of the foreclosure.

The important constituent phantasy of the psychic drive antagonism is that, in the primordial state, a lack experienced by the ego can solely be compensated through fusional appropriation of the primary object, insofar as the means of compensating for the lack can only lie in the primary object. For an outside of the primary object, an alternative to it, does not exist in this earliest constitution before object constancy, where, as said, the primary object is the totality of the activated perceptual situation and insofar the all-that-is. When the primary ego experiences the lack within itself, this lack can only be satisfied out of the primary object. Apart from that, it must be recognized and stated that also the primary ego in this primordial structural condition is as yet not tied to its real conditions and limitations, in particular not yet tied to the body, hence the primal attachment of the ego to the body is not yet accomplished. The primary ego consists solely of the actively perceiving pole of the act of perception and therefore represents a totality which is parallel to the one as expressed in the imago of the primary object. The primal attachment of the ego to the body thus corresponds to the attachment of the primary object to the human other which introduces, on the side of the object, the condition and consecutively the dependency into the omnipotent primary narcissistic cosmos as the price to pay for the gratification of needs. When Freud therefore in 1923 in the second chapter of "The Ego and the Id" says that "the ego is first and foremost a body-ego" (p. 27), then this does not reflect the primordial constitution, but the state after the establishment of the primal attachment of the ego to the body.

If then the suspension of the lack by necessity is located in the primary object of the still unmodulated primary narcissistic constitution, this primary object must then represent the plenitude of possible gratification. In this first constitution of the psyche the primary object then, by definition, is that which is being positively posited, positively given. It is the pre-ambivalent object, the basic affirmation of life in its psychic dimension. After the primal attachment to human contact and thus to orality this leads to the meaning and importance of the breast as the good object.

In the situation of the psychogenic encapsulation autism, the case now seems to arise that based on accidental circumstances the felt pressure of the unpleasure of lack and thus the pressure towards fusion become so enormous that, as a drive dynamical emergency reaction, a refusal to fuse manifests out of the imago of the primary object itself in order to counter the threat of ego dissolution in a fusional realization. Thus the primary object becomes a traumatic not-me object in Frances

Tustin's sense. This means that the phantasy to compensate the experience of lack via the fusion of ego and primary object collapses, and in this way the traumatically premature experience of separation from the primary object occurs which Tustin named as cause for the infantile psychogenic autism, expressed in her formula of the "not-me object": The primary object can no longer be incorporated into the ego by way of the ego-cosmic, primary narcissistic fulfillment phantasy. Thus also the experience of dependency from this not-me object becomes, as Tustin emphasizes, a premature, and insofar traumatic experience. For as long as the ego entertains the phantasy of fusional, ego-cosmic control over a primary object that represents fulfillment of satisfaction, dependency is clearly no issue.

The triggering of the infantile psychogenic autism therefore is not about a primary object as a representation of lack, but about a primary object that rejects fusion. The prohibition of fusion confronts the primary ego here in the primary object itself and out of it, as this primary object cannot yet be split because the stage of representational object constancy has not yet been reached so that the prohibition of fusion cannot be expressed via the split. The consequence of this traumatic disillusion, in the psychogenic autism of the encapsulation type, is the foreclosure of the not-me object. The not-me object is thus a—traumatic—manifestation of the anti-fusional principle on which the maintenance of the dimension of psychic life rests. From these considerations follows that the specific psychogenic anxiety of the pre-schizoid phase of psychic development must be that of the manifestation of this traumatic not-me object. That this anxiety has a factual basis is evidenced in the clinical picture of the psychogenic encapsulation autism. One might conclude here that the dynamic reason for establishing the paranoid-schizoid object splitting after reaching the developmental phase of representational object constancy is to counter, in this way, the danger of foreclosure of the imago of the primary object which results from the dynamic antagonism of the two drives. The reality of this danger is evidenced by the encapsulation autism in which mental development is arrested immediately after the start.

Frances Tustin's description, as set out earlier, that the autistic child in its turn remains, as she calls it, in an "imitative fusion" with the primary object, does not preclude this argumentation. As her descriptions clearly show, this is not about an actual fusional process: Tustin employs the term "fusion" descriptively here, in the sense of a defensive operation, with the help of which the child attempts, by camouflaging all natural limitations of sensory experience and all boundaries between ego and object through imitation, to suspend the traumatic experience of the not-me object, that is to say the rejection of the fusion that the not-me object expresses. Underlying this process is no splitting of the primary object into a fusional merging aspect and a non-fusional not-me aspect, no modification of a good-bad split, as a splitting of the object imago, as said, is not yet possible at this level of functioning; but rather, the imitative fusion serves the denial of and the undoing of the manifestation of the not-me dimension of the primary object, that is to say, the denial precisely of the failure of the fusional project. It is, therefore, a reaction. Genetically speaking these are processes on a timeline: first there is the traumatic experience and the resulting foreclosure of that conception of the primary object which is involved in this experience. After that follows an experience with the primary object, which due to the missing object constancy is isolated from the previous experience, and reactively leads to the imitatory fusion in defense against the traumatic experience.

However, as both experiences—before representational object constancy is attained—take place in a psychical constitution in which

PSYCHOGENIC ENCAPSULATED AUTISM

time and thus also timely succession are not yet experienced and the respective active representation of the primary object on the level of subjective experiencing is the all-that-is outside of which nothing exists, these two experiences that are genetically successive and held together in the common traumatic context, are pulled together and consolidated into one uniform experiencing within which the primary object is at the same time foreclosed in its totality, and the ego enters—also in totality—into the pathognomonic imitative fusion with it. The end result can then be the foreclosure of the traumatic not-me object, as expressed in the relationship with the compensatory autistic object, simultaneously and side-by-side with the imitatory fusional relationship. This constitutes the clinical picture of the psychogenic infantile autism of the encapsulation type. There is no splitting mechanism underlying it.

Through this constellation two things become evident:

1. Primary experiencing in fact takes place in timelessness.
2. The primary object, in this first phase of mental life, has in fact this character of totality and globality which I have summarised in the formulation of the "all-that-is" outside of which nothing exists.

Proof is offered insofar as, for one thing as far as concerns timelessness, in the symptomatology of the encapsulated infantile autism the mutually exclusive simultaneous occurrence of foreclosure of the primary object and imitative fusion with it cannot be explained otherwise.

Then again, the character of totality and globality of the inner perception of the primary object in this primary constitution of the psyche leads to these two psychic movements that actually contradict each other—foreclosure and imitative fusion—to paradoxically co-exist peacefully and undisturbedly side by side due to the totality claim of

121

both, because this unconditional experience of absoluteness leads to a situation where contradiction and mutual exclusion are not finding a representation. The resulting quality of totality of the symptomatology spans the whole spectrum of experience, with its character definitely blocking development as a whole.

This is the metapsychologically stringent explanation of this first form of psychical illness, and in reverse, I consider this very succession or, later, side-by-side of the foreclosure of the traumatic not-me version of the primary object and the reactive imitative fusion with its non-traumatic form of manifestation as clinical evidence for the correctness of my reflections on the existence of a pre-schizoid phase, for such parallelity of contradictory relations with the object is only possible before the background of a not yet established object constancy, so that successive states of the relationship to the primary object cannot be compared yet with each other and thus be recognized as incompatible.

In terms of theory, this is a metapsychological conclusion of prime importance. It is the gain we can draw out of our understanding of this earliest form of psychic pathology, proving that our inferences about mental functioning at the primordial level are correct.

The open question of the genesis of the primary psychogenic autism has thus become clarified to the extent that the traumatic manifestation of the not-me object is not the direct consequence of an external influence, but that of a psychic materialization of the anti-fusional principle of the life drive within the imago of the primary object itself, which results from the dynamic opposition of the drives and which represents an extreme emergency reaction in order to prevent the imminent collapse of the dimension of the psychical in a concrete fusional realization. This overly strong fusional movement though may have been triggered by a frustrating outer event or by a fateful external constellation, but does not have to be. The moment of causation may just as well be found in non-transparent internal regulation complications.

In this sense I consider, further, the encapsulated psychogenic autism as the clinical evidence for the actual existence of that psychical power, given from the beginning of mental life, which I call the life drive, and as evidence that the psychic struggle which the antagonism of the drives is about centers on the subject of the fusion with the primary object: this is, in this sense, a compelling result from the double aspect of the pathognomonic symptomatology, that on the one hand the traumatizing event consists in the manifestation of the not-me object refusing to fuse, and that on the other hand, the circumstance that this not-me object is in fact about the fusion theme, is evidenced by the autist's development of the symptoms of the imitatory merging in a compensatory way, the only meaning of which is to deny and annul the traumatic refusal to fuse through the imitative and repetitive mechanisms. Before the backdrop of these premises the enormous dynamic and economic force of the life drive proves itself, as well as the force of the antagonistic drive dynamics in the context of which it manifests itself, namely by its ability to produce a clinical symptomatology like that of the primary encapsulated autism. The unconditional impact of this primordial drive dynamism is the result of a structural situation in which neither the primary ego nor the primary object are bound by their real circumstances and conditions as yet, but exist solely out of the sensory poles of perception.

To carry this argumentation even further, I had already pointed out in the beginning chapters of this work when discussing the situation before representational object constancy is reached, that the counteractive measures of the life drive against the fusional tendency of the death drive—in a situation where the object imago cannot be split yet and therefore a negative, denying, bad representation because

123

of its globality and totality is not compatible with life—can only express themselves by creating an unavoidable pressure towards change of the existing overall situation, in the confrontation with the psychic experience of lack. Meanwhile we have seen that this is so at least inasfar as the life drive does not traumatically express itself, as it would in the encapsulated autism, in the manifestation of the anti-fusional not-me object. I have proposed to regard this pressure for change of the existing overall situation, behind which we have the fear of the manifestation of the traumatic not-me object, as the constitutive moment of the life drive dynamic in the psyche, which later on with the onset of attachment to the human object associates itself with the biological drive determinants—orality for a start. For the death drive, in its turn, the root of the drive moment would be found in the concrete and concretistic direction towards the primary narcissistic, ego-cosmic fusion with the primary object, from which need satisfaction or suspension of the lack, respectively, is being expected, but which from another perspective endangers the existence of the ego and thus of the whole dimension of the psychical.

In the further course of development the death drive with its fusional aim follows those object cathexes which the life drive prescribes along the lines of psychosexuality. Psychosexuality, with its phases as psychoanalysis describes them, is therefore not immediately biologically determined and thus by its nature unconditional invariant of mental life, but it is linked to the accomplishment of the primal attachment, that is to say, to the binding of the primary object to the human other, whereby, to remind the reader, the primary object must be thought of as purely intrapsychic-coenesthetic, originating from the sensory structural givens of the human brain.

If the fixation point of the psychogenic encapsulated autism, as Tustin writes, must be assumed before the primal attachment to the

PSYCHOGENIC ENCAPSULATED AUTISM

human object comes about and thus before the initialisation of the biologically determined psychosexuality, it would have to follow from this that in the intact state of the autistic encapsulation there are no direct sexual drive manifestations. The autostimulative moments which might be misunderstood as autoerotic activities, have, as described, a meaning that corresponds to the autistic object, namely to block the autistic hole in a delusional fashion.

Tustin writes: "(...) in the early states of treatment, when the pathological autism is being disturbed, several elements come into operation at one and the same time, in a confused and disorderly fashion. These come from different areas of the personality, so that anal, phallic and oral elements interpenetrate each other" (1981, p. 174). Tustin, in this context, perusing surgical terminology, speaks about "compressed and impacted stages of development". In the encapsulated autism the normal sexual drive development does not find a mental representation due to the foreclosure of the primary object, and hence does not take place. Only with the therapeutic abolishment of this foreclosure, the sexual drive theme manages to break through in its compressed and impacted form, so Tustin, into the dimension of the psychical for the first time and is being represented as psychic content.

The structure-forming antagonism of the psychical drives in the sense as I attempt to present it in this work—namely the formulation of the death drive in the phantasy of the fusion with the object that compensates the lack and insofar satisfies, and the reactive phantasmatisation of the life drive which culminates in the castrative consequence of the Oedipus complex—comes to a standstill in the encapsulated form of autism in the very first steps. Instead, we see a defensive imitative merging with the primary object, at a purely sensory level, before the formation of representational object constancy, while the primary object, in its objectal not-me dimension separated from the ego is being foreclosed and excluded from mental representation.

13

The integration of sensory opposites and representational object constancy

further point in the discussion of the encapsulated autism which seems important to me under the aspects of my conceptualization concerns the integration of sensory opposites. Before the background of the clinic of the conditions in encapsulated and confusional autists which keep the psychical circumstances of the beginning of life fixated in a time warp-like fashion, Tustin vividly describes that and in how far the primary psychic functioning is a purely sensory one and proceeds first of all from the unmodulated sensory opposites. I would like to stress that this emphasis on the sensory system also corresponds to my own starting point, when I speak about the fact that after the unfolding of the poles of perception, the primary object consists solely and exclusively in the sensory afferences which are bound together in a unified representation only through temporal contiguity. I have described that, in this psychic state that is tied to two-dimensionality, there are no phantasies in the actual sense, or mental content, as they require object constancy on the one hand, and an inner space on the other, and thus lead away from immediate sensory perception. For constancy of the representation of the object over time is the prerequisite for the development of phantasies with this object and about it; and the concept of the inner space is lastly a consequence of the break-through to the position outside in the depressive position, which, via the taking up of the reflexive distance of the ego towards itself opens up the third dimension and, via the process of projection and re-identification of the primary identification makes the idea of an inner space possible. In that respect experiencing in the pre-schizoid phase is necessarily bound to the immediate sensory perception. This is a one-to-one situation which Tustin puts forth in the case of the encapsulated autists.

Tustin, in this context, points out in particular that autistic children have not managed the basic integration of sensual opposites—that is to say hot-cold, soft-hard, light-dark—and that this failure has led to a, in her words, "binary split", a bisection of their body-self.

She relates this failure to the exclusion of the traumatic not-me object, that is—in the case of the encapsulated autists—to the foreclosure of the primary object, as the early "auto-sensual breast-mother" (Tustin) would have to achieve the integration of the sensual opposites, something made impossible by the foreclosure. Tustin regards this failure of sensory integration as directly responsible, on the one hand, for the fact that the encapsulated child experiences his own as well as someone else's body as inanimate, on the other hand for his being bound to two-dimensionality, that is to say, for lacking perception of corporeality and thus of the inner space. She demonstrates that the feeling of space develops from learning to cope with the sensory gradations, insofar as these represent the basis for distance perception.

She writes: "(...) his responses to a world which is scarcely differentiated from his body remain based on bodily rhythms and crude sensations, which become bizarre, rigid and perseverative. Thus childhood psychosis, in the first instance, seems to be a disturbance of primary sensuousness which has prevented the development of normal emotional relationships.

These rigid, perseverative auto-sensual reactions have been termed *pathological autism*. Pathological autism is a system of *protective manoeuvres*, the function of which is to prevent or to massively diminish contact with the 'not-me' outside world. Such contacts seem to threaten bodily disintegration and annihilation. The delusion is that these manoeuvres prevent the disaster. In the elemental sensation-dominated states of pathological autism, unbearable panic, rage, anguish and ecstasy hold sway. In such states perceptions are so inhibited or distorted that the child may appear to have impairment of sight or hearing. If this inhibition or distortion of perception is continued for a considerable period of time, it seems possible that it may even be replicated at an organic level" (1981, p. 254; italics F.T.).

"In psychotherapy with these young children, it is usually clear that the binary split in the body-self occurred in terms of primary sensuous contraries such as hard and soft, rough and smooth, light and dark, etc. In the Encapsulated children these contraries are not felt to be connected with each other and cannot be experienced together. Thus, experiences are sharply separated from each other and become segmented into discrete entities which are not connected with each other. Such compartmentalising replaces normal differentiation, and prevents the bringing together of contraries so that they can modify each other. Such Encapsulated children live in a state of acute extremes; for example, they feel that they have a hard back and a soft front, and a hard head and a soft bottom, and that there is nothing inside which links these two extremes together. They are kept apart and controlled by the encapsulation. The child is trapped in a two-dimensional state of awareness. In rare states of occasional awareness of bodily separateness there is a soft 'me' and a hard 'not-me', which threatens to hurt their soft vulnerability. In order to shut out this hard 'not-me', 'me' and 'not-me' are partitioned off from each other and kept rigidly apart, to be controlled by the encapsulation in which mother and child seem fused" (1981, p. 61).

And again Tustin: "In all types of childhood psychosis in which psychogenic elements predominate, the patient needs to be helped to sort out compressed, impacted sensuous dispositions. As basic sensuous *distinctions* are made (for example, between 'hot' and 'cold', 'hard' and 'soft', 'rough' and 'smooth', 'light' and 'dark', 'nice' and 'nasty', 'sweet' and 'bitter', 'thick' and 'thin', 'full' and 'empty'), basic sensory integrations begin to take place. The psychotic child has missed this stage in infancy. When this occurs in treatment, it feels like a life and death struggle. The transference situation is very intense and the child has to feel that the therapist cares whether he lives or dies and that he will be firm and strong in protecting and taking care of him" (1981, p. 175; italics F.T.).

The problem with this integration is that that part of these contraries, respectively, which feels aversive to the autistic child has fallen under the foreclosure of the not-me object. Therefore the evocation of these antagonists by the analyst provokes the fear connected with the foreclosed object, which Tustin equates with Bion's (1962) "nameless dread". If one tries to answer the question in which manner these basal sensory integration tasks constitutive for the further development of the psyche normally come about, one is directed back again, in my opinion, to the theme of the primary object in the pre-schizoid phase before representational object constancy is reached, where the object, as outlined again above, is the only thing that is given and positively posited. I assume that it is the central task of this pre-ambivalent primary object to serve as a catalyst and container for this sensory integration. Thus we are dealing with a basal, early form of the containing function: containment and an archaic, sensorily defined alpha function are being exercised solely intra-psychically by the inner primary object. In any case it is precisely this task which fails when the primary object of this developmental stage falls under the autistic foreclosure.

Carrying on with this train of thought one arrives at the formula that, in Winnicott's term, it would be the task of a good enough mother and 'environment mother' at this stage of development to prevent the appearance of a frustration tension which is so overexerting that the pre-ambivalent object breaks down in a manifestation of the traumatic not-me object and must be foreclosed against. If mother and environment mother are able to fulfill this task, the basal sensory integration via the pre-ambivalent primary object can happen, the drive dynamic can constitute itself via the good-bad split of the object, the primal attachment and thus the coupling to the biological, sexual and aggressive drive constituents can take place, and further psychical development is thus 'under way'.

A consequence of the non-integration of the sensory contraries in the enclosed autistic child is, in any case, a phenomenon described by Tustin and many other authors which have worked with such children, namely the immediate side-by-side of extreme fear and ecstatic enraptured states, whereby the latter result from the positive poles of the unintegrated sensory contraries, but structurally may also have to do with the primary object of the pre-schizoid phase always having to be considered as the positive given, as I have worked out further above. Thus autistic children paradoxically display, next to extreme fits of panic and temper tantrums, states of absolute rapture which they describe, when they start to speak during the treatment, as experiences of pure beauty.

Obviously, herein also lies the cause for a deep resistance of these children against the treatment, which also forces them, through the rescindment of the foreclosure, to modulate the sensory contraries and thus to lose this ecstatic layer and form of sensory experiencing. The child can only take this step if it is clear about the fact that renouncing the ecstasy and rapture would also equal overcoming his archaic fears.

I need not emphasize what the uncovering and understanding of these interrelationships means of course also for our understanding of the experiencing of the newborn in normal development, inasfar as we must proceed from the assumption that the latter, due to the need to solve the same task—that is to say integration of sensory contraries—up to a certain degree knows the same conditions which in the encapsulated autistic child have remained fixated in their unilateral excesses. If in the psychoanalytic tradition the fiction of the intrauterine nirwana state of bliss has played such a big role and produced a series of theoretically untenable ideas, then these intuitive convictions which are often defended so tenaciously and acrimoniously in the discussions, possibly find their justification here—albeit only representing one side of the coin.

In order to call to the reader's attention the other side of the coin—but also its ecstatic counterpart—let's hear it in Tustin's words again: "At each milestone in his psychological development, and at each daily crisis, the Encapsulated child experiences again the terror of failure and helplessness aroused by his first disastrous encounters with the 'not-me'. With gaping mouth he gives again the gulp and gasp of horror as the 'black hole' of the unknown 'not-me' yawns before him. Psychological growth seems to mean taking a step into the unfathomable darkness down which he will fall endlessly to his doom. This experience comes into the dreams of normal and neurotic people, but the Encapsulated child lacks the capacity to dream. The primordial stuff of dreams is his waking reality. In his relatively undifferentiated state, agonies and ecstasies come together like an electric shock" (1981, pp. 151).

"When such children can talk, they tell of the 'ugliness' of the tantrum. For them, beauty seems to be associated with ecstasy, ugliness with tantrums. I have come to realise that, for these elemental children, the ecstasy of beauty is associated with moments of bodily completeness in which there is an experience of ecstatic fusion with the 'earth mother'. These childrens' despairing search for an 'extra bit' to their bodies seems to be part of their need for perfect sensuous completeness (which means that it is perpetually present and available). Gradually, as therapy progresses, they come to see that a sense of satisfying completeness does not come from auto-sensual experiences nor from material objects used to plug the gap" (1981, p. 236).

I think that what is clearly expressed in these words—referring, as said, to a pathological state in which certain aspects of the primary, archaic constitution of the psyche have survived in a form preserved through the illness—is, in particular, the theme of the fusional yearning with respect to the object which in the present work plays such a central role as the motif of the death drive, as well as the moment of extreme endangerment which the psyche encounters in pursuit of this motif. For whatever reasons, the fusional yearning in these autistic children obviously had been so strong at a particular point in time that a traumatic manifestation of the fusional prohibition out of the imago of the primary object itself occurred. It appears that the autistic pathology has not only preserved the sensory context of psychological functioning at this particular time, but also the fusional yearning itself, as well as the horror that it gave rise to and which—due to the globality and totality of the experiencing associated with this stage of development and with which this horror is therefore itself experienced—had to lead to a global and total foreclosure of the object imago. With respect to the horror, reference be made again here to the consideration that this horror is basically not representable in the psychological constitution before object constancy is reached, as the child who cannot hold a good experience from memory against it would otherwise be exposed to a totally aversive universe. The horror which the encapsulated autistic children express is thus directly linked with the trauma; it is the trauma. The pathology of the encapsulated autism thus consists in the conservation of the complete traumatic situation: sensory context, fusional yearning, and traumatic horror.

Above I had indicated that the global foreclosure of the primary object for structural reasons seems to be bound to the pre-schizoid phase, as after the occurrence of the good-bad split of the object one of the aspects of the object would always remain outside of the foreclosure. With the foregoing discussion in mind, one could ask whether, insofar, the foreclosure is really only possible at this level of functioning of the pre-schizoid phase, as the psychical here has not yet gone beyond the immediate sensory experience and is still bound to two-dimensionality. In other words, there is no inner mental space as yet which could contain thoughts and phantasies, contents with the complexity and network characteristics inherent to them. That it is, therefore, only possible under this condition of the as yet complete binding to the sensory system to erect a kind of firewall, as the encapsulated autistic child does, in order to exclude from experience certain sensory constellations which the child experiences as traumatic.

As said, I regard the pathology of the encapsulated infantile autism as clinical proof for the existence of a pre-schizoid phase or position, which initially I had postulated for theoretical reasons. As the clinic of the encapsulated autism shows, the psychic experiencing during this time is bound to an unmediated two-dimensional sensory system. The sensuous experience under this constitution is to be considered as that which is positively posited, positively given, as the constitutive moment is the not yet existing awareness of time, so that there is no representational constancy of the object yet through which a psychological condition of the primary object at the present time A could be compared with a previous, remembered condition of a time moment B. The consequence of this is an absolute globality and totality of experience which I have captured with the formulation that the primary object at this point of development is the all-that-is for the primary ego, outside of which nothing exists. This leads to the impossibility of experiencing a negative, aversive version of the primary object at this point in time, as otherwise the ego would be confronted with a negative, bad cosmos, which as a maximally traumatic experience cannot be conceived as compatible with life. It must be the case therefore, that the psychic experiencing, which only just constituted itself through the separation of the poles of perception, is collapsing anew over and over again, if the level of aversiveness rises above a certain mark.

This important thought about the processing of aversive tension must be discussed in greater detail: If at the pre-schizoid level the experience of lack becomes too intense and if the deterrence with reference to a fusional movement towards the primary object becomes at least strong enough to prevent the manifestation of a not-me object, then the total psychical dimension of experience, the dimension of the psychical as such is probably simply "shut off" and the organism, due to the lack of adequate psychic modes of processing, as an emergency reaction goes back to functioning on the purely biological level again. From this perspective, one could regard the development which begins with representational object constancy and consists in the good-bad split of the object and the establishment of the paranoid-schizoid and depressive positions as an event which serves above all one goal: to develop the psychical possibility to contain and process need-tension and thus to develop <u>frustration tolerance</u>, so that the dimension of the

135

psychical can be maintained with continuitiy. Building up the mental apparatus thus has a double purpose, namely to make frustration processable intra-psychically, in a manner that a breakdown of the dimension of the psychical, due to either structural overload or fusional realization which would make the poles of perception collapse, will be prevented.

The primary pre-schizoid order is over, in any case, as soon as the representation of the object can be maintained over time and thus the good-bad split of the object can occur. This means the negative, aversive experience becomes representable, because a memory of a good experience can be held against it which then secures psychic survival. This is equally categorial a leap in the structural level of psychic life as the leap, later on during the crisis of the depressive position, to the position outside, the latter making the splitting constitution of the psyche obsolete. I have set out that this last leap receives its revolutionary meaning by it opening up access to reality, the child leaving the structurally psychotic constitution of the psyche. In my hypothesis, this leads to the fact that the functioning of the psyche according to the split mode, which continues to exist, becomes structurally unconscious due to its incompatibility with the new mode of reality-appropriate time-space identity of the object imago and thus becomes the core of the id.

That the splitting mechanism upholds its function, comes from the fact that, in my view, the unification of the object imago, the suspension of the splitting, results from a certain work demand on the ego, namely the taking up of a reflexive distance towards itself, where the ego looks at its own experiencing, comparing its current state with previous states, thus drawing on its own experience for the first time. The ego thus introduces a split within itself, which makes the realization of a fusional experiencing impossible as long as this split is being maintained, so that with it object splitting as a principle of counteracting the fusion can be given up.

One has to assume, however, that this particular distancing work of the ego, i.e. the taking up of the 'position outside of the drive phantasma', is not operating the whole time or not totally functioning, and that therefore the ego, in parallel, always remains in the functioning mode of the identity with its own experiencing, that is to say, is not in the reflexive distance mode, and insofar functions both consciously and unconsciously at the same time, whereby the unconscious functioning is bound to the splitting constitution.

It is obvious that making the leap to representational object constancy contains as elemental a change in the mode of functioning of the ego as does its later change to the position outside. With the introduction of object constancy, the functional level of the good-bad split of the object imago becomes possible, the child enters the world of the splitting-mode of the paranoid-schizoid and the depressive positions. With the position outside, on the other hand, this splitting mode is overcome and the child gains access to reality. With the position outside the differentiation between a conscious and an unconscious functioning of the ego arises, and together with it an elemental categorial leap occurs which in particular introduces the category of consciousness as such, "the fact of consciousness" which Freud (1938, p. 157) referred to as "without parallel, which defies all explanation or description".

On the other hand, with the breakthrough to object constancy the infantile ego leaves the level of unconditional binding to immediate sensual experiencing as it is preserved in the encapsulated autism, for it is the decisive moment concerning the level of functioning of the ego that the ego is then able to create phantasies. Phantasies are tied to the maintenance of an object representation over time, successive object representations are linked to each other through the phantasy. It need not be stressed that, in adult life, this very ability to create phantasies constitutes the psychical functioning in the first place.

Which leaves the question of whether, concerning the pre-schizoid mode, we are dealing with a phase or a position. For the paranoid-schizoid and the depressive modes this question has been answered: as soon as the ego gives up or takes back the reflexive functional mode of the split within itself, it returns to the functional mode of the good-bad split of the object representation. Concerning the object representation it has been described many times that and how mental life consists in a permanent change between splitting and non-splitting modes, and the paranoid-schizoid and depressive positions. This is why Melanie Klein preferred the term position to that of phase, as in the chronological sequence of the psychosexual phases. Is it imaginable that there is a similar oscillation also between the pre-schizoid mode and the splitting positions? One is tempted to say: no, for it may well be assumed that the dimension of time, once grasped, and thus the maintenance, over time, of an object representation which is no longer directly present, in other words, memory, cannot be reversed. The question is, however, if this is really so; or if perhaps this underestimates the fluidity of cerebral functioning. Also for maintaining representational object constancy a specific work demand, an endeavor of the ego, is necessary—precisely this memory performance—which as such under certain conditions or at certain overly regressive levels of functioning can collapse or be given up. This may have to be left open. In any case, it is conceivable that there is a link here to the psychosomatic illnesses and the clinical concepts of operational thinking and of alexithymia with their emphasis on predominantly sensory experiencing, which would speak for the fact that the ego can function in parallel at both levels of constancy and non-constancy of the object conception. Tustin (1981) at least

138

propounds this view when she writes: "The relevance of the foregoing hypotheses to *Psychosomatic Disorders* and *Hypochondria* will be fairly obvious. For various reasons, sensuousness has become unduly directed towards bodily organs and processes. This has remained unregulated and untransformed into dreams, fantasies and play. One function of the psychosomatic illness seems to be to release and deal with the violence associated with unregulated sensuality, as well as to give form and shape to formless, raw autistic elements" (p. 240; italics F.T.).

In order to bring this debate about the encapsulated form of infantile autism to a close, I would conclude that the central pathogenic process seems to lie in the foreclosure of the pre-ambivalent primary object which is traumatically experienced as removed from the ego's omnipotent control, as resisting fusion, as, in other words, a not-me object.

14

Frances Tustin and the theoretical fiction of a normal objectless autistic phase

At this point I would like to make a brief historical excursion important for the central thoughts of this work. In her original publications, following mainstream psychoanalysis of the time, Tustin regarded and described infantile pathological autism as a regression or arrest, respectively, with reference to an assumed normal autistic phase of development. A few years before her death she explicitly clarified this view as erroneous and revised it in two publications that received much attention (1991, 1994):

"I should like to think about an error made by many psychoanalytic therapists (including myself), to which I drew attention in a paper published in *The International Journal of Psycho-Analysis* as recently as 1991. In that paper I pointed out that observational studies of babies by workers from many countries (...) had shown conclusively that there is not a normal infantile stage of primary autism to which the pathology of childhood autism could be a regression. This has been the mainstream hypothesis concerning the aetiology of childhood autism to which many psychoanalytic therapists have subscribed, especially in the United States and in Europe. This flawed hypothesis, based on faulty premises, has been like an invasive virus in that it has permeated and distorted clinical and theoretical formulations" (1994, p. 3).

"I began to see that, as an infant, the child had felt so unified with the mother that abrupt and painful breaking of this sense of dual unity, when inevitably they became aware of their bodily separatedness from the mother, had seemed like the loss of part of their body which, until then, had seemed to be part of the mother's body. This disruption during the suckling phase of infancy had seemed catastrophic for both mother and child. They both felt left with a bodily hole. The trauma of this violent wrenching apart precipitated autistic reactions in the child. I began to realise that, in seeing this perpetuated state of unified 'at-oneness' with the mother as a *normal* situation in early infancy, we had been extrapolating from a *pathological* situation and mistakenly seeing it as a normal one. This was an error we must be careful not to repeat. I now realise that the infantile state that was being re-evoked in the clinical situation was an *abnormal* one. I have come to see that autism is a protective reaction that develops to deal with the stress associated with a traumatic disruption of an *abnormal* perpetuated state of adhesive unity with the mother—*autism being a reaction that is specific to trauma*. It is a two-stage illness. First, there is the perpetuation of dual unity, and then the traumatic disruption of this and the stress that this arouses" (1994, p. 14, italics F.T.).

In other words, there are two errors that Tustin describes here, namely one, the assumption of a normal phase of the fusional "unified at-oneness" of mother and child, and secondly, that there is a normal autistic phase. This corresponds to my conceptualization according to which, on the one hand, the phantasma of the fusional union with the object is the manifestation of the death drive and thus no normal phase; and on the other hand, a normal autistic phase is not possible inasmuch as the dimension of the psychical comes about with the moment of the separation of subject and object of sensory perception, that is to say, with the moment of the constitution of the ego and the

142

psychical object. The theory of a normal objectless autistic phase is therefore a fiction.

15

Annihilatory aggression and primary envy

In order to return from this special investigation of an isolated syndrome, childhood encapsulated autism, back to my outline of general psychopathology, I will have to follow up, finally, with a reflection on the unconditional aggression aiming at annihilation of the object.

One of the consequences of the thoughts presented in this work is that access to reality, that is to say, overcoming the early paranoid splitting of the object, results from the ego taking up the position outside the drive phantasma. Through this the fusional merging of ego and primary object is being prevented and thus the manifestation of the death drive made impossible. Therefore object splitting as the early mode of defense against the death drive can be relinquished. The real object, the reality dimension of the object, when looked at from its psychical background, is thus intimately linked with Eros as the drive to safeguard the ego. Eros simultaneously guarantees the safety of the ego as well as its access to reality.

The sexual route of the striving for fulfillment of the death drive consists in the attempt to achieve fusional union with the primary object—that is, the object as such—in the midst of reality, via the path of incest with the mother, at the level of the unconscious phantasma. As this attempt fails because of the Oedipus complex and the threat of castration, the death drive is able to break away from the sexual, oedipal project of its fulfillment in reality via the real object, and can attack the real object itself with the aim, through its destruction and annihilation, to return to the imagination of the 'pure' primary object of the splitting condition and behind this, of the pre-ambivalent object of the pre-schizoid phase, which is the original promise of fulfillment of the death drive. The aim, therefore, is the return to the level of the 'subjective object' as I had called it further up.

Thus this attack at the same time aims to suspend the position of the ego outside the drive phantasma, inasfar as this latter contains the break of the 'romantic' union of the ego with itself and in this very way opens up the path to reality. The death drive attacks the reality dimension of the object, at the same time as it also attacks the position outside and the father imago deriving from it, the threat of castration, in actual fact the Oedipus complex itself. This is the background before which Bion (1970) in *Attention and Interpretation* writes about the hate for reality and the hate for cognitive functions that allow us to perceive reality—that is to say, the hate for the position outside and the self-reflexive ability that comes with it, as well as the ability for symbol formation that it also gives rise to. Both are prerequisites for thinking at the reality level of the ego that is no longer concretely bound to two-dimensionality and immediate sensuality. Similarly, what may arise before this background of the attack on thinking is a lack of self-recognition and conscious self-perception—and precisely not as the correlate of a deficient intellect—and in addition, hate for the dimension of consciousness itself, which, in order to shut off consciousness, may even include suicidal impulses. And of course the attack on the reality dimension of the object is also directed against genital sexuality and gender difference, both of which are intimately linked with the theme of reality.

Of importance in this context is that from the attack of the death drive against the reality dimension of the object arises not only the formal disorganization of the object representation, the fragmentation and dissolution of its time-space identity, but also coldness, emptiness and meaninglessness of relationships and of the experiencing of the world. This coldness and emptiness regarding relationships results from the attack against the real object in its dimension as the carrier of emotional meaning. Typically we find here also massive manifestations of blind repetition compulsion, one further fundamental characteristic of the death drive, via which it attempts to force the illusion of fusional union with the object, the illusion of eternal presence, the dissolution of causality and finality, the suspension of the passing of time. Most impressively this can be seen in the stereotypical repetitive movements of the encapsulated autistic child. The annihilatory death drive which turns against the reality dimension of the object, must go on turning against any form of mental development inasfar as it alienates the death drive from the illusory possibility of the realization of its intention to return to the level of the primary pre-ambivalent object and the fusion with it.

Hence it becomes totally plausible when Freud describes the death drive as that force the aim of which it is to dissolve complex units. Only that the ultimate goal of this drive is not directly the reduction of tension to zero and the regression to the anorganic state, but the creation of a mental constitution in which those obstacles are dissolved which hinder the realization of the narcissistic fusion with the primary object. Of course, an ego which is under the influence of an annihilatory aggression against the reality aspect of the object representation must basically be regarded as being in a psychotic regression. Bion (1957, 1962) describes that the psychotic ego which attacks reality is also able to direct this attack against its own functions and against its organs of perception of this reality. The mythical example for this position is Oedipus blinding himself.

In a case presentation Fonagy (2009) held the view that the fragmented, disorganized, self—and hetero-destructive, negativistic, cognition-aversive tendencies subject to a blind repetition compulsion in the psyche of one of his patients, who, from my point of view, underwent such annihilatory regression, represent the contents of a neurobiologically given and chaotically destructive unconscious that are not normally intended to ever become conscious, but which by 'accidental' mirroring had become contents of the 'psychoanalytic' unconscious and from there were able to determine the patient's experiencing and behavior. As said, I consider these manifestations to be within a dynamic process carried by a death drive that desires realization.

In addition, the death drive, in a very fundamental sense, can attack the attachment of the primary object to psychosexuality occurring in the early oral phase, in the first days of life, via the partial object of the breast, which is the foundation of the attachment to the human object. For it is via this 'error'—from the point of view of the annihilatory death drive—of the attachment to the sexual object that the constitutive illusion of the Oedipus complex came about. One might, therefore, express the fundamental complication this way: that the ego in the annihilatory, destructive regression follows the attraction of the primary narcissistic constitution of the pre-schizoid phase, in which the primary ego, in its delusional experiencing, still had omnipotent fusional control over the as yet unsplit primary object, with reference to which an outside could not yet be imagined, and where the attachment of the primary to the sexual object, the breast had not occurred yet.

The mythical image of this aggressive turn against the overall course of mental development is matricide, which in fact is the murder of the reality mother, of the reality dimension of the mother, and behind this of the sexual mother, the murder of the mother as a sexual object. This is the mythological codification for the dissolution of the attachment to the human object, and that is why in Greek mythology matricide has been designated as the ultimate crime which entails the curse of the Erynnis.

One could say that the death drive, in this attack on the real object, recognizes and attacks the fundamental trick of nature, by which in the position outside reality is won at the same time as a realization of the death drive is made impossible, so that the ego basically faces the impossible alternative to relinquish either reality, or the realization of the death drive. From the point of view of the death drive, the sexual Oedipus complex consists in the attempt to solve this dilemma. This attempt finally fails with the experience of castration, and one of the possibilities to react to this failure is to abandon the attachment to sexuality itself and to attempt a violent reversal of the whole process.

This complication is the unconscious origin of the violence aimed at the destruction of the real object. The annihilatory violence is therefore an attack against the attachment to the real object and to sexuality. Béla Grunberger (1983) calls this the anubic aggression. In the same vein André Green (1999) in *The Work of the Negative* describes an annihilatory, deobjectalizing activity of the death drive and Janine Chasseguet-Smirgel (2003) a dimension of murder and also of suicide behind which there is the annihilation of the object and object relatedness as such.

Hans-Volker Werthmann (2006) has published a psychoanalytic investigation of the case of the so-called 'Cannibal of Rotenburg', which belongs in this thematic context. To his subtle reflections I would add the thesis that this act of cannibalism was a compromise formation between, on the one hand, the wish for annihilatory suspension of the object in the above-described sense, and its concretistic-depressive restitution via oral ingestion, which is the attempt to prevent the psychotic breakdown.

Within the classic descriptions of psychosexual development one could, for the rest, also identify a link to the first phase of the anal sadistic stage as described by Abraham (1924), in which he sees anal evacuation in the context of the phantasy of the destruction of the object. In the transition from this first to the second, retentive stage of anality he then draws the line between psychotic and neurotic kinds of regression. But the regression with respect to the representation of the object in the case of the annihilatory aggression reaches even further back, goes beyond the destructive anality that Abraham puts in the foreground, which here is only a means to a regressive end. Psychosexuality contains strongly cathected themes of dissolution and destruction of the object, both in anality and orality, and the structural regression with relation to the object representation which is carried by the death drive, orientates itself by these milestones of ontogenesis and phylogenesis which appear one after the other.

It is, however, undeniable that the most important concept in this context is that of Melanie Klein (1957) which she describes as primary envy. This envy which Klein regards as the elementary destructive force per se is directed against the good of the good object, if and insofar as this object evades the omnipotent control of the subject. It is obvious that this envy is the complementary piece to the fusional impulse of the death drive, which becomes effective as soon as this impulse meets with resistance with respect to its fulfillment imagination. It represents a massive threat for the ego, inasfar as it threatens to destroy the inner and/or real objects of the ego. Klein's concept has been further developed especially by Rosenfeld in his famous paper on destructive narcissism of 1971, which Steiner, with reference to the envy theme, summarizes as follows: "(...) the basic problem remains central to our understanding of the deepest roots of severe pathology. It postulates the universal emergence of internal sources of destructiveness manifested as primitive envy and threatening to destroy the individual from within. The part of the ego containing such impulses and phantasies is split off and evacuated by projective identification and in this way attributed to others. In the process, paranoid anxieties are created as the envious, destructive impulses are felt to attack the ego from without and a variety of defences are mounted in order to deal with this process" (1993, p. 45).

It is important, however, to be theoretically exact here. Primary envy is not identical with what I described above as the aggression that attacks the reality dimension of the object and, in this sense, is annihilatory. This aggression is directed against the process of structure formation, especially against the position outside, which opens up the access to the reality dimension of the object, but which also makes the fusional realization definitely impossible. This annihilatory aggression, conceptualized in this way, attempts to reverse the process of structure formation in order to, ideally, recreate the apparent preconditions for the fusion through the return to the primary-narcissistic suspension of space and time. But in any case the reality constitution of the object and its corollaries—consciousness, thinking, genital sexuality, gender difference, the concept of development—are the predominant themes of this aggression.

Primary envy, in turn, is a different force. It arises out of the position of an ego that no longer sees the possibility to incorporate the object into its ego-cosmic primary narcissistic omnipotence and which therefore engages in a furious campaign of destruction against this object which is eluding the ego's grasp. This is envy. Envy, therefore, is actually the expression of the death drive that is despairing because its aim cannot be fulfilled. In this sense it is the essentially suicidal force.

One could say that it is primary envy, conceptualized in this manner, that is behind the foreclosure of the primary object in the case of the psychogenic encapsulated autism.

In order to give a clear theoretical formulation: I have described further above that the prohibition of fusion and thus the life drive in the pre-schizoid phase—that is, in the phase before representational object constancy is reached and thus before the good-bad split of the object—can only articulate itself by the primary object itself refusing to fuse, in other words, by withdrawing from the ego when a fusional realization is attempted by the ego. In its traumatic maximal effect this is the experience of the not-me object, which Frances Tustin described as the cause and origin of the psychogenic encapsulation autism. Against this primary object that refuses fusion and withdraws from the ego, and that simultaneously is the sum of all that which the ego lacks, the primary envy is directed. This is indeed the primary form of manifestation of aggression, inasfar as it relates to the object's withdrawing as the primary form of expression of the antifusional principle of the life drive and reacts to it.

In any case, it becomes clear now that the annihilatory aggression described above and primary envy are not identical, but that they lie on a continuum of destructive regression: Annihilatory aggression can turn into primary envy, if in the course of the structural regression, which it engages in, it meets with the experience that fusion cannot be realized, not even under conditions of a suspended reality. In this way it becomes clear that the early development (only talking about it here) is indeed a trip between Scylla and Charybdis: on the one hand, the fusion between the primary ego and the primary object must be prevented at all cost, in order to prevent the collapse of the poles of perception and thus the self-annulment of the dimension of the psychical. On the other hand, the equally elementary danger of primary envy threatens, by which the primary ego attempts to destroy its object, inasfar as the object withdraws from the ego and refuses itself.

As far as development from here on is concerned, one has to say that primary envy as the archaic reaction of the ego to the primary object withdrawing from fusion, just like all forms of psychic expression once developed, remains active also after the transition to the good-bad split of the object, that is to say, after the establishment of representational object constancy and is now directing itself against the bad split object, so much so as the latter now represents and carries the defense against the fusion movement of the death drive, in other words, blocks the access to the good object. What we in the clinic recognize and dread as manifestations of primary envy in adults and children alike, draws its impact and dangerousness from its provenance out of the pre-schizoid phase, that is, from the phase of primary narcissism with its characteristics of globality and totality. As already touched on further above, it is evident that this envy is in a complementary relationship to the vision of fulfillment of the fusional death drive: it becomes effective to the degree that the death drive—or, respectively, the ego that is its ally—always and ever finds itself barred from establishing the primary narcissistic union with the object.

This envy is defended against through projection and projective identification, and significantly contributes to the threatening aspect of the bad object of the paranoid-schizoid and depressive position. The intensity of the destructive affect which is connected with this envy is experienced by the ego as threatening so much that it and the personality parts associated with it must be split off and projected, and in this manner, as stated, paradoxically contribute considerably to the experienced threatening character of the bad persecutory split object (cf. Rosenfeld, 1971), although the dynamic significance of the latter is to specifically prevent the fusion, whereupon the envy reacts. The

153

envy is so to speak against its own will, that is to say against its original intention, fed into the circuit of deterrence of the life drive via which the fusion is prevented and against the prevention of which the envy in fact reacts. To me, this appears to be a very essential process, insofar as through it the elementary destructive force of the primary envy, though not neutralized, is at least diverted in a direction that is fundamentally supporting psychic development.

Anyway, these considerations on the genesis of primary envy and annihilatory aggression imply that aggression, even in its most fundamental dimension, and consequent to the thoughts presented in this work, cannot be regarded as an independent drive but rather, that it has to be accorded the status of a possible complication in the ego's processing of the death drive, in this respect not unlike those specific maladjustments, faults and errors of the ego, which as described above, produce the major nosological categories.

16

Sublimation, ego-ideal and the dissolution of the traumatic nature of the ego

One of the most important further conclusions which results, according to my description, from the structural binding of the antagonism of the drives refers to the concept of sublimation. It can now be understood as the self-renunciation of the ego with regard to the temptation of incestuous corruption of the primal scene, which optimally results from the ego's dealing with the oedipal conflict and the meaning of the threat of castration. This sublimational ego has learnt that the threat of castration is not directed against its own interests but rather preserves them, by safeguarding the ego against the only danger threatening it from within, namely the fusional incest. In the sublimation the ego implicitly acknowledges the father imago as the, so to speak, operative imago of the safety of the ego, as a manifestation of the, by necessity, anti-fusional nature of the ego itself.

To remind the reader: The core of the father imago is the self-reflective position of the ego outside the drive phantasma which implies a split within the ego, contrasting the directly experiencing ego with its self-reflective function. This split renders a fusion with the primary object structurally impossible insofar fusion, as a global and total process, is only possible on the basis of a unitary ego, and in this way makes the good-bad split of the object as the early mode of defense against the fusional danger obsolete. This dynamical meaning of the father imago is psychically expressed in the image of the primal scene where the father unites with the mother without getting lost in fusion, <u>because he is the antifusionary principle</u>.

The constitution of the father imago as the antifusionary principle is founded, as said, on the self-reflective split of the ego within itself. Seen like this, the father imago defines the nature of the ego as that of a basic non-identity with itself and contains the warning for the ego not to try to be identical with the father, not to try to possess the phallus as the expression and means of his power and potency to ban the fusional danger, as on the phantasmatic plane, this would mean to reverse the self-reflective split within the ego and to confront the ego anew with the unmodulated splitting of the object and the consecutive loss of reality access. This is the essential meaning of the threat of castration which I, for this reason, have designated as the phallic threat of castration, as it is the threat of losing, in the appropriation, the antifusional capacity and potency of the phallus as the phantasmatic condensation and dynamic attribute of the apotropaic power of the father.

When in the process of sublimation these implications and meanings of the primal scene imagination have been worked through and understood by the ego, and the ego has accepted the necessity to give up its wish to intrude into the primal scene and to incestuously corrupt it, the primal scene in its above delineated sense stands out as the phantasmatic, imaginative definition of the security of the ego from the only danger that threatens it from within, i.e. the danger of fusion with the imago, the representation of the object. In this sense, this imago of the primal scene which the ego explicitly stays out of, is <u>the sublimational ego-ideal</u>. This sublimational movement is therefore

156

the solution of the oedipal conflict arising from its very structure itself. In it, the primary traumatisation of the ego from the confrontation with its inherent threat of annihilation as the consequence of its unavoidable fusional desire dissolves. The traumatic nature of the ego which I have described would come to an end in it.

While in the neurotic constellation the Oedipus complex must perish as it is being repressed into the id by the threat of castration in order to, in this way, safeguard the non-identity of ego and phallus and prevent the fusional incest, sublimation offers an alternative here. As the primal scene imago in the case of the sublimational constitution of the ego no longer represents the fusional danger for this ego, but to the contrary shows itself in its true nature as the imago of the safety of the ego, the primal scene must no longer be withdrawn from the realm of the ego and relegated to the id, but can be installed—as the quasi-definitional imago of the ego—in the form of the sublimational ego-ideal, as a 'grade in the ego', in modification of Freud who, within the framework of his structural theory, had addressed the term ego-ideal both in "The Ego and the Id" (1923), and in the "New Introductory Lectures on Psychoanalysis" (1932) as a grade in the superego.

This sublimational ego-ideal in this view represents the completion of the structural development of the psyche, because it defines the antifusional nature of the ego and in this way protects it against the danger arising from within itself.

The ego-ideal is constituted by the final internalization of the relationship to the oedipal objects. The core of the ego-ideal is the imago of the primal scene in a version where the ego has withdrawn out of it, that is, has relinquished its incestuous demand. It is this renunciation that makes internalization possible, as the wish for satisfaction through the real object has been given up. To put it differently, the final internalization is not possible as long as the wish for satisfaction has not been given up. In this version the primal scene is therefore the phantasmatic definition of the antifusional life drive, and thus of the safety of the ego.

In a parallel way, Michael Feldman writes on the subject in his paper on the Oedipus complex: "If the patient negotiates the Oedipus complex in a relatively healthy way, he has an internal model of an intercourse that is, on balance, a creative activity. This seems to be directly connected with the development of the patient's capacity to allow thoughts and ideas to interact in a kind of healthy intercourse" (1989, p. 120).

Janine Chasseguet-Smirgel (1975) described the ego-ideal as a pathological factor, as an engram of the narcissistic position, which she identifies with precisely the striving towards the fusional incest with the mother. For me, this striving has become the content, the expression of the death drive on the oedipal plane. Nevertheless, I am grateful for her lucid examination which has stimulated my own thoughts.

The primal scene imagination, integrated into the ego in the sublimational ego-ideal, is in fact dynamically unconscious, as it is, for one thing, too close to the incest phantasy and, for the other, the death drive with its quality of temptation continues to remain active of course, also under the conditions of a sublimated state of the psyche. For the death drive is the immediate psychic consequence of physiological lack and the unpleasure resulting from it. Its binding is the continuous and fundamental work demand of the psyche. For the fulfilment of this work demand, which falls to the ego, a sublimational ego-ideal only provides the optimal conditions in as far as in it, the formula, so to speak, for the resolution of the oedipal conflict is laid down.

The meaning of the ego-ideal is thus less one of agency but rather of position. It is the definition of a certain potential level of functioning of the psyche, or of the ego, respectively.

One has to be clear about it here that the death drive, in its basic motivation, is not in any way bad or reprehensible, even if, parallel to the degree it brings the ego under its spell, it generates psychic pathology. It is the aim of the death drive to reach a state of total emotional calmness via establishing union with the object in which the ability to suspend need-tension, that is to say lack and unpleasure, is seen to reside. This motive as such is beyond reproach. The problem lies in the fact that its realization by fusion with the object/the imago of the object would lead to a self-annulment of the ego and thus of the dimension of the psychical.

17

Ego, father imago and the Christian myth

As already briefly sketched further above, one surprise application of the thoughts presented in this work refers to the mythos of the Christian religion. The basic tenet of the New Testament is about a theology of the relationship of Jesus Christ to the God of the Old Testament: Jesus is the son of God, the logos that became flesh, God himself who incarnated in him in human form and who in this human form has defined his relationship to the God who simultaneously remains outside this incarnation, as that of the Son to the Father. Within a perspective which understands the mythos as a representation of the inner world, Christ thus declares himself as the ego insofar as the ego is always 'the child of ...'.

Such a view of religion and of mythos as projected metapsychology is also shared by Freud (1904) in *The Psychopathology of Everyday Life*: "... a large part of the mythological view of the world, which extends a long way into the most modern religions, *is nothing but psychology projected into the external world.* The obscure recognition (the endopsychic perception, as it were) of psychical factors and relations in the unconscious is mirrored (...) in the construction of a *supernatural reality*, which is destined to be changed back once more by science into the *psychology of the unconscious.* One could venture (...) to transform *metaphysics* into *metapsychology*" (p. 258-259, italics Freud).

161

The Christian mythos thus reveals itself as a religion which has as its subject the relationship with the father, with the father imago. This meaning of the Christian religious myth as a specific father-son, that is to say, father-ego religion is highlighted by the fact that the God of the Old Testament is only referred to as Father in a handful of very rare passages. W. Marchel (1966) and J. Jeremias (1965) were only able to detect twenty such references, while the address as Father occurs far over one hundred times in the Gospel of John alone.

This relationship of the ego to the father imago is accurately described by the religion mythologem when it refers to Christ as both wholly God and wholly human at the same time. The meaning of this dogmatic definition is clearly exemplified in the temptations of the devil, but also in the death on the cross itself, inasmuch as Christ, as wholly human, observes the limitations that apply to humans without at the same time invoking his God-nature in order to override the laws of reality. By doing so Christ declares that his relationship to the Father is one of an identical non-identity: he is of the same essence as the Father, but as a human, as ego, he must not lay claim to the identity with the Father.

As a structural pattern, the above ties in with my deduction exactly, according to which the father imago in its core—which is the position of the ego outside the drive phantasma—is a split-off part of the ego, by which the ego protects itself against the only danger threatening it from within, namely its fusional self-annulment. In the father imago, therefore, the ego's nature, so characteristically based on non-fusion, becomes expressed. The father imago is a part of the ego that has become objective and absolute, the task of which is, from this moment on, to carry and represent the ego's own law and to sanction its transgression.

It is true that ego and father imago are of the same essence, but in order to not annul the effect and power of the father imago again, which as we know is based on the distancing of the ego from itself, the ego must not equate itself with it. Anyway, it is clear from this perspective to what degree the conflict with the heretic movement of Arianism, which occupied the first centuries after Christ so passionately, touched the core of the psychological content of the message of Christ: Arian's intention was, as is known, to replace the identity of Christ with God—wholly human and wholly God—with the mere similarity (homousy vs. homeousy).

The paradox expressed in the Christian religious myth is that the Son, by internalizing the necessity of renunciation as conveyed by the father imago, to the degree of this specific internalization becomes identical with the father principle itself, that he indeed represents and possesses the phallus, the phallic potency. This identity with the Father thus contains the deepest knowledge about the necessary and indissoluble non-identity. In other words, the identity with the Father, the father principle consists, by definition, of this integrated non-identity. I think it may astonish, rightfully so, if one considers the precision with which the religious mythologem has captured this context in the formula of the simultaneous identity—"Anyone who has seen me has seen the Father" (John 14:9)—and non-identity of God-Father and God-Son.

Coming from the other end, we could say that God becoming man in the Son, on the intrapsychic plane of the Oedipal relationship of the ego to the parental images, contains, charmingly so, an offer of reconciliation to the son by the prohibiting father of the Oedipal superego who excludes from the primal scene: inasfar as the Father becomes Son himself, in order to demonstrate the binding nature of the threat of castration, the renunciation with regard to the primal scene, which he as Son must also accept. This means the self-binding of the Father as Son to the Oedipal law, in as much as this law is not an unjust exclusion, but the law of the safety of the ego. In this way the mythos of Christ completes the mythos of Oedipus and describes as the core of the message of redemption the Oedipal law, namely as the psychic requirement of freedom and 'salvation' of the ego, in the sense of the protection against the only danger which threatens the ego from within.

Seen in this way the holy name of God acquires a deep meaning, which the latter had revealed to Moses from the burning thornbush (Ex. 3: 13-15): "Ehyeh hasher eyeh", "I Am that I Am", also translatable as "I Am the 'I-Am'", or precisely, "I Am the I that Is".

Out of interest I wish to point out that the Old Testamentarians are discussing alternative translations, in addition to the above classical translation which the Greek version also reflects with "I am the Being". According to Werner H. Schmidt (1983) the translation "I will be that I will be" can be etymologically upheld, also. Manfred Görg (1997) translates: "I am that I will be" and by doing so expresses the timelessness, the suspension of time.

Incidentally, the deep and meaningful reference to the primal scene of the Christ mythos is also documented in the *Constitutio Apostolica 'Munificentissimus Deus'* of Pius XII, as C.G. Jung (1952) had already pointed out. This *Constitutio*, issued in 1950, despite its revolutionary theological importance garnered little attention outside of the Catholic theological realm. In this by character dogmatic proclamation of the Assumption of Mary, which in fact expands the divine trinity to a quaternity, we read that Mary has been united as the bride with the Son, and as Sophia with the divinity, in the heavenly bridal chamber (thalamus). The female principle, the imago of the mother, was thereby put on an equal footing with the trinity which in itself forms a unit, and which in this way was completed to form the primal scene imagination.

In symbolic condensation, this Constitutio Apostolica contains the theory of the sublimative ego-ideal which I presented in the previous chapter, insofar as the ego—Christ—which has integrated the father, that is to say, has accepted the non-identity with the father, is able to carry out the primal scene union with the mother without losing itself in the fusion. For the recognition of the non-identity with the father implies the renunciation of even trying to establish the fusional identity with the mother as the paradigmatic object, for this fusion would only be (seemingly) possible under the protection of the appropriated phallus of the father. In this way, Christ stands for the ego which has overcome the death drive. The incest—the union with Mary as the bride in the heavenly bridal chamber—becomes possible, because it is no longer fusional and thus no longer holds the danger of ego dissolution; or because, to formulate the paradox, it is no longer incestuous.

In sum: in the context of this work I have described the primordial constitution of the psyche where, in the state of timelessness, the primary ego is surrounded by a primary object, outside of which nothing is conceivable and which insofar constitutes the all-that-is for the primary ego. With the appearance of the first need-tension and thus the first wish, which is based on the suspension of this need, the ego attempts to put itself in one with this surrounding all-that-is object, to fuse into union with it, for the suspension of this need must of necessity be founded in this object as there is nothing else otherwise. Regrettably, however, this striving for the establishment of unity is immediately the death drive, for this union, once established, would lead to a collapse of the newly opened up dimension of the psychical.

These formulations clearly show their closeness to the descriptions of mystical experience. It is, therefore, the first task of the psyche to resist this mystical pull, as this pull—when the ego gives in to it without previously having understood the constitutive significance and meaning of the Oedipus complex as the safeguard for living in the world—leads straight into psychopathology. In my opinion, it is this fact of the unavoidable Oedipalization which is being formulated in the Christ mythos from within the center of the very world of religious thinking and which, with uncanny precision, meets the findings and conclusions of psychoanalysis.

18

The death drive as the mode of functioning of the primary narcissistic ego

In order to return from the heavenly heights to the psychoanalytic everyday I would like to discuss one more clinically very important implication, which is a consequence of the drive concept as I have presented it. If I conceptualize the death drive as the striving that originates in the primordial condition of the human psyche in that it constitutes itself from the separation of the poles of perception; that is to say—on the basis of a certain ontogenetic stage of maturation of the central nervous system—from the emergence of subject and object of perception, the perceiving primary ego and the perceived primary object; if the death drive, before this backdrop, consists in the involuntary and inescapable tendency of the primary ego, in case of a physiological tension of unpleasure, to look for compensation for the feeling of lack through the fusional appropriation of the primary object, as this is the only thing given apart from itself and thus compensation for the lack can only come from it; if the problem with this totally comprehensible and natural tendency consists in the fact that with its consummation, the barely arisen new dimension of the psychical would again collapse, as it consists only in maintaining the tension of separation between subject and object of perception and springs from this separation; therefore, if this is so, the death drive in essence is the drive of negation of the separation from the object. I do not need to redraw, one more time, the path on which the life drive finds its ways and means to counteract this ominous striving, and on this path finds opportunity to bring about the formation of the complete structure of the human psyche. In any case, the final expression of these counteractive measures precipitates in the Oedipal conflictual constellation.

The aim of the death drive, which is to suspend the separation from the object, remains the same at all stages of mental development and structure formation. The various forms of psychopathology consist in the various attempts of the death drive and of the ego coalescing with it, to enforce this aim of the drive. The central phantasmatic expression and common denominator of all these attempts is the attack on the Oedipal father as the instance that prohibits and prevents the fusional incest with the mother. I would like to stress in this context, however, that this is always and in every single case about suspending the separation from the object.

The death drive thus is the power that negates the primary object's objectal character which is independent from the ego; it is the deobjectalizing drive. This has immediate consequences for the theory of the depressive position. The classical concept (Klein 1935, 1940) sees the depressive position as the complication according to which the clear and unquestioned object splitting of the paranoid-schizoid position can no longer be maintained within a psychical constitution which, in principle, has not yet overcome the good-bad split of the object, leading to the complication that the ego, under the influence of its own panic, in its attacks on the bad object also damages the good object and—in its phantasmatic experiencing—destroys it. In the positive case when the depressive position is successfully worked through and overcome, this leads to the double movement of, on the one hand, mourning for the apparently damaged and destroyed lost object—the source of the good, of satisfaction, of the suspension of lack-, and on the other hand, to phantasmatic efforts towards its reparation.

The process of mourning is thereby thought of (cf. Steiner, 1993, following Freud 1917) as fundamentally occurring in two steps, namely, one, in the immediate reaction to the loss, in the denial of that loss and in the attempt to possess the object internally and to preserve it, to keep it safe. In this context a further category of splitting processes occurs within the framework of the depressive position, in order to accomplish this particular protection of the object, also from one's own destructive attacks. This, too, must fail with the experience that the ego cannot provide this protection. The second step of the mourning process then consists in acknowledging the loss and the existence of the object independent from the ego. That is to say, here a situation arises in which as a result of the conflictuous complication of the depressive position the independence and autonomy of the object is being acknowledged.

If one was to consider this formulation before the backdrop of my thoughts regarding the meaning and the psychodynamics of both psychic drives, it becomes evident that, with this perspective, something far more fundamental is happening than has been outlined in the already heavyweight formulas of the classical concept: the death drive is being forced, namely in and through the process of mourning, for the very first time, to withdraw its aim which is directed towards the absolute, omnipotent possession of the object. Or rather, one must formulate this more exactly, as the drive would be no drive if it desisted from its aim: the ego, for the first time, is being forced to realize that its old pact with the death drive in the attempt to establish the primary narcissistic union with the object, is not self-evident and natural, good and right, but rather, to the contrary, that the life-maintaining object, at the level of the drive phantasies, while pursuing this aim, has become badly damaged and perhaps even destroyed. Thus the ego, in its collaboration with the death drive which as said appeared so natural, for the first time encounters a definite no go, a genuine prohibition, and the crisis of the depressive position, in this sense, is a prefiguration of the later crisis of the Oedipal conflict, the intentional task of the latter being to finally bind the death drive structurally, once and for all.

In the crisis of the depressive position with its theme of injuring and destroying the object, and, in consequence, of the enforced acknowledgement of the separation from it through the process of mourning, two themes are, for the first time, simultaneously addressed and psychically captured: one, implicitly, the theme of deobjectalization (and in this sense destruction) of the object which is the theme of the death drive, and two, and above all, the theme of a necessary separation of ego and object.

The depressive crisis into which the early object splitting leads in consequence of the unavoidable developmentally given insight into the fundamental time-space unity of the object, thus has to be considered a brilliant move of nature in order to divide the ego and the death drive. The success of this move then immediately shows by the ego developing, as a result of working through the successive depressive crises, the 'position outside the drive phantasma', that is to say, the ego is taking up a reflexive distance towards itself for the first time. This reflexive distance consists in a splitting of the ego within itself, through which, as I have shown, object splitting as mode of defense against the fusional danger that results from the death drive is overcome. The position outside becomes the seed and core of the father imago and thus the origin of the Oedipal constellation, the task of which, as said, is to bind the death drive once and for all. The psychic structuring process may therefore be regarded as one in which the psychic separation of the ego from the object becomes codified. This separation is the basis of mental life, and therefore also the basis of mental health.

At this point one should spend some thought on what I have referred to here and consistently throughout this work, as psychical drive. Just above, I have formulated it in the way that the crisis of the depressive position serves to divide the ego and the death drive, that is to say, to make clear to the ego that its own interest, namely keeping up the relationship to the life-maintaining object, is not congruent with the fusional and insofar deobjectalizing drive aim of the death drive. My mental conception, in this formulation, is to treat this as if the ego and the death drive until that time, so to speak, form a coalition, a pact, as the ego has not yet become aware of the contradiction of its own nature to that of the death drive. One may ask, however, if this is actually so or whether in the earliest constitution in which the primary ego, in a state of lack, wants to incorporate into itself and merge with, in a primary narcissistic way, the primary object as the only thing existing outside of itself, and thus as the only conceivable source that could suspend this lack: whether this primary ego is not simply identical with the death drive.

The ego, as a separate motivational structure, would thus only detach from the death drive with the crisis of the depressive position. In other words, that which we further on call the death drive, would designate the early form of functioning of the ego, in which the ego confronted the object still totally recklessly without any regard and where the only task was to suspend need-tension and in this sense achieve blissfulness. That which we call drive in the psyche would thus conserve the impetus and momentum of the primary narcissism of the primary narcissistic world, i.e. of the pre-schizoid phase.

I do not consider it unlikely that this is indeed so. This means that the ego, as the agency that we know, only begins to develop when it struggles with the question of the preservation of the object; that is to say, the ego having the experience that it, as concerns its structural identity, gets the best protection for itself through an object whose identity in turn is protected. This experience is then being laid down structurally in the position outside, and especially in the father imago developing from it, which embodies and exemplifies the anti-fusional principle. The death drive, the primary form of functioning of the ego, would therefore result immediately out of the system property of the human brain, according to which the direct sensual perception is the first form of functioning of this organ that can build up representations and is thus in principle capable of displaying the quality of being conscious. The whole structure-forming process of the psyche that psychoanalysis describes has, from then on, no further task than to make the ego, the subject of perception, understand, that the condition of its structural safety is different from its desire for an instant fusional merging with the other pole of the perceptual function, the object.

The life drive, then, would have to be regarded in its turn as the force, which represents the natural law based system property of this newly arisen dimension of the psychical. This means it must be assumed that when this new dimension comes into being through the poles of perception separating out, that is to say with the constitution of the primary ego and the primary object, that there exists a kind of system consciousness of the fact that the realization of the aim of the death drive of fusing the primary ego with the primary object would lead to the reannulment of this newly arisen dimension. This tendency of the psychical to preserve itself would oppose the realization of the death drive and lead to the development of the mental apparatus, by which the death drive—we should rather say: the primary narcissistic ego—is being bound. The life drive is the dynamically effective principle that from the very beginning represents the fact that the ego and the representation of the primary object must be kept separated, to prevent the ego from getting lost in the fusion. I have therefore referred to Eros or the life drive as the drive of ego protection. The theme of the life drive is that the safety of the object from the fusional attacks of the death drive simultaneously means, and is in fact, the safety of the ego. Insofar as the life drive represents and protects the object and is about this secret relationship of mutual safety between ego and object, it is not inappropriate to designate it with the alternative term Eros.

The energetic potential of the Eros or life drive captured in this way, if one was to follow this thought, paradoxically ensues directly from that of the death drive, that is to say, from the existential necessity to hold up against the death drive's primary-narcissistic impact. One could say that without the death drive, there would be no life drive, either; that the life drive has its raison d'être in the death drive. Without death drive there would therefore be no psychic structure formation and thus no formation of the specifically human quality of a self-reflexive consciousness in the sense of the position outside. Sexuality, the physical sexual drive, is only later linked to these drive dynamics of the psyche via the primal attachment to the human object, and then becomes the arena for the manifestation of both psychical drives that finally leads to the fully developed Oedipal conflict constellation, the aim and objective of which is to structurally bind the death drive once and for all. That this attachment to physical sexuality, to the human object, is reversible or may not happen, respectively, is known from cases of the most severe psychopathology.

As unusual as the formulation might sound, there is, however, upon closer inspection, something to be said for such identification of the primary ego's functional form with the death drive, inasfar as in our investigation we have repeatedly reached the point where we can see that earlier forms of functioning of the ego remain alive in the psyche. The most spectacular case in this respect is certainly the form of functioning of the identity of the ego with the drive phantasma which is the functional background of the paranoid-schizoid and depressive constitutions of the psyche and which is related to object splitting as the mode of defense against the death drive. I have argued that this form of functioning remains in existence in parallel when the position of the ego outside the drive phantasma is reached and that it forms the structural core of the unconscious of the id, while the 'position outside' opens the door to time-space identity of the object and thus to reality and forms the basis of the function of explicit consciousness (i.e. as opposed to unconsciousness). Here, too, the ego has left behind its earlier onionskin, whereby this latter remains totally intact as to its function. In other words, the ego functions continuously both in its identity and non-identity constitution, only that we refer to the identity constitution no longer as ego but as id.

We fare not better, as it seems, with the death drive: we have also here succumbed to a reification, by designating the force which we call death drive in this very manner, and in this way have blocked our view and now cannot see that the death drive is the surviving form of functioning of the primary ego. The cause for this is to be seen, most certainly, in the enormous dynamic power and as-it-were wildness which nolens volens must be ascribed to the death drive and which, as a result, appears to make this classification as a drive unavoidable. In my opinion this dynamic potential comes from the fact that the death drive has its roots precisely in the primary constitution of the psyche, in which the power of desire has not yet been curbed by any reality conditions, and the primary ego in confrontation with the primary object—which in its turn in this earliest constitution, before representational object constancy, was the all-that-is—was faced with the seeming possibility to enlarge itself to the ego-cosmic ego. There is no greater power of seduction. I have described the pertaining existential situation at length in the beginning chapters.

The continued existence of the good-bad split of the object in that part of the psyche that, also after establishment of the position outside, keeps functioning in the mode of the identity of the ego with the drive phantasma thus also means the parallel keeping up of two different and mutually incompatible object conceptualizations, namely one, the splitting concept of the object, and two, the concept of time-space identity of the object, with which access to reality is given. One can ask if something similar is also the case with respect to the object conceptualization of the pre-schizoid position, in which, before the establishment of representational object constancy, the experiencing of the object is still exclusively bound to immediate sensory stimulation, as I have set out in detail in the context of the infantile encapsulation autism. Above, after citing Tustin, I have discussed the hypothesis that there is possibly a close link between the continued unconscious existence of this form of experiencing and the psychosomatic illnesses. If my above deduction of the death drive from the dynamic circumstances of this earliest constitution is correct, the death drive in its characteristics has a lot to do with its being bound to the immediate sensory experience. This, too, is a hypothesis which unquestionably has a lot going for it.

Unlike the object conceptualization of the splitting world and that of the time-space identity of the object, both of which differ in that they show a radical and unreconcilable rift between them, the object conceptualization of the pre-schizoid phase or position and that of the representational constancy of the object are not quite so different as to their essence. What is being added with object constancy is first of all 'only' the ability to split, that is to say, the ability resulting from the new capacity to maintain the representation over time—in plain language: resulting from the new capacity to remember—to counter the representation of the good, need-satisfying object with that of a bad, persecuting object. Consequently one can assume that the transition from the object conceptualization of the pre-schizoid phase to that of the level of splitting is a fluid one.

The central difference here consists in the form of function of the ego: in the pre-schizoid phase, which is that of primary narcissism, the ego, on the affirmative side of experiencing, is able to experience itself as completely unrestricted. It is under the absolute omnipotence of thought and under the illusion that it possesses the ability to aggrandize itself into an ego-cosmic ego through omnipotent control over the object and fusion with it. This illusion comes to an abrupt end through the appearance of the bad, persecuting splitting object. I assume that this primary narcissistic form of how the ego experiences and of its motivationality remains existent and conserves what we subsequently call the death drive. If, therefore, in the transition from the splitting constitution to the position outside the conceptualization of the object undergoes dramatic changes, when time-space identity develops out of the split object, then, in the transition from the pre-schizoid to the splitting constitution, the conceptualization of the ego changes: the ego of the primary narcissism which posits itself as absolute turns into the attacked ego of the paranoid-schizoid position which fights for its existence, and, although it tries to maintain the old megalomania, goes more and more on the defensive until it eventually fails in the depressive position.

In the larger context around these issues the question of projective identification will still have to be discussed again. John Steiner (1993) worked out that what has to be taken back in mourning, chiefly and all in all—in the depressive position and elsewhere—are the projective identifications which the subject has put into the lost object and through which it is connected to it. As has been said elsewhere in this work, the projective identifications can be regarded as particular fusional movements via which the ego attempts to force a fusional connection with the object. In Steiner's words: "One of the consequences of projective identification is that the subject relates to the object not as a separate person with his own characteristics but as if he is relating to himself. He may ignore aspects of the object which do not fit the projection or he may control and force or persuade the object to enact the role required of him." (1993, p. 42). And: "We can see that projective identification gives rise to a state in which true separateness is not experienced. This state of mind provides relief from anxiety and from frustration as well as from envy, and is idealized." (op. cit. p. 44). Sohn (1985) describes, as an extreme, narcissistic organizations in which the massive use of projective identifications leads to the subject having the feeling to become the object and to possess all that is good and the properties of the object, so that the object is very concretely being taken into possession.

This so-to-speak narcissisalizing trait of projective identification applies irrespective of the fact that the projective identifications largely serve defensive purposes, that is to say, are there to enable the evacuation of unloved parts of the personality. If one takes into account that through the fusion with the primary object, wholly and largely, relief is to be provided for the experience of lack by equating the object, as the source of complemental plenitude, as the source of suspension of the lack, with the ego, it would be completely along these lines if these parts of the ego that are in one way or other tainted by the experience of deficiency or lack, were evacuated into the object. At the same time, the connection with these parts is maintained, since with the same movement the aim of fusion is to be reached. If one cannot equate the good, the object, in a global fusional movement with the ego, so as to suspend the lack, one can at least try to relocate the lack, the negative in parts into the object and thus simultaneously bind the object to the ego. This also clarifies the theoretical question of why the ego may want to get rid of an aversive content, on the one hand, by evacuating it into the object, and on the other, may not want to give up the connection with it.

Projective identification in the sense of the above evacuation and defense, which simultaneously establishes a fusional connection with the object, and thus undercuts the separation between ego/subject and object, is, therefore, the main mode of operating of a death drive which sees itself barred from fulfillment via the large-format primary narcissistic fusion between the primary ego and the primary object. In a similar sense, John Steiner (1993, p. 61) writes: "Today, as we recognize the central role of projective identification in the creation of pathological object relations (....)", thus designating the striving for suspension of the separation from the object as the motor of psychopathology.

Hence this is probably the place for a basic reflection on the character of psychopathology in general, under the perspective of the drive concept presented in this work. It is, however, not so easy to not drift off into generalizations so that the impression of banality arises. Lastly, what would have to be said as the sum of all my reflections, is that any form of psychopathology must be regarded as a form of activity of the death drive. Under the definition which I have given the death drive this means, however, that psychopathology, in whichever form, goes back to the attempt to suspend the separation between the ego and the object—the object imago or the representation of the object, respectively. This, too, the question of separation or non-separation of ego and object as a determining factor of mental illness is by itself no new theme. It is new, however, to regard this theme as the sole and exclusive axis around which psychic structure formation revolves and from the systemic error susceptibilities of which the individual forms of psychopathology systematically and describably develop. I have endeavored to give examples for this in the individual clinical investigations of this work (hysteria, psychogenic encapsulated autism, annihilatory aggression).

John Steiner, in a work that has impressed me much and from which I have cited frequently for this reason, has formulated a theory of 'psychic retreats', which in its turn already covers a very wide field of psychopathology. He conceptualizes these psychic retreats as fallback positions, be it in the form of concretely thought of inner places or as special forms of organization of defensive processes or as a special construct of internal object relations or as a combination of all of these. As to their content, they are characterized, for one thing, by a denial of the separation from the object, and for another, by a simultaneous acknowledgement and non-acknowledgement of reality, which is what carries this denial. He calls this simultaneous acknowledgement and non-acknowledgement the 'narcissistic perversion', following Freud's work on fetishism of 1927. The points in common with my view are obvious here.

The theme is too broad for me to even attempt to comprehensively deal with it, not even in approximation. But I would like to raise the question of whether or not each form of psychic illness can be regarded as a specific psychic retreat; as a form of resistance and defense which attempts to enforce the aim of the death drive after all, or at least to not give up the claim to its realization (as in grudge, resentment and remorse—all of them retreats described by Steiner). Each and every psychic illness would then be a retreat, a place of mentally withdrawing in the sense of a, in each case, specific evasion from the necessity of acknowledging the separation from the object. With every form of such an evasion from separation comes with necessity, as I have described, both a simultaneous acknowledgement and non-acknowledgement of reality, in the sense of a simultaneous evasion and non-evasion from the position outside; in any case above the psychotic level of functioning.

I think, however, that the withdrawal or retreat characteristic of psychopathology under the precondition of my death drive model can be described even more exactly: at the basis of it is, in each single case, the maintenance of an absolutely posited and as-it-were relentless egocentric satisfaction claim of the ego with respect to the object, which in its core is an attack against the object and actually an attack against the primal scene, against the excludedness from the primal scene. The retreat theme—narcissistic in this sense—consists in the fact that the ego, under the fiction of deprivation, of lack, feels that it is being attacked and thinks it has to secure its survival by attacking the object and, in the phantasmatic background, by pursuing its incorporation into the ego. The ego is thereby not courageous enough to allow the insight that the psychical condition of its secured existence lies in the intangibility of the object; that the ego by withdrawing from the primal scene defines its own structural safety.

The deprivations and needs, imagined or real, hereby support the fiction of entitlement of the death drive to face the object with the mentality of an animal of prey, in order to counter the fear. What is misunderstood here is that the psychic, structural condition, that is to say, the cause of fear lies in the attack on the object imago because through it the structural delimitation between ego and object imago is attacked and threatens to collapse. Through this attack, the ego wants to enforce fusion and ignores the fact that it would itself be suspended in fusion. Therefore, the delimitation between ego and object is being secured through the—in this sense—psychogenic fear. For this reason, the acknowledgement of this delimitation is the condition for freedom from fear; in any case as far as the latter has intrinsically psychic reasons.

Hence the alternative designation of the life drive as Eros has a deep meaning, for it is Eros which highlights the object in its inviolability and wholeness, in its splendor, and celebrates it, and through this affirms life. Lastly this is the theme of the arts, insofar as they are in search of beauty as the moment in which the truth of the object speaks. The psychic retreat of pathology is therefore the retreat from the object to the ego, it is the narcissistic movement.

One more theme I would like to touch on in the context of these general considerations, as it is of importance for our psychotherapeutic-psychoanalytic conception of man, for the image we have of our own science and profession, and thus for the consideration of our own existence. We are used to seeing the psyche as an infinity, as a field that is inexhaustible. Not much will change here, on one side, for the occurring cases of combinatory possibility of circumstances and personalities continue to be unfathomable. On the other side, the basal structure of the human psyche, before the background of my reflections, is given a comprehensible and describable framework. This means a change of our view of the human being and frees up capacities, as a certain problem—that of this basal structure—can be deemed as solved.

19

Theoretical refutation of Freud´s death drive concept

pplying the thoughts presented in this work finally leads to one further important implication, inasfar as I am of the opinion that from them a formal theoretical refutation of Freud's death drive concept may be deduced.

In his formulation of the death drive, Freud started out with the clinical manifestations of repetition compulsion and repetition phenomena, of sadism and masochism, of the negative therapeutic reaction, ambivalence and regression, self-destruction, melancholia and depression. All these phenomena are, also in my view, forms of expression of the death drive: they are linked by the fight against objectality, that is to say, the fight against the objectal character of the object, in the sense of that particular quality of the object imago which opposes the fusion with the ego and which the life drive maintains and defends. Freud who for his part saw in the death drive fundamentally the drive towards self-destruction, writes in *The Economic Problem of Masochism*: "The libido has the task of making the destroying instinct innocuous, and it fulfills the task by diverting that instinct to a great extent outwards—soon with the help of a special organic system, the muscular apparatus—towards objects in the external world" (1924, p. 163).

For clarification, the death drive for Freud was in this way connected with the aim of destruction, and its primary and fundamental object for him is the self of the subject in its physical and psychical identity. Life, therefore, is only possible for Freud insofar as this death drive is being deviated from the self and directed "towards objects in the external world". Thus this contains a change of object. Contrary to that, I would maintain that the death drive is directed against or towards the object <u>from the beginning</u>. More exactly, it is directed against the separateness of the ego vis-à-vis the imago of the primary object, against the necessary separation of subject and object of perception. The aim of the death drive is the suspension of the tension of unpleasure by fusing with the object. This aim has nothing to do with a primary aggression either against the self or the object.

This leads to the, in my view, theoretically crucial insight that the direction of the death drive towards the external world is no more than the result of the reality access which comes about through the overcoming of the good-bad split of the object as the primary form of defending against the death drive. Through this new feature the erstwhile purely intrapsychic, subjectively defined imago of the primary object is brought into alignment with the representation of the external real object. Before as after, the death drive is directed towards the object, this object, however, is first the primary, subjective object of the splitting constitution, later with the overcoming of the sole rule of the splitting constitution through the acquisition of the position outside, the outer reality can be recognized and perceived as such, and then—and only then—can the death drive be directed towards the external object.

The quality and the object, the content and the aim of the death drive do not change in any way or form through its direction to the external world, in particular, there is no change from auto-aggression to hetero-aggression, that is to say no change of object takes place, which incidentally would also imply a change in aim. Underlying this is a theoretical misunderstanding with serious consequences: the equation of the death drive with destruction, for one, could only ever have been made on the faulty assumption of an object change, whereby destruction according to Freud enforces this object change so as to prevent the self-destruction of the subject. In this way it was misunderstood that this drive is basically neither directed against the self nor against the object, but against the moment of separation. The death drive is not per se the "destroying instinct".

Only before the backdrop of the hypostasis of an object change which, so it seems, necessarily results from the empirical, descriptive observation of the direction of the aggression towards the external, was Freud able to link the death drive theoretically with aggression. This object change enabled him to deduce heteroaggression from the outward diversion, necessary for maintaining life, of a destructive tendency derived from the organic that seemingly was originally directed against the subject itself. Without this conclusion of an unavoidable object change Freud's concept of the death drive lacks in its axiomatic deduction, inasfar as then the genesis of aggression can no longer be deduced from the death drive's aim of self-destruction.

If this objection against Freud's assumed object change is justified, Freud's conceptualization of the death drive would be refuted for theoretical reasons. This provides the theoretical legitimacy for thoughts like the ones I have presented, which fundamentally reformulate the concept of the death drive. In any case, however, Freud's basic assumption of a dualistic drive structure, in which sexuality can no longer one-sidedly be assigned to one of the two drive poles, is also in my view correct and inevitable.

185

Without the object change that Freud assumed as necessary in his theory formulation, the death drive would have to be equated directly with "inborn" aggression—irrespective of whether it is directed against the object or the subject—which in the years after his death, under the, as-it-were, application of it from pragmatic points of view, became the course of things. As discussed further above, the aggression directed towards the annihilation of the real object, an aggression which can also lead as far as suicide against the self, is, in my view, one of the possible fates of the death drive, but not the expression of its innermost very own nature. Freud would never have accepted a reduction of the death drive to a general inborn aggression, as with certainty it would have appeared to him as an intolerable theoretical shortcoming to speak of an aggressive drive without any indication out of which necessity within the subject, within the subjective psyche, such aggression conceptualized as a primary drive might possibly arise.

For him this necessity lay in the demand for work to maintain a multicellular organism, and related with it the unpleasure which leads to the wish to suspend this multicellular organization, whereby this "destroying instinct" then—with the implication of object change—must be diverted to the exterior world in order to guarantee the maintenance of life. With the absence of object change, however, this deduction of the death drive becomes untenable.

The reduction of the death drive to aggression, in my view, does not do justice to the circumstance that the theme of the death drive is the fight against the separation from the object. The external appearances of this fight can be either aggressive or sexual, so that the same applies for aggression as for sexuality, namely that it is the medium of expression for both drives.

That Freud could assume such a qualitative change of the death drive with respect to its direction towards the external—in other words, object change—has to do with the historic moment that the formation of a theory of early psychic development had not yet happened. To be specific, the theory that was subsequently formulated by Melanie Klein and her school about the primary stages of psychic structure formation in the splitting constitution. Only this theory, to summarize again, has made it possible to show that the external direction of aggression does not necessarily imply an object change from self to object, but rather, that the early good-bad split of the object imago prevents the mental conceptualization of the real object. Only the overcoming of this good-bad split makes access to reality possible, by having the effect that the now no longer split imago of the object can be brought into alignment with the representation of the real object. With this we have—amongst other things—the external direction of the aggression, which, however, before and after is directed to the psychological object; the primary aim of which is therefore not, as Freud had assumed as necessary, the destructive dissolution of the multicellular subject. In consequence, aggression loses that central meaning which it would have if its diversion to the exterior world was linked with the question of being or not being of the subject. Aggression is not at the center of the death drive.

One of the concerns of this work is to provide conclusive evidence, via a general metapsychological integration, for the explicative potential of the broader theoretical perspective that came about with Melanie Klein's discovery.

20

Considerations under a theory of science perspective

Some considerations on the status of this work from a theory of science perspective shall be added here. In the abstract of his paper on the definition of psychoanalysis in terms of the theory of science, Bernd Nissen (2010) writes that scientific precision can only be attained by incorporating scientific tenets and concepts into theories and meta-theories. With my present theoretical outline I have attempted to argue the claim that the position of psychoanalysis as a theory, in terms of the theory of science, is that of an a priori science like logic and mathematics. It operates as a logical procedure defined and determined by the laws of psychical functioning as discovered and described by psychoanalysis, via inference, deduction and proof, and in this sense escapes positivist determinism's one-sided empirical concept of science.

This may at first seem like a bold claim. In any case, it puts everything with which we were raised in our psychoanalytic-scientific socialization on its head. Had it not always been pointed out to us that psychoanalytic theory formation had a probabilistic character and represented a hypothetical generalization from certain clinical findings in the sense of scientific metaphors and examples of behavior? In my opinion, this only applies to a particular stage in the development of our science, in which a gradual enrichment with respect to particular theory fragments has taken place. In my view this stage has meanwhile reached a degree of saturation that makes it possible to reverse the process and put a logical structure, a logical order underneath the existing theory fragments, combining those fragments into a uniform theory.

In this sense I try to show that the a-priori basic thought from which, and this is the hypothesis to be proven, the complete structure formation of the psyche and its pathological deviations can be inferred in a discipline-specific step-by-step argumentation is the following that with the moment in which the first sensory perceptions become possible, based on the ontogenetic maturation of the central nervous system, these perceptions by definition have a bi-polar structure: they consist of the pole of the perceiving subject and the pole of the perceived itself, that is to say, the representation. I assume that in psychoanalytic terms the perceiving subject is directly the archaic, primordial ego, that which is perceived—the representation—is the archaic, primordial object. The other claim which, like the primary hypothesis would have to be proven deductively through the explanatory capacity of these assumptions, is that this is in fact the starting point of psychic life in its total potential impact if though for that matter still at a level that is very primitive in terms of structure formation.

I furnish proof by way of logical argumentation that such a simple system, with the addition of need-tension, instantly and unavoidably meets with problems which constitute the conflictual nature of human psychic life: prompted by need-tension the primary ego attempts to incorporate the primary sensory object into the sphere of its own identity, as in a world that consists only of the early ego and the first object, the only possibility to suspend the unpleasure—that is the sensation of a lack in the sphere of the ego—is localized in the object, as there is nothing else besides this primary object that could be considered 'outside', and because suspension of the lack in the ego must come from the outside. For the ego cannot suspend the lack from within itself, otherwise the ego would not feel any lack.

This psychic movement is the beginning of mental activity in the sense of an archaic, sensorily determined wish. It leads to a constitutive conflict, as in the intended fusion of the ego with the object the bi-polar world of internal perception would again collapse, a world that has only just unfolded and out of which the dimension of the psychical is about to develop. This unavoidable fusional movement is therefore in my definition the core of the death drive, the ontic power that opposes it, the power that wants to maintain and secure the dimension of the psychical which is just yet coming into being, the life drive. Both drives are, therefore, according to this understanding, purely psychical productions.

This primordial sense-based object initially has nothing to do with a human counterpart. It is the precipitate of not yet assigned co-enaesthetic stimuli, which pêle mêle may stem from the external world and could also be of a proprioceptive, enteroceptive or central nervous system-related nature and are only held together by their contiguity in time. The dimension of space, let alone inner space, does not yet exist; the sensory opposites are not modulated yet. These archaic objects of sensory perception are most likely related to those still inanimate object formations which we know from the autistic cosmos. From them, in the process of primal attachment, the imago of the human object, initially as part object, gradually forms. Via primary identification, psychical qualities are ascribed to this human imago that is coming into being, qualities that correspond to those in the subject and by which the expectation is put into this imago, at the level of pre-conceptional assignment, that it is able to contain the psychism of the subject, the child.

191

In this way, through primary identification, life is, so to speak, breathed into the imago of the human object that is coming into being. Thus it becomes the primary object in the sense of the classical terminology, that is to say, the representation which later, when it is a fully formed image, will be the mother. At the basis of it are, however, inanimate object representations which stem directly from sensory perception and the residues of which we see in the strangeness of the object formations of the autistic perception, which we probably all have gone through.

With the primary identification then projective identification is launched, and with it, the original and archaic mode and mechanism of communication. With this definition of the drives that centers on object constitution and the relationship to the object, clinical manifestations which in recent years have begun to occupy us, like the autistic and autistoid phenomena and, in general, pathologies of withdrawal, become major themes in the discussion of psychodynamics. Then again, this topic of the psychic drives, insofar as there is proof of their determining organizing activity at every level of psychopathology and at every level of structure formation, is evidence, from my point of view, of the fact that the question of the relationship between ego and object is the central theme of the psyche. The qualification as a drive has a direct bearing on the all-pervading character of this theme.

This is the core of my argumentation, from which all else logically unfolds. Proceeding from here, I begin by showing how the development of the splitting world described by Melanie Klein is the unavoidably logical consequence of this primordial situation, and on which paths this splitting world is overcome through the development of the self-reflexive position of the ego outside the drive phantasma. This is the position of the third. I have shown how, in the process of this overcoming, the dimension of the unconscious of the id constitutes itself structurally, and how this unconscious is thus not, for example, an expression of an assumed continuum of the psychical toward the somatic, but the precipitate of early experiencing at the splitting level, which, with the breakthrough to the time-space identity of the object because of the categorial leap that goes with it, is consciously no longer conceivable.

From there I followed up with, on the one hand, a theoretical explanation of the psychogenic autism as the first form of psychic illness, have, on the other hand, attempted to show that the Oedipus complex is the final form of elaboration of this conflict of the drives and represents, in its structurally fully developed form, a definite binding of the death drive. I have also shown in what way the various forms of psychopathology as specific deviations on this path can be precisely located theoretically. I would also like to point out that such theoretical fundamentals allow for a meshing of psychoanalysis with neurobiological research, for in this way we proceed as a basic theorem from a simple representational model of strictly sensory perception, which is compatible with neurological models of encoding.

Inasfar as the discipline-specific logical implementation of the a priori primary hypothesis proves to be able to describe the totality of the psychical and can, in this capacity, thus be considered deductively proven, the conclusion can be drawn, in retrospect, to assume the beginning of psychic life—of which we cannot gain any direct evidence— as in fact corresponding to the basis theorem: that psychic life begins with the ability of the central nervous system to form representations which are perceived by the subject, whereby this perception constitutes the ego function. This would then, through a theoretical deduction and inference procedure deductively prove that the beginning of psychic life does not consist in a fusional state of total or partial undifferentiatedness of ego and object representation. This may appear so at the phenomenal level, but at the level of endopsychic experiencing it has no reality.

The subversive moment in this theory formation is to allow the thought that the entire complex internal world which psychoanalysis has discovered and studied in the past one hundred and more years, including the phenomenon of the unconscious, could result as a logical consequence from a simple basic fact such as the theory of perception axiom of the confrontation between the perceiving subject and the object of perception, that is, the thing itself that is perceived. But if this should indeed be so, then psychoanalysis would have a theory available on the origin, structure, and functioning of the psyche, which in principle cannot be shaken any longer because it rests on a most simple basic fact. We would have arrived at a point in our theory formation where we could claim to formulate the natural laws that apply to the area of the psyche, not only mere hypotheses which in case of doubt are subjected to varying opinions. I think we should have the courage to consider this possibility. Regarding such a development, we would not be alone in the field of history of science. After all, the course of physics, for example, as the basic discipline of the natural sciences was exactly the same: from tools to theories.

Building on the thoughts of Janine Chasseguet-Smirgel on the fusional meaning of the oedipal incest wish towards the mother, I started out with linking the classic Oedipus complex with the positions of Melanie Klein under the premise of a modified definition of Freud's last drive theory in which the danger psychically threatening the ego is seen in its suspension through fusion, with the life drive opposing this. From there, by way of logical inference, I worked my way forward not only to formulations on the resolution of the Oedipal conflict and to the ego-ideal as the formation in which this resolution is laid down structurally, but also, looking back, was asking the question of

194

how the antagonism of the drives so defined might have come about. This question then led to the theory of perception axiom. Thus I did not proceed from this axiom as, so to speak, primary hypothesis. I proceeded instead, together with Chasseguet-Smirgel and other respected authors, from an alternative conception of the known clinic and the classic theory formation deriving from it.

The system psyche thus rests on representation. The representations are the screen, the membrane that separates the psyche from the soma. The central danger for this system lies in the suspension through fusion of the perceptual distance between the ego and the representation—i.e. the distance of non-identity between perceiver and perceived that belongs to the logical system properties of the act of perception, as this fusion would mean the collapse, the self-suspension, of the system. We are here dealing with the internal perception in the sense in which Freud, in *The Interpretation of Dreams*, spoke of consciousness as the sense-organ for the perception of psychical qualities. The ego is under the illusion to be able to escape unpleasure and suffering, to find salvation, by suspending this separation from the representation of the object. This conflict is reflected in the antagonism of the psychical drives. It is the biological task of the Oedipus complex to bind this system danger inherent in the psyche.

We do not know the information deposited in the system properties of the brain with which the individual is born. What can be said, however, before the background of the deductive proof of my basis theorem is that the structures described by psychoanalysis are building up starting with the formation of the first representation with which a sensory event is registered, encoded, in the central nervous system. More is not needed. The psyche, therefore, as a system, is bound to the representations. Only that which passes through this process of encoding in the course of representation formation, or has such a representation process as its base, is psychic content. Also, all information which, as the case may be, is stored in the system properties of the brain, must, for its psychic activation, first elicit a process of representation formation. This is the reason why, for example, the pre-conceptions that Bion describes need events for their activation through which they can then express themselves. It may well be, however, that these pre-conceptions (and other inborn information) have an attracting effect for the constellation of such events. The representations are originally purely sensory, or hallucinatory-sensory; see also the world of psychogenic autism. They only gain a symbolic, that is, symbolising dimension through the position outside, in the course of the depressive position.

In my view, the decisive argument in the framework of a discussion from the point of theory of science is that, while drafting this theoretical attempt, I found myself moving back and forth between, on the one hand, the known clinical and theoretical knowledge of psychoanalysis and, on the other, a logical deduction from my primary hypothesis, and again and again was confronted with the fact that the logical conclusions corresponded to our clinically secured particular theories very exactly. It has been this fact which gradually led me to think that a possibility of truth could be ascribed to my approach. This is, therefore, an a priori theory formation guided and controlled by the clinic.

If I am right with the above, then we would have a consistent theory of psychoanalysis which, in my view, corresponds to what Nissen (2010) has demanded as a necessary desideratum in order to counter positivistic determinism with our own and equally valid position from a theory of science perspective. According to Nissen's explanations, and if we related this to our theoretical framework of ideas sofar, we would be dealing with a theory replacement in line with the criteria put forth by Lakatos (1970): "The replacement of a theory takes place at the earliest, according to Lakatos, if in a comparison between two theories T and T' the following conditions are fulfilled: T' when compared to T has a surplus content, the proven tenets of T are contained in T' and parts of the surplus content of T' are proven. Hence, growth can take place also without refutations: ´the few crucial excess-verifying instances are decisive` (Lakatos 1970, p. 121)." Nissen, 2010, p. 607; transl. P.Z.).

I agree with Nissen that this independent position in terms of the theory of science *in praxis* would have to consist in a constant communication movement between our partial clinical findings and the a priori secured body of theory, whereby, for one thing, the logical stringency principle of theory makes a maximized conceptual and theoretical clarity possible for the formulation of the clinical finding, and for another, the clinical finding either confirms the theory or forces an analysis of the apparent or actual divergence. As initially already touched on, Nissen in this context speaks of "*scientific tenets and statements not conceivable without a theoretical integration.* Therefore reflections on the structure of scientific theories have shown that scientific tenets are only meaningful when they are integrated into a theoretical structure" (op. cit. p. 606, italics B. N.; transl. P.Z.).

In addition to this inductive path, there is on the other hand—as Nissen has described as well—the deductive path of derivation of certain clinical postulates or hypotheses from the theory itself. In my draft for instance, I have taken this path when, in order to explain psychogenic autism, I have deduced the assumption of a regular pre-schizoid phase, or position, respectively. Along the same lines, the theory would require that the specifically demanded connection between father imago/position outside and access to reality must be empirically proven or falsified. In my opinion this central interface would offer the opportunity for proof that could be operationalized, and which, if positive, would furnish evidence for the complete psychoanalytic theory formation on Oedipality, for which this connection is constitutive.

One of the potentially most important deductions is also an understanding of the annihilatory aggression as the most elementary form of expression of the death drive, directed towards the dissolution of the reality-bound object representation. The death drive here attempts to enforce the fusional realization, by, after futile beleaguering of the Oedipus complex, attacking the reality dimension of the representation of the object which is founded in the position outside as that manifestation of the life drive, which, in the sense of the unrepealable delimitation, prevents the fusion.

Proof through verification in psychoanalysis then consists, for one thing, in the comparison with the total corpus of clinical findings which are deemed secured; for another, in the examination of the correlation with the leading theory which in its turn has undergone a logical falsification test, and in particular instances has been proven deductively as well as inductively. Nissen poignantly describes how this interplay of theory and clinic, in the face of the complex-dynamic character of the subject of our research establishes an independent and unique psychoanalytic criterion for science which can stand up to the gold-standard of randomized control.

Apart from that, I would like to remind the reader that psychoanalysis has shown that the ability for cognition and the ability to perceive reality are not there from birth, but are psychic capacities that have been acquired in very specific ways. At the same time these are not esoteric pastimes of psychoanalysis, but rather, the clarification of these questions, like access to cognition and access to reality, is identical with the question about the origin of psychopathology, that is to say, it is identical with the central subject of psychoanalysis. Inasfar as the empirical sciences deal with the application of cognition to their subject areas, and as far as they depend on the fact that this cognition function refers to a correct perception of the reality aspect of its subject, the natural sciences, from a theory of science perspective, are in a relationship of dependence with psychoanalysis. For psychoanalysis shows how the mental instruments, which enable us to do science in the sense of positivistic determinism, come into existence at all. Thus it is that stage of scientificity in which science self-reflexively focuses on itself.

In any case, this would justify why psychoanalysis, totally in line with its nature, in terms of the theory of science would have to occupy a different position than the, in this respect, banal empirical sciences, as-it were. Wittgenstein (1922) formulates this in the *Tractatus* in proposition 5632 thus: "The subject does not belong to the world but it is a limit of the world". This, in fact, is the position of psychoanalysis in terms of the theory of science. Hence it is justified, in my view, in defining itself as a mixture of a priori theory and empirical clinic.

An important practical aspect is the professional policy aspect which would have to be assigned to a general theory of psychoanalysis that was endorsed in terms of the theory of science. This would be an effective argument against the introduction of a uniform "general" psychotherapy that is purely pragmatic, and would be equally effective regarding the identity-defining delineation against other psychotherapeutic procedures. Psychoanalysis might, on this basis, defend itself against being lumped together with the so-called "dynamic" modalities, insofar as they are pragmatic vulgarizations and particularizations of psychoanalytic fundamental positions. Psychoanalysis would be the only procedure with a consistent theory formation in terms of the theory of science, and with a consistent practice of verification and falsification independent from evidence-based research according to the pattern of the controlled randomization standard. Therefore this possibility should be closely examined. As Nissen stated in the last sentence of his paper: "Psychoanalysis must determine its scientific standards and be on the offensive representing them. Everything else would be its demise" (op. cit. pp. 619; transl. P.Z.).

Up to now, the pragmatic alternative to a logically formulated metapsychology has been to define our field via a limited number of central assumptions. The problem is that this is quite useless in terms of the theory of science or in terms of professional policy. The only chance in both respects is to dismiss randomized controlled trial research as the only valid criterion, as the gold-standard of scientificity for the area of psychotherapy. Nissen has shown that there is the possibility, in principle, to do this. And I maintain: it can be done.

This does not mean, of course, that we should not engage in clinical empirical research of the randomized control standard. This is absolutely necessary to advance the discipline and to use the results to test and validate our theory, in the sense delineated above. But the center of our scientific identity lies in the consistency of our theory.

21

Metapsychological discussion

Finally I would like to give my view on the question of what we gain with a metapsychology altered in the ways described, with respect to the understanding of the framework within which psychical processes play out. I divide this statement into five subject areas:

a

Firstly, the model presented in this work allows for putting forth a theoretical line of reasoning about the importance of the Oedipus complex and the related structural givens of the psyche which in its causality is principally independent from taking recourse to the supporting evidence of the clinic, but which is carried and confirmed by such evidence in the sense of an argumentation of proof. Such theory formation which by way of logical consistency arrives at a general theory is the prerequisite for psychoanalysis to be able to find basic acceptance under the rules of the causal concept of science, and which it then inevitably also must be able to find, by fulfilling these criteria of science. It is, therefore, in my view, as I have presented in greater detail above, the condition for the survival of psychoanalysis as a science. In other words, it is what the scientific world demands of us, and rightly so. The theory of psychoanalysis thus becomes teachable without restrictions.

As far as concerns oedipality as the structure giving theme of the human psyche, my considerations can be further expanded on in two directions: on the one hand, I have set out the paths of internal childhood development consisting in the formation of the oedipal phantasmatization. This phantasmatization, according to its own inner laws, by necessity leads to its dissolution by repression in the confrontation with the phallic threat of castration. In this way the particularly human phenomenon of psychosexual latency comes about, in agreement with Freud's respective formulations in the third of the *Essays on the Theory of Sexuality* of 1905. Like Freud, I also consider it the task of latency to have the defensive boundaries established against the oedipal objects to the degree that, when genital sexual development sets in in puberty, the sexual interest is no longer directed towards the oedipal but the displaced objects. From my theory formation it can therefore be inferred that this dissolution by repression—and thus latency—is a logically inescapable structural consequence, provided that the oedipal conflict constellation has been correctly established.

Latency, therefore, is no biological fact, but one purely contingent on phantasma. This fact entails that derailments of development in the infantile working through of oedipality may lead to latency not or not sufficiently being established, or, to the contrary, may develop such repressive impact that it also withstands the hormonal and maturational push of puberty and may even continue into adult life, as it were, unbroken. Both are known clinical phenomena of child and adolescent psychoanalysis which have a high diagnostic significance. In latency the power and impact of the phantasmatic side of human existence shows itself, and especially the power of the oedipal conflict constellation, to the degree that this central crisis of the ontogenesis of the psyche directly affects psychosexuality which in its course appears totally caused by biology, but is not therefore, in this, so very important place.

The other direction I would like to expand on is the statement that Freud's 1926 and up to this day still very controversial distinction made in *Some Psychical Consequences of the Anatomical Distinction between the Sexes* into an infantile phallic and, starting with puberty, a genital phase of sexual development, is correct in my view, only that—speaking for the boy—I would not link the overvaluation of the phallus during the infantile oedipal phase to the boy's own genitals, but to the father's, and that I deduce the overestimation of one's own genitals from the death-drive related oedipal phantasy of the identificatory appropriation of the phallus of the father. Thus what we are dealing with here in this identificatory appropriation is a manifestation of the death drive.

For the girl the same applies mutatis mutandis, insofar as for her, too, the phallus of the father, under the influence of the death drive, represents the central means for the realization of the fusion with the mother. The formulation of an infantile phallic phase in this sense applies for both sexes, and this had also been Freud's position.

The dissolution of the Oedipus complex by repression includes the receding of the phallic theme and opens up the way for the genital cathexis of puberty, inasfar as this development is not blocked or changed by irregularities in the oedipal working through.

In other words, I consider the clinical facts which Freud had referred to as givens, despite the critique that has meanwhile been expressed about Freud's phallic monism. I think that this criticism, as well as Freud's formulation itself, is based on the error that the phallic primacy is about the genitals of the boy, that is to say, the (male) ego. In truth, however, it is about the phallus of the father which has the same meaning for both sexes. Even the male child never fails to recognize the female genitals; what is more, they are in fact the goal of the oedipal, incestuous wishes. Where the existence of the female, penis-less genitals is being disavowed, this is already a consequence of the phallic threat of castration and the expression of the disavowal of this threat. But the phallic primacy of the oedipal phase exists; it is a clinical reality. The phallic theme is the pivotal point of oedipality.

b

With reference to my metapsychological accounting, I am further of the opinion that the theoretical complications of the classical definition of the drive, especially as concerns its unclear delineation towards the somatic, are being corrected in the proposed reformulation. The most important difference to the classical view is the relationship to the object. Of the object as one of the elements in the drive equation, Freud writes in his *Instincts and Their Vicissitudes* (1915, p. 122): "It is what is most variable about an instinct and is not originally connected with it, but becomes assigned to it only in consequence of being peculiarly fitted to make satisfaction possible."

This formulation of Freud's has two levels of meaning. For one, it refers to the object as that element of the drive equation which is "what is most variable about an instinct" insofar as it is the very means which makes satisfaction possible, but which has nothing to do with the nature of the drive as such which consists of the aim to discharge the tension arising at the source of the drive. The second level of meaning of this variability refers to the fact that the objects may change, while source and aim are fixed.

If one was to separate out the sexual drive into a motivation either governed by the death drive or by the life drive, fighting each other within the sexual theme, then what definitely applies for the present theory formation is that it is the juxtaposition of ego and object, of subject and object of sensory perception, that constitutes the dynamics of the drives in the first place. The object as constituting factor of the drive is, in this sense, as invariable as the ego. The variability of <u>sexual</u> objects along the lines of the second of the above-distinguished meaning levels, emphasized by Freud since his *Three Essays on the Theory of Sexuality* (1905), if one was to exclude external displacement vicissitudes, has its fundamental cause in the phantasmatic complications of the relationship between ego and inner object which I have described systematically in this work. This variability results from the dynamic character of both drives, that is to say, from the aim of either the death drive or the life drive, respectively, regarding the real sexual object, which, in turn, goes along with different object conceptions or refers to different objects in the first place.

In my perspective, therefore, things are such that I see the fight over the control of the object as the constitutive moment of the dynamic character of the drives. The genesis of both drives results from the relationship of tension between ego and object and from the phantasmatic alternatives this relationship contains. According to this relationship, the <u>place</u> of the object in the drive equation is absolutely invariable. The only variable thing is the content assigned to it. In other words everything revolves around the internal object which has its root in the primary object and is opposing the ego. The ego and the internal object, the subject and object of sensory perception, are, in their juxtaposition, the two columns that support the inner world.

In order to sum up the subject matter of this work under the aspect of the controversy around the drive concept, I hope to have shown two things:

1. The drives can be understood in a purely intrapsychical manner, namely as the expression of the fundamental question of survival of the ego in the confrontation with the object.

2. This definition attests to their ability to accommodate also the most severe forms of psychopathology without taking recourse to, for instance, a biologically motivated striving for destruction and fragmentation of living units. Sexuality, in this context, is to be seen as the medium within which both drives articulate themselves phantasmatically. In the same manner, aggression may serve the aims of the life drive as well as those of the death drive.

The nature of the psychic drives is therefore explicitly mental, that is to say, we are dealing with a particular theme with circumscribed content in the interaction between ego and object, namely the question of the control over the object. This theme has an intensity and dynamism that maximally involves the whole spectrum of human passion; it is the psychic content of the human form of sexuality. One might ask, however, whether a phenomenon with such a focus on the mental, on circumscribed content, and in this sense, of a highly motivational nature, can still be called a drive. This objection can be countered with the argument, what in the psyche may be more rightfully called a drive if not a theme that possesses the fullest dynamic potential and builds the whole structure of the psyche, produces the categorical distinction between the unconsciousness of the structural id and consciousness, and the regular and lawful aberrations of which cause the variations of psychopathology.

I maintain that the adequate description for such a range of performance can only be the notion of the drive. The phenomenon must therefore be seen the other way round, namely that the drive-quality in the human psyche, as said, is of an explicit mental nature.

In the beginning chapters of this work I have set out that, in my view, the specific dynamic moment of the drive in the psyche originates out of the unrepresentability of the bad, persecuting object in the pre-schizoid phase, before representational object constancy is established at all, and for that reason is the primary manifestation of the life drive. (As a reminder, I regard the bad object of the paranoid-schizoid and the depressive levels of splitting, in its strictly psychodynamic basic foundation, as the counterreaction of the life drive to the fusional impulse of the death drive and to the correspondingly idealized object representation).

In the pre-schizoid phase, instead of the unrepresentable bad object, we have the imperative, absolute pressure for change of the existing overall situation. This is the drive moment of the Eros—insofar strictly psychically conceptualized—which in this way rests on non-representation imbued with high dynamic energy, or, for that matter, representation of a dynamic void which propels the psychic structure forming process. The corresponding drive moment of the death drive, in contrast, always consists of the very concrete and sensory pressure to unify the ego and the object. The dynamic moment of the life drive would thus owe its existence to the pre-schizoid phase and preserve its conditions.

I therefore assume not a corporeal, but a purely psychogenic nature of the psychic drives. Without the formation of these psychical drives the hormonal and instinctual impulses, which originate in the body, would have no leverage on the psyche, no representation and thus no possibility to become psychically effective and real. That this is more than a theoretical construction, and in fact a clinical potentiality is proven by the existence of the encapsulated form of psychogenic autism, in which there is no evidence of objectal sexual drive manifestations. The consequence of these considerations would be to fundamentally reformulate the definition of the drive as far as it applies to the territory of the human psyche.

Remember that also Freud, in his *Three Essays*, defined the drive as a psychical representation: "By an 'instinct' is provisionally to be understood the psychical representative of an endosomatic, continuously flowing source of stimulation, ..." (1905, p. 167). This as contrast to the one-sided view that Freud saw the drive as that part of our biological endowment which, so to speak, protrudes directly into the psyche. This is only one side of the coin.

In order to once again rephrase the problem of the interrelationship between physical sexuality and psychical drive exactly, I proceed from the assumption, in this case fully in accordance with the anaclitic model of object choice, that in orality, through its biologically conditioned experiences of satisfaction which, next to the satisfaction of the immediate need, also comprise feelings of safety-giving sensory stimulations and contact experiences, the representation of the primary object becomes bound to sexual sensuality and thus to the human object. This is the primal attachment. In the encapsulated form of psychogenic autism this attachment does not come about. Then again it is exactly this attachment which is being attacked in the annihilatory aggression, at first by attacking the external object of the position outside, but then with an attack on the attachment to sexuality as such. Both processes clinically demonstrate that the attachment to the human object and thus to sexuality is no biological given, but the result of a psychical, mental process, which not only may not come about, but is also reversible.

The sexual sensuousness and the oedipality developing out of it is the language in which, under the condition of the attachment to the human object, the structure-forming phantasmas of the life drive and the death drive articulate themselves. Sexuality, thus, is not the drive par excellence, but the result of the coupling to the biological determinants of the enormous forces released from the tension of the relationship of ego and internal object. Correspondingly, the same applies to aggression, the impact of which feeds off of the attempts at implementation of the aims of both the life drive and the death drive. Here, too, aggression only peruses the available, as the case may be, biologically determined instinctual patterns and uses the reservoir of the somatic, but its psychical dynamism is supplied from somewhere else.

The dynamic forces of the theatre of the human drives are, by their very nature, psychogenic, and are only added on to the biological dispositions. This is the reason why the human drive manifestations can be far more radical than foreseen in the biological instinctual processes, and why they can directly oppose the biological regulatory mechanisms of maintenance of the self and of the species.

This is about the relationship, therefore, of the motivational mental drive structure of the psyche, the challenge and task of which is to safeguard the ego, to its somatic substrate, that is to say, to the overall complex of the physical, humoral, neurobiological, and, as the case may be, instinct-oriented conditions within which the psyche is situated. In my opinion, this relationship can be delineated exactly, it is the world of the internal stimulus-producing outside which has an effect on the ego in its constitutive basic function as the organ and subject of perception, and the stimuli that come from this internal outside are processed by the ego according to its own laws as I have described. The prime paradigm here would be sexuality, the physical sexual drive, the impetus of which is psychically being organized within the framework of the unconscious phantasmatization of the life and death drives and thus within the oedipal context and structure. In this understanding these stimuli coming from the internal outside, in their basic nature

209

would not be different from those coming from the external outside world of the extra-corporeal reality.

I have, further, on the basis of these considerations developed the thesis that that which we call the psychic death drive is the preserved form of functioning of the primary narcissistic ego of the pre-schizoid phase, before representational constancy of the object is reached, and where object splitting is not yet possible, and where the object, experienced in absolute totality and as the only means to suspend all and any need, is the only thing facing the primary ego: the all-that-is, outside of which there is nothing. The ego, under need-tension, is filled with the desire to bring this primary object under its omnipotent control and to merge with it, in order to aggrandize itself in this fusion to the primary narcissistic ego-cosmic ego. This early ego, which is not yet bound to the body and not yet challenged and put into its place by the splitting of the object, i.e. by the appearance of the bad object, is, I would assume, what we later refer to as the death drive. This strictly psychically conceived death drive thus preserves the motivational structure of the primary narcissistic primordial ego. As I have been discussing further up, one can, in parallel, deduce the dynamic criterion of the life drive to push towards a change in the prevalent overall situation also from the pre-schizoid constitution and its structural conditions, to the degree that the dynamic moment of both drives depicts and preserves their genetic initial situation.

c

In this sense, thirdly, the ability to form representations which centrally depict an afferent stimulus, seems to be a kind of immaterial barrier to brain activity, similar to the blood-brain barrier as it were, whereby starting from a certain morphogenetic level of brain structures, due to the system properties of the human organ brain, the formation of representations sets in constituting a categorial leap that creates a closed system, the representational world. This is thus that area of the total structure brain where, on the basis of representational, phantasmatically organized structure formation, as I have tried to sketch in this work, self-reflexive awareness originates.

English language usage distinguishes between psyche and mind. In this sense, Antonio Damasio (2004), in his keynote address at the IPA Congress in New Orleans, differentiated between 'emotion' and 'feeling'.

This representational barrier which, as it were, constitutes the 'mind', shows in my opinion also under this perspective that 'in the depths of the soul' there is no fluent transition whatsoever from the somatic to the mental, but that, as said, the stimuli from the body—and also those from other areas of the brain—meet the mental system as a special category of external stimuli leading to the formation of representations, the processing of which—in plain words: the phantasy formation—in its turn may feedback onto the somatic substrate. Only that can become psychic content which has formed a representation—no matter whether this be Panksepp's primary and secondary emotions or whatever else approaches the psyche from other areas of the brain as, so to speak, internal outer world. Evidently, this conceptual model, too, thereby shows a connection, and interaction, between soma and mind, but it seems to me that the concept of a representational barrier is scientifically more correct and also more appropriate than that of a fluent transition.

I think that what I have presented in this work is, strictly speaking, a 'theory of mind', whereas the notion of the psyche would also include the overall complex of the neurobiological-hormonal-instinctive and genetic parameters. Before the backdrop of the considerations presented here one can say that the 'mind', the mental, is that dimension which arises because the conditions of existence and the essential characteristics of the ego as the agent of the perceiving function—conditions and characteristics that have the quality of a natural law—emerge in the confrontation with phantasmatic movements in which this ego, unbeknownst to itself, enters into conflict with its own nature. It is my aspiration to show that that which manifests as illness in the psyche, and equally so the condition for mental health and for the creative, articulate themselves within a specific terminology and within particular themes, and that the structure of it can only be understood and directly influenced and changed within this terminology and these themes.

If it is the ambitious goal of neuropsychology to come up with a "theory of the mind"-mapping, that is to say, a mapping of the mental, then psychoanalysis can support this effort by pointing out that the internal neuronal complexity of the brain with its 10 to the power of 150 synaptic connections, as calculated by Gerhard Roth, leads, on the mental plain, next to its purely physiological-neurological tasks, to the formation of a representational world which regulates the relationship of the experiencing ego to the perceived object according to binding rules. An external stimulus, as far as its mental processing is concerned, does, so to speak, not meet directly with a specific neuronal tissue, but it meets with the total representational matrix in its complex circuitry. The specific nature of this representational matrix decides over mental illness or mental health, and the stimulus coming from the outside is being received according to the givens of this representational world. This representational world is the field of psychoanalysis.

The crucial phenomenon, in any case, is the one that the brain is giving itself a representational basic structure, which directly results from the system properties of the representation-bound perception and thus experience. This form of perception, which is tied to representation is, in its turn, the precipitate of the morphological properties and structure of the brain. Each and every study of brain function must reckon with this autonomous basic structure which is the structural frame within which mental functioning occurs and consciousness originates. Mental functioning outside of this frame is not possible; this frame is the coordinate system. The key to understanding this basic structure is the oedipal theme.

d

The approach presented in this work, fourthly, opens up the possibility to develop a theoretical conception of how the basic mental concept of an inner world comes about from the divergence of the two operational modes of psychic functioning. The functioning of the mental apparatus, which genetically comes before access to reality, generates, as has been set out, a form of functioning on the level of the good-bad split of the object imago which, due to the splitting, is not in contact with reality. If then, with the position outside, access to reality is gained, and the splitting of the object imago is overcome, the prior form of functioning of splitting of the object at the level of the identity of the ego with the drive phantasma is maintained and creates the quality of the structural unconscious.

I presume that the incompatibility and friction of the primary and continued coexisting form of functioning of the splitting of the object imago with the reality-adapted functioning, at the level of the position outside, is responsible for the occurrence of the existential, compelling experience—endopsychic awareness—of the existence of an internal world which obeys its own laws. This unresolvable contradiction and the continuous conflictual tension it gives rise to would have to be considered as the trigger point for the struggle with the specificity of the psychical human condition. For completeness I like to add that as the precursor of the splitting positions—i.e. the paranoid-schizoid position and the depressive position—one has to assume, on top of this, the pre-schizoid phase or position, with its yet again very different functional characteristics, which contrasts with the functional level of reality access in a much cruder way still.

What I have described in this work are the phantasmatic constituents of this inner world, the mental space. It is only through them that this space evolves and forms; it consists in them. I would maintain that the range of themes which this work discusses reflects the structural framework of this mental space in a complete, exhaustive sense, as these themes result from the lawful development and differentiation of a particular basic constellation, namely the confrontation of subject and object of sensory perception. This basic constellation, because of the nature of the conflict it expresses, requires a very specific phantasmatico-structural resolution, which manifests itself in the resolution of the oedipal conflict.

As this whole development is based on a logical and causal necessity, it should be accorded the status of a natural law which specifically governs the formation and the functional structuring of the psyche, more exactly, of the mental. To the degree that, as stated, all variants that are factually possible have been described, there is no plus ultra that is not covered by the themes of this work. Thus, within the framework of this approach, the human condition comes full circle.

The themes and structural positions which I have attempted to describe in this work could thus be understood as the living phantasmatic coordinate system of the space of human consciousness, the 'mind', which includes functionally conscious as well as functionally unconscious content. This coordinate system is the background matrix for the subjective, personal constructions the individual ego uses to build its life and inner world. What the analyst must uncover, clarify, and interpretatively change in the material and in the transference of the patient is essentially this matrix.

Before this background I also understand my work as an explicit plea for the high-frequency, four-hour and five-hour a week analysis. Especially the high-frequency analysis with its corollaries of abstinence and technical neutrality is capable of energetically charging this background grid of mental life—the mental structure screen, the mental membrane—in a way that this matrix, which is predominantly oedipal, becomes visible and can be worked on. The coming about of this phenomenon designates the definitional area of psychoanalysis as a therapeutic procedure. One can only speak of psychoanalysis where this criterion is met.

What I advocate here is, therefore, a radical constructivism: the inner world, the dimension of the psychical, is a phantasmatically erected, constructed world. How important this statement is can be measured by the dimension of the psychical being, the place where consciousness originates and plays out, and so the total rational access of man to reality, to the world, is bound to the existence of this dimension. In the words of Shakespeare:

> We are such stuff as dreams are made on,
> And our little life is rounded with a sleep.
> *The Tempest, Act 4, 1*

e

For the rest and under the point of view of a metapsychological résumé, it remains to be said that the psyche, before the backdrop of this theoretical conception, becomes conceivable as a completely self-contained system, which develops and unfolds on the basis of the phylogenetic development of the cerebral cortex and its system properties from the mere function of perception. I have shown that all forms of pathology can be described as the lawful forms of aberration of this system. That perception plays this central role appears to me as theoretically extraordinarily fitting, insofar as this indeed represents the simplest conceivable axiom. If psychoanalytic theory formation, the basis of which is, on the other hand, the clinical facts, could be based on this axiom consistently, and if this was successful, it would be quasi unassailable from a theory of science point of view.

Of importance to me is that I believe to have provided evidence that even such seemingly elementarily organic and physical manifestations like those that we call drives can be explained from the primary narcissistic way of functioning of the psyche, and in the same manner that the id can be justified as the expression and precipitate of the early form of functioning of the ego which always remains active, in parallel with secondary process oriented and self-reflexive later forms of functioning. In other words, it is not necessary to assume a fluid transition of the id into the somatic, as Freud had done, in order to explain the archaic character of the id or, for that matter, of the drives. There is hardly something more archaic than what we may get to know as the mental form of functioning of the encapsulated autists, and we must assume that these modes of functioning are kept up at the unconscious level in each of us, and are simultaneously active in addition to the higher and later forms of functioning.

One further important consequence of these considerations is that, insofar as all psychical forms of functioning and all forms of pathology may be explained from the genetic succession of the self-organization of this system and from its lawful forms of aberrations, the reverse conclusion is that the representation-forming cerebral cortex, on which this system is based, is to be regarded as a tabula rasa following no other laws than those which result from the system of perception itself. There are no other provable intrinsic factors, in my view, which determine the fundamental structure formation of the psyche which culminates in the Oedipus complex.

Everything that is added in terms of influences, stimuli from the general body, or from other parts of the brain, is internal outer world which can only become effective psychically, if and when representations—as consequences of perception—are formed, but which then are processed and organized according to the structural laws of the psyche. The exploration of these structural laws is the domain and territory of psychoanalysis.

22

Conclusions

I n conclusion, in order to elaborate on the practical or factual gain from the theoretical considerations presented in this work, I would list the following, in my opinion, critically important points of view:

1. I hold the thoughts of a pre-schizoid phase to be an important theoretical innovation. These thoughts define primary narcissism not as an objectless state, but as a condition which also includes the primary, pre-ambivalent object in its absolute meaning; as the all-that-is, outside of which nothing exists. The leading illusion is the delusion of omnipotent, fusional control of the ego over the object. I have attempted to show that this theory of the pre-schizoid phase is the clinical key to the understanding of the encapsulated form of infantile autism, and reversely, that the conditions in this genetically earliest form of psychopathology may be considered to be clinical proof for the existence of a pre-schizoid phase.

2. These considerations on the pre-schizoid phase have resulted in the thesis to regard that which I described as the psychic death drive, as the preserved and maintained motivational structure of the primary narcissistic ego of this pre-schizoid phase. The death drive would thus be identical with the primordial ego. In the same manner, according to these considerations, the dynamic

potential of the life drive stems from its unrepresentability in the pre-schizoid phase, i.e. before representational object constancy and thus the possibility of the good-bad split of the object is reached. As a consequence of this unrepresentability, it can only express itself via the unconditional pressure for change of the prevalent overall situation, insofar as this situation is determined by the death drive, and thus fusional in nature. The characteristic moment of both mental drives therefore derives from the conditions present at their origin in the pre-schizoid phase. The specific character of the primary-narcissistic ego which cannot experience itself other than absolute, because it is, at this early stage, not yet conditioned, neither intra-psychically, nor through the not-yet-occurred attachment to the body, would thus have to be considered the foundation of what we call the psychical drives.

3. From the fact of the foreclosure of the relationship to the primary object in the encapsulated autism; from the reflections on the origin of the part-object of the breast out of the coupling of the primary object with that sensory stimulation in which oral need satisfaction finds its expression; from the description of annihilatory aggression as, lastly, the attempt to dissolve this coupling again, and within it, the coupling of the death drive to sexuality, results an exact metapsychological formulation of the mechanism of primal attachment. The proof of the clinical validity of this formulation, again, can be found in the conditions of the encapsulated form of autism and in the realization of the above aim of annihilatory aggression.

4. Further on, from the description of the dynamic interrelation of the drives results a metapsychologically precise understanding of the meaning of the father imago, in particular concerning the relationship between reality access and father imago. The concept

as such is in agreement with the well-known pathology of the father imago as to the various forms of psychic illnesses and, in addition, opens up the possibility to empirically prove or falsify the specific connection between father imago/position outside and reality access. In my opinion this central interface would offer the opportunity to furnish an operationalizable proof, which, if in the affirmative, would prove the complete psychoanalytic theory formation on oedipality, for which this connection is constitutive.

5. The meaning as presented in this work of the dynamic conflict of the drives allows for an understanding of the Oedipus complex as the expression of the fight over the structural safety of the ego. In this sense the sublimated ego-ideal can be understood as the phantasmatic definition of this structural safety of the ego, as imago of a conception of the primal scene from which the ego has withdrawn, with the insight that this withdrawal is the condition for overcoming the only danger threatening it from within. For this reason the sublimated ego-ideal is the structural resolution of the oedipal conflict. It must be regarded as a potential level of functioning, as position, not as a firm acquisition.

6. Finally, what follows from my considerations is a theoretical refutation of Freud's death drive concept. This refutation is conclusive, in my eyes, even if one prefers not to go along with the other theoretical formulations of this work, as long as one accepts the validity of the primary splitting conception of the object, which was worked out by Melanie Klein and her school and which today arguably must be regarded as general theoretical standard.

GLOSSARY

List of items

Anality

Anality, under the aspect of the themes dealt with in this work, fundamentally consists in the struggle with the moment of control over the object, especially via the development of the concept of the means—that is to say of the tool that is linked with voluntary motor functions—which then lays the foundation for the imagination of the phallus.

Even though Melanie Klein (cf. 1945) assumes the activity of the internal image of the phallus already in the first months of life, this early phallus in her opinion is initially still very orally defined and derives directly from the experience of the breast as something hard—the nipple—which is enclosed by something soft, thus lacks the specific quality as the tool and the means with the help of which the father enters into contact with the mother in the primal scene.

Annihilitatory aggression, primary envy

One of the consequences of the thoughts presented in this work is that access to reality, that is to say, overcoming the early paranoid splitting of the object, results from the ego taking up the position outside the drive phantasma *(see there)*. Through this, the fusional merging of ego and primary object *(see there)* is being prevented and thus the manifestation of the death drive made impossible. Therefore object splitting as the early mode of defense against the death drive *(see there)* can be relinquished. The real object, the reality dimension of the

226

object, when looked at from its psychical background, is thus intimately linked with Eros as the drive to safeguard the ego. Eros simultaneously guarantees the safety of the ego, as well as its access to reality.

The sexual route of the striving for fulfillment of the death drive consists in the attempt to achieve fusional union with the primary object—that is, the object as such—in the midst of reality, via the path of incest with the mother (*see there*), at the level of the unconscious phantasma. As this attempt fails because of the Oedipus complex (*see there*) and the threat of castration (*see there*), the death drive is able to break away from the sexual, oedipal project of its fulfillment in reality via the real object, and can attack the real object itself with the aim, through its destruction and annihilation, to return to the imagination of the 'pure' primary object of the splitting condition and behind this, of the pre-ambivalent object (*see there*) of the pre-schizoid phase (see there), which is the original promise of fulfillment of the death drive. The aim, therefore, is the return to the level of the 'subjective object' (*see there*).

Thus this attack aims to suspend the position of the ego outside the drive phantasma, inasfar as this latter opens up the path to reality. The death drive attacks the reality dimension of the object, at the same time as it also attacks the position outside and the father imago (*see there*) deriving from it, the threat of castration, in actual fact the Oedipus complex itself. This is the background before which Bion (1970) in *Attention and Interpretation* writes about the hate for reality and the hate for cognitive functions that allow us to perceive reality—that is to say, the hate for the position outside and the self-reflexive ability that comes with it, as well as the ability for symbol formation that it also gives rise to. Both are prerequisites for thinking at the reality level of the ego that is no longer concretely bound to two-dimensionality and immediate sensuality. Similarly, what may arise before this background of the attack on thinking is a lack of self-recognition and conscious self-perception and in addition, hate for the dimension of consciousness itself, which, in order to shut off consciousness, may even include suicidal impulses. And of course the attack on the reality dimension of the object is also directed against genital sexuality and gender difference, both of which are intimately linked with the theme of reality (*see: Hysteria*).

Of importance in this context is that from the attack of the death drive against the reality dimension of the object arises not only the formal disorganization of the object representation, the fragmentation and dissolution of its time-space identity, but also coldness, emptiness and meaninglessness of relationships and of the experiencing of the world. This coldness and emptiness regarding relationships results from the attack against the real object in its dimension as the carrier of emotional meaning. Typically we find here also massive manifestations of blind repetition compulsion, one further fundamental characteristic of the death drive, via which it attempts to force the illusion of fusional union with the object, the illusion of eternal presence, the dissolution of causality and finality, the suspension of the passing of time. Most impressively this can be seen in the stereotypical repetitive movements of the encapsulated autistic child. The annihilatory death drive which turns against the reality dimension of the object, must go on turning against any form of mental development inasfar as it alienates the death drive from the illusory possibility of the realization of its intention to return to the level of the primary pre-ambivalent object and the fusion with it.

In addition, the death drive, in a very fundamental sense, can attack the attachment (*see there*) of the primary object to psychosexuality (*see there*) occurring in the early oral phase, in the first days of life, via the partial object (*see there*) of the breast, which is the foundation of the attachment to the human object. For it is via this 'error'—from the point of view of the annihilatory death drive—of the attachment to the sexual object that the constitutive illusion of the Oedipus complex came about. One might, therefore, express the fundamental complication this way: that the ego in the annihilatory, destructive regression follows the attraction of the primary narcissistic (*see there*) constitution of the pre-schizoid phase, in which the primary ego, in its delusional experiencing, still had omnipotent fusional control over the as yet unsplit primary object, with reference to which an outside could not yet be imagined, and where the attachment of the primary to the sexual object, the breast had not occurred yet.

One could say that the death drive, in this attack on the real object, recognizes and attacks the fundamental trick of nature, by which in the position outside reality is won at the same time as a realization of the death drive is made impossible, so that the ego basically faces the impossible alternative to relinquish either reality, or the realization of the death drive. From the point of view of the death drive, the sexual Oedipus complex consists in the attempt to solve this dilemma. This attempt finally fails with the experience of castration, and one of the possibilities to react to this failure is to abandon the attachment to sexuality itself and to attempt a violent reversal of the whole process. This complication is the unconscious origin of the violence aimed at the destruction of the real object. The annihilatory violence is therefore an attack against the attachment to the real object and to sexuality. Psychosexuality contains strongly cathected themes of dissolution and destruction of the object, both in anality and orality, and the structural regression with relation to the object representation which is carried by the death drive, orientates itself by these milestones of ontogenesis and phylogenesis which appear one after the other.

It is, however, undeniable that the most important concept in this context is that of Melanie Klein (1957) which she describes as primary envy. This envy which Klein regards as the elementary destructive force per se is directed against the good of the good object, if and insofar as this object evades the omnipotent control of the subject. It is obvious that this envy is the complementary piece to the fusional impulse of the death drive, which becomes effective as soon as this impulse meets with resistance with respect to its imagination of fulfillment. It represents a massive threat for the ego, inasfar as it threatens to destroy the inner and/or real objects of the ego.

It is important, however, to be theoretically exact here. Primary envy is not identical with what I described above as the aggression that attacks the reality dimension of the object and, in this sense, is annihilatory. This aggression is directed against the process of structure formation, especially against the position outside, which opens up the access to the reality dimension of the object, but which also makes the fusional realization definitely impossible. This annihilatory aggression, conceptualized in this way, attempts to reverse the process of structure formation in order to, ideally, recreate the apparent preconditions for the fusion through the return to the primary-narcissistic suspension of space and time. But in any case the reality constitution of the object and its corollaries—consciousness, thinking, genital sexuality, gender difference, the concept of development—are the predominant themes of this aggression.

Primary envy, in turn, is a different force. It arises out of the position of an ego that no longer sees the possibility to incorporate the object into its ego-cosmic primary narcissistic omnipotence and which therefore engages in a furious campaign of destruction against this object which is eluding the ego's grasp. This is envy. Envy, therefore, is actually the expression of the death drive that is despairing because its aim cannot be fulfilled. In this sense it is the essentially suicidal force. One could say that it is primary envy, conceptualized in this manner, that is behind the foreclosure of the primary object in the case of the psychogenic encapsulated autism.

In order to give a clear theoretical formulation: In the context of my examination of encapsulated psychogenic autism, I have described that the prohibition of fusion and thus the life drive in the pre-schizoid phase—that is, in the phase before representational object constancy is reached and thus before the good-bad split of the object—can only articulate itself by the primary object itself refusing to fuse, in other words, by withdrawing from the ego when a fusional realization is attempted by the ego. In its traumatic maximal effect this is the experience of the not-me object, which Frances Tustin described as the cause and origin of the psychogenic encapsulation autism. Against this primary object that refuses fusion and withdraws from the ego, and that simultaneously is the sum of all that which the ego lacks, primary envy in its pure and early form is directed. This is indeed the primary form of manifestation of aggression, inasfar as it relates to the object's withdrawing as the primary form of expression of the antifusional principle of the life drive and reacts to it. Annihilatory aggression described above and primary envy are not identical, but they lie on a continuum of destructive regression: Annihilatory aggression can turn into primary envy, if in the course of the structural regression, which it engages in, it meets with the experience that fusion cannot be realized, not even under conditions of a suspended reality.

What we in the clinic recognize and dread as manifestations of primary envy in adults and children alike, draws its impact and dangerousness from its provenance out of the pre-schizoid phase, that is, from the phase of primary narcissism with its characteristics of globality and totality. As already touched on further above, it is evident that this envy is in a complementary relationship to the vision of fulfillment of the fusional death drive: it becomes effective to the degree that the death drive—or, respectively, the ego that is its ally—always and ever finds itself barred from establishing the primary narcissistic union with the object.

These considerations on the genesis of primary envy and annihilatory aggression imply that aggression, even in its most fundamental dimension, and consequent to the thoughts presented in this work, cannot be regarded as an independent drive but rather, that it has to be accorded the status of a possible complication in the ego's processing of the death drive, in this respect not unlike those specific maladjustments, faults and errors of the ego, which as described above, produce the major nosological categories.

Primal attachment
    See: Part object, split object, primal attachment; the reality breast

Primal attachment, psychosexuality and drive dynamics

I have pointed out when discussing the situation before representational object constancy (see there) is reached, that the counteractive measures of the life drive (see there) against the fusional tendency of the death drive (see there)—in a situation where the object imago cannot be split yet and therefore a negative, denying, bad representation because of its globality and totality is not compatible with life—can only express themselves by creating an unavoidable pressure towards change of the existing overall situation, in the confrontation with the psychic experience of lack. I have, further, shown that this is so at least inasfar as the life drive does not traumatically express itself, as it would in the encapsulated autism, in the manifestation of the anti-fusional not-me object. I have proposed to regard this pressure for change of the existing

232

overall situation, behind which we have the fear of the manifestation of the traumatic not-me object, as the constitutive moment of the life drive dynamic in the psyche, which later on with the onset of attachment to the human object associates itself with the biological drive determinants—orality for a start. For the death drive, in its turn, the root of the drive moment would be found in the concrete and concretistic direction towards the primary narcissistic, ego-cosmic fusion *(see there)* with the primary object *(see there)*, from which need satisfaction or suspension of the lack, respectively, is being expected, but which from another perspective endangers the existence of the ego and thus of the whole dimension of the psychical.

In the further course of development, the death drive with its fusional aim follows those object cathexes which the life drive prescribes along the lines of psychosexuality. Psychosexuality with its phases as psychoanalysis describes them is therefore no immediately biologically determined and thus by its nature unconditional invariant of mental life, but it is linked to the accomplishment of the primal attachment, that is to say, to the binding of the primary object to the human other, whereby the primary object must be thought of, in the first place, as purely intrapsychic-coenesthetic, originating from the sensory structural givens of the human brain.

If the fixation point of the psychogenic encapsulated autism *(see there)*, as it starts before the onset of the feeding situation, must be assumed before the primal attachment to the human object comes about and thus before the initialisation of the biologically determined psychosexuality, it would have to follow from this that in the intact state of the autistic encapsulation there are no direct sexual drive manifestations. In the encapsulated autism the normal sexual drive development does not find a mental representation due to the foreclosure of the primary object, and hence does not take place. This is in correspondence with the general symptomatology of encapsulated autism. The autostimulative moments which might be misunderstood as autoerotic activities, have a meaning that is in parallel to the autistic object, namely to block the autistic hole in a delusional fashion.

If I consider the primal attachment of the, in the first place, purely endopsychic imago of the primary object to the human other and thus to psychosexuality as a specific step to be taken within the course of psychic development—and which may fail, as encapsulated autism shows, the same goes for the primal attachment of the primary ego (*see there*) to the body: the primary ego, too, firstly has to be seen as an abstract entity so to speak that consists in the subjective pole of the act of perception (*see there*) and that draws its primary narcissistic (*see there*) absolute and unconditional power that answers to the primary object´s quality of being the all-that-is, from its not being conditioned by the primal attachment to the body which only comes about in correspondence to the primary object´s primal attachment to the human other and, thus, to psychosexuality.

I consider the encapsulated psychogenic autism as the clinical evidence for the actual existence of that psychical power, given from the beginning of mental life, which I call the life drive, and as evidence that the psychic struggle which the antagonism of the drives is about centers on the subject of the fusion with the primary object: this is, in this sense, a compelling result from the double aspect of the pathognomonic symptomatology of encapsulated autism, that on the one hand the traumatizing event consists in the manifestation of the not-me object refusing to fuse, and that on the other hand, the circumstance that this not-me object is in fact about the fusion theme, is evidenced by the autist's development of the symptoms of the imitatory merging in a compensatory way, the only meaning of which is to deny and annul the traumatic refusal to fuse through the imitative and repetitive mechanisms.

234

The structure-forming antagonism of the psychical drives as I attempt to present it in this work—namely the formulation of the death drive in the phantasy of the fusion with the object that compensates the lack and insofar satisfies, and the reactive phantasmatization of the life drive which culminates in the castrative consequence of the Oedipus complex—comes to a standstill in the encapsulated form of autism in the very first steps. Instead, we see a defensive imitative merging with the primary object, at a purely sensory level, before the formation of representational object constancy, while the primary object, in its objectal not-me dimension separated from the ego, is being foreclosed and excluded from mental representation.

Autism, psychogenic encapsulated

Psychogenic encapsulated autism is the genetically earliest mental illness. Within psychogenic autism Frances Tustin (1972, 1981) describes two forms of the illness, the encapsulation type and the confusional type, whereby she regards the encapsulated form as the earlier one, the first signs and symptoms showing already at or shortly after birth. Therefore, the circumstances of the ego's relationship with the primary object (see there) and the complications arising from this represent themselves directly in this disease.

Both forms of the illness, according to Tustin, have their cause in the fact that the newborn experiences the primary object in a premature and traumatic way as outside the reach of its own omnipotent control, as not-me object. The encapsulation type reacts to this trauma—or sequence of traumas—by breaking off all contact with the object, and he does that before the primary attachment (see there) is established, by excluding the object from psychic perception and withdrawing into a delusional state of encapsulation. The confusional type of autism does not break off connection with the primary object, but the child attempts to engulf the object and/or enter it, to become entangled with it, by using archaic-concretistic pre-forms of projective identification (see there) in order to, in this way, delusionally reverse the separation which was experienced as traumatic.

In my terms, the trauma of the premature not-me experience of the object signifies the loss of the primary narcissistic illusion of omnipotent control over the primary object, that is to say, the loss of the illusion, more precisely of the delusion, to be able to absorb the experience of lack psychically via control of the object as the source to remedy and suspend this lack. The ego would then be exposed to the physiological experience of this lack, without protection. The autistic pathology is the attempt of a counterreaction to this unbearable state.

These children do not establish contact with their parents or other people. They avoid eye contact, are mute as a rule and not clean. In Tustin's words: "Since his first traumatic experience of bodily separateness, the child has had virtually no sense of bodily separateness. (...). (.). For most of the time the child behaves as if fused with the outside world, and outside objects are experienced as a prolongation of his bodily sensations or movements. In his state of imitative fusion, everything is experienced as "me", (...).(..) the 'not-me' is quickly made into 'me', by feeling that it is part of his body and under his control" (1981, p. 29). Tustin clarifies that we are dealing with a defensive formation against the traumatic not-me experience here. The crucial point here is that this is about the <u>simulation</u> of fusional merging (see: fusion) via the path of imitation. The imitative fusion serves as defense against the traumatic perception about the separation from the object, is thus a pathological distortion in the sense of a rigid denial and reaction formation, the undoing of the manifestation of the not-me dimension of the primary object, that is to say, the denial precisely of the failure of the fusional project.

236

Tustin describes the mechanisms which the autistic child uses to maintain the state of imitative fusion, whereby these mechanisms at the same time preserve the kind of perception of this earliest period in life when this primitive mode of defense of imitative fusion developed. Hence these mechanisms provide invaluable insight into the quality of perception (see there) within a psychical constitution which as yet does not know a differentiation between inside and outside, between animate and inanimate, between one's own body and the real object, and where perception is still directly identical with experiencing, as at this time neither object constancy (see there) and thus memory, nor the ability of symbol formation connected with the position outside (see there), have been acquired.

"As a reaction to this unbearable disturbance, he cultivates the illusion that he is fused with hard objects. By his withdrawal he feels he turns his hard back to protect his soft front. The encapsulation mechanisms also protect his vulnerable softness.

This total encapsulation to form the delusion of a protective shell is characteristic of global, undifferentiated states and is a primary pathological autistic manoeuvre" (Tustin 1981, pp. 29).

The decisive point in the formation of the encapsulated autistic pathology is that these children experience the trauma of the not-me quality of the primary object as a hole in their own bodies, as this is how the traumatic collapse of the primary narcissistic illusion of omnipotent control over the object expresses itself. As the encapsulated children experience themselves and the object as inanimate, they experience this collapse as a hole, and they develop the delusional phantasy to close the hole with a kind of ritual thing called the autistic object, which an autistic child always carries on him.

In the encapsulated autist, the theme of the autistic hole is not only expression of the traumatic not-me experience alone, but more

237

importantly and in particular, it is the expression of the post-traumatic active exclusion, foreclosure of the primary object from the psychic space. This exclusion concerns that manifestation of the primary object where the latter has become the traumatic not-me object. The traumatic events of which we speak here take place before the point in time when representational object constancy is reached. Therefore we have a succession of, on the one hand, foreclosure, and on the other, imitative fusion, as the reaction to the trauma. The autistic encapsulation serves to protect from this not-me object and represents a definitive separation, a dividing wall towards it.

The problem with autistic objects is, that they so to speak enshrine the foreclosure of the not-me object, the autistic child putting them in the place of lack caused by the traumatic loss of the primary object, so that the autistic hole is being filled and closed, thus providing the child with the delusional illusion of intactness. Tustin emphasizes that no phantasy or meaning in the normal sense is connected with the autistic object, as the autistic psychotic child is yet unable to achieve a psychical feat like the formation of phantasies or symbolic meanings. The autistic object is selected on a purely sensory, sensual basis according to criteria of contour, surface texture, shape, etc. The task of this autistic object is to compensate and close the sensory deficit of the autistic hole by way of sensory analogies and formal similarities that are, for this reason, central to these children. The problem with autistic objects (and likewise with the sensory autostimulations which serve the same function) is that they replace the foreclosed primary object in a delusional manner. With this, psychic development comes to a complete standstill at a very early stage.

The autistic object bars access to the world definitively and absolutely, and, without therapeutic help, once and for all: for the autistic object, as said, is put in place of the primary object in its meaning as the foreclosed traumatic not-me object, whereas in compensation, an imitatory fusional relationship is being entered into with the non-traumatic manifestation of the primary object, which in its turn negates the ego-independent objectal character of the primary object. In doing so any human relationship, as an object relationship that is, is given up by the autistic child, or does not even come about, because the encapsulation of the autist takes place before the primal attachment even occurs.

Seeing, hearing, and smelling are translated into tactile experiences by the autistic child, as these sensory modalities are the distance perception modalities. By suspending their proper character and coenesthetically incorporating them into the tactile register, the autist also here turns against perceiving the separation of the source of excitation from his own body, or the immediate ego, and thus against the perceptual basis of the recognition of the separation from the object. This suspension of the perception of distance directly affects the experience of dimensionality—the third dimension, space, must not be experienced. Thus an inside and outside are not available, in the same way as the differentiation of the criteria of animate and inanimate would imply the recognition of an existence separate from the ego, and therefore is ruled out.

Tustin writes: "The Encapsulated child lives in a two-dimensional world. He is preoccupied with surfaces, textures and shapes. If he gets inside an object, for him it is not the getting *inside* which is significant— he is not aware of that as such—it is the sensation of being covered up, of being sheltered and protected which matters. He is forever seeking analogies and identities in terms of shapes. Things which seem dissimilar to us are equated by him on the basis of their sharing some characteristics which is important to the child" (1981, p. 42).

Tustin understands the pathognomic compulsory and perseverative search leading to these autistic sensation shapes—a search for formal analogies and artificial identities that dissolve the real boundaries of things—as the expression of the striving to suspend the differentiation between the self and the object. This she also bases on her understanding that the suspension of the differentiation between things is a characteristic of the anti-objectal quality of the fusional tendency. In this sense, this is an expansion of the imitative fusion.

Tustin points out that because the psychic functioning of these children is tied to two-dimensionality, no concept of an internal psychic space, or mind, can develop, which might contain thoughts, feelings, phantasies and memories, but which is also the basis for psychic mechanisms like projection, introjection, or projective identification. As no concept of their own inner space (see there) exists, such space cannot be ascribed to the object through the process of primary identification (see there) either, and from there be reintrojected again, a situation that supports the lacking differentiation between an animate and an inanimate world. Imitative behaviour, echopraxia and echolalia, and the obsessive search of these children for formal analogies in their turn support the sensorial binding to tactile experience of a two-dimensional kind which ignores the boundaries between real things. They are the mechanisms of foreclosure, or of the exclusion of the perception of the not-me, respectively. By that they secondarily support the lack of the concept of an inner space, in the person itself and in the object.

Tustin pointedly notes that the motive of the fusional striving of autistic children is the maintenance, or restitution, respectively, of omnipotent control over the object. The bodily sensations mediated through the autistic object and also through the autostimulation give the child the feeling "(...) he had a perfect mother always with him who gave him ecstatic and instant sensual satisfaction" (Tustin 1981, pp. 103). As a consequence, the encapsulated autistic child does not acquire the frustration tolerance which is the 'conditio sine qua non' for the reflexive distance of the ego in relation to its own states in the position outside, and thus for gradually acquiring the capacity for symbol formation, and for any higher functioning of the mind.

The missing frustration tolerance also expresses itself in the equally pathognomonic tendency of encapsulated autistic children to display raging anger tantrums and panic attacks. In Tustin's words: "The constant use of Autistic Objects means that the psychotic child has little possibility of learning to tolerate frustration and to develop a more realistic evaluation of inner and outer stimuli which are felt to be life-threatening. When frustration impinges, tantrums pound through muscle and vein and cause the child to fear total annihilation. To counteract this deadly terror he clutches a hard Autistic Object. He never learns to deal with bodily and mental irritation in a considered, thinking way" (1981, p. 110).

When Tustin speaks of the "unhealthy" and "wayward" omnipotence of autistic children and further, that they "in an autistic state (...) are unaware of their actual weakness and neediness", these are not, in my opinion, pathological changes of an original state, no matter what that state may be like. In fact, Tustin describes the global and total experiencing in the pre-schizoid phase, in which the primary object is the all-that-is, outside of which nothing exists, and where, equally so, the ego in complete contrast to its real neotenous helplessness and weakness, experiences itself as not limited and not conditioned, because it does not yet experience its real boundaries and is not identified with them yet. I have identified this as that state which Freud had in mind when he described the constitution of primary narcissism; only that in my opinion, as I have outlined, the primary

241

object which takes up the total space of psychic experiencing would be included in this constitution. The encapsulation autism preserves this primary narcissistic constitution and conveys an impression of the tremendous psychic impact which results when neither object nor ego are subjected to any kind of condition or real limitation. It is from this totality and globality that the formative power derives which this primordial constitution has for the further life of the psyche.

The autistic child has no inner concept of bodily growth, psychical development, or even healing. Tustin: "The *unintegrated* Encapsulated type of psychotic child experiences it (the body) as an inanimate thing; (...). (He) experiences bodily separateness from the outside world as a 'hole' (...). Since the psychotic child has no knowledge of growth and healing, the hole is a 'hole' and remains a 'hole' (.)" (1981 p. 179).

In other words, in these children the splitting dynamics of the paranoid-schizoid and depressive (*see there*) positions do not take place, the central results of which are the acquisition of psychical concepts like growth, development, and healing. That this splitting does not come about is simply the consequence of the circumstance that the pathogenic trauma takes place before the point in time when representational object constancy is acquired and therefore a split of the object representation cannot yet be performed.

Tustin places the start of the traumatic not-me experience of the encapsulated autistic child very early, in the first few days of mental life, perhaps interpartally, perhaps even still in the womb. She states that the primal attachment in any case has not yet occurred. "The encapsulated child has experienced bodily separateness from the mother precociously. This may have been before he was put to the breast (or bottle experienced as breast)" (1981 p. 164). And she says that the encapsulated children are "usually reported as being withdrawn from birth or just after birth" (1981, p. 37).

I have pointed out that the splitting of the imago of the primary object is only conceivable as of the time when a rudimentary memory function—in other words a rudimentary representational object constancy—is present, where the ego simultaneously with calling up a negative, bad split image, can *in principle* maintain the memory of the good object. The splitting presupposes the parallel maintaining of the representation of the good and bad objects in time, and consists in it. Only when the condition of object constancy is met, is the splitting of the object representation possible. The breakthrough to the perception of time via the maintenance of a past experience of the object in memory constitutes the definitional content of representational object constancy.

Said the other way around, an outside of the primary object, an alternative to it, does not exist in this earliest constitution before object constancy, where, as said, the primary object is the totality of the activated perceptual situation and insofar the all-that-is. If then the suspension of the lack by necessity has to be located in the primary object of the still unmodulated primary narcissistic constitution, this primary object must then represent the plenitude of possible gratification, and the ego, under pressure of unpleasure, must seek the fusional identity with it. This is the pre-ambivalent object.

In the situation of the psychogenic encapsulation autism, the case now seems to arise that based on accidental circumstances the felt pressure of the unpleasure of lack and thus the pressure towards fusion become so enormous that, as a drive dynamical emergency reaction, a refusal to fuse manifests out of the imago of the primary object itself in order to counter the threat of ego dissolution in a fusional realization. Thus the primary object becomes a traumatic not-me object in Frances Tustin's sense. This means that the phantasy to compensate the experience of lack via the fusion of ego and primary object collapses, and in this way the traumatically premature experience of separation from the primary object occurs which Tustin named as cause for the infantile psychogenic autism, expressed in her formula of the "not-me object": The primary object can no longer be incorporated into the ego by way of the ego-cosmic, primary narcissistic fulfillment phantasy. Thus also the experience of dependency from this not-me object becomes, as Tustin emphasizes, a premature, and insofar traumatic experience. For as long as the ego entertains the phantasy of fusional, ego-cosmic control over a primary object that represents fulfillment of satisfaction, dependency is clearly no issue.

The triggering of the infantile psychogenic autism therefore is not about a primary object as a representation of lack, but about a primary object that rejects fusion. The prohibition of fusion confronts the primary ego here in the primary object itself and out of it, as this primary object cannot yet be split because the stage of representational object constancy has not yet been reached so that the prohibition of fusion cannot be expressed via the split. The consequence of this traumatic disillusion, in the psychogenic autism of the encapsulation type, is the foreclosure of the not-me object. The not-me object is thus a traumatic manifestation of the anti-fusional principle on which the maintenance of the dimension of psychic life rests. From these considerations follows that the specific psychogenic anxiety of the pre-schizoid phase (see there) of psychic development must be that of the manifestation of this traumatic not-me object. That this anxiety has a factual basis is evidenced in the clinical picture of the psychogenic encapsulation autism. One might conclude here that the dynamic reason for establishing the paranoid-schizoid object splitting after reaching the developmental phase of representational object constancy is to counter, in this way, the danger of foreclosure of the imago of the primary object which results from the dynamic antagonism of the two drives. The reality of this danger is evidenced by the encapsulation autism in which mental development is arrested immediately after the start.

It is important to note that in the psychodynamics of primary psychogenic encapsulated autism, there are no splitting mechanisms in the sense of the good-bad split of the paranoid-schizoid position involved. Instead there is a succession, and later a side-by-side of mutually contradictory, or somehow exclusive, global states as, on the one hand, the autistic foreclosure of the traumatic primary object (the not-me object) that leaves a hole which is filled by the autistic object; and, on the other hand, the imitative fusional practices and manoeuvres that serve to deny the trauma of the manifestation of the antifusional not-me object. Both states of mind are, as said, running counter to each other but do not imply a split neither of the ego nor of the primary object. The possibility of their coexistence signifies a psychical constitution before representational object constancy is attained, that is a constitution in which time and comparison of different states of mind in time are not yet experienced, and therefore, the respective activated representation of the primary object on the level of subjective experiencing is the all-that-is outside of which nothing exists. Under this condition, these two states of mind are pulled together and consolidated into one uniform experience by the common traumatic context, within which the primary object is at the same time foreclosed in its totality and the ego enters—also in totality—into the pathognomonic imitative fusion with it. This constitutes the clinical picture of the psychogenic infantile autism of the encapsulation type. There is no splitting mechanism underlying it.

The character of totality and globality of the inner perception of the primary object in this primary constitution of the psyche leads to these two psychic movements that actually contradict each other—

foreclosure and imitative fusion—to paradoxically co-exist peacefully and undisturbedly side by side due to the totality claim of both, because this unconditional experience of absoluteness leads to a situation where contradiction and mutual exclusion are not finding a representation. The resulting quality of totality of the symptomatology spans the whole spectrum of experience, with its character definitely blocking development as a whole.

Through this constellation two things become evident:

1. Primary experiencing in fact takes place in timelessness.
2. The primary object, in this first phase of mental life, has in fact this character of totality and globality which I have summarized in the formulation of the "all-that-is" outside of which nothing exists.

This is the metapsychologically stringent explanation of this first form of psychical illness, and in reverse, I consider this very succession or, later, side-by-side of the foreclosure of the traumatic not-me version of the primary object and the reactive imitative fusion with its non-traumatic form of manifestation as clinical evidence for the correctness of my reflections on the existence of a pre-schizoid phase, for such parallelity of contradictory relations with the object is only possible before the background of a not yet established object constancy, so that successive states of the relationship to the primary object cannot be compared yet with each other and thus be recognized as incompatible.

In terms of theory, this is a metapsychological conclusion of prime importance. It is the gain we can draw out of our understanding of this earliest form of psychic pathology, proving that our inferences about mental functioning at the primordial level are correct.

The open question of the genesis of the primary psychogenic autism has thus become clarified to the extent that the traumatic manifestation of the not-me object is not the direct consequence of an external influence, but that of a psychic materialization of the anti-fusional principle of the life drive within the imago of the primary object itself, which results from the dynamic opposition of the drives and which represents an extreme emergency reaction in order to prevent the imminent collapse of the dimension of the psychical in a concrete fusional realization.

In this sense I consider, further, the encapsulated psychogenic autism as the clinical evidence for the actual existence of that psychical power, given from the beginning of mental life, which I call the life drive, and as evidence that the psychic struggle which the antagonism of the drives is about centers on the subject of the fusion with the primary object: this is, in this sense, a compelling result from the double aspect of the pathognomonic symptomatology of encapsulated autism, that on the one hand the traumatizing event consists in the manifestation of the not-me object refusing to fuse, and that, on the other hand, the circumstance that this not-me object is in fact about the fusion theme, is evidenced by the autist's development of the symptoms of the imitatory merging in a compensatory way, the only meaning of which is to deny and annul the traumatic refusal to fuse through the imitative and repetitive mechanisms.

The structure-forming antagonism of the psychical drives as I attempt to present it in this work—namely the formulation of the death drive in the phantasy of the fusion with the object that compensates the lack and insofar satisfies, and the reactive phantasmatization of the life drive which culminates in the castrative consequence of the Oedipus complex—comes to a standstill in the encapsulated form of autism in the very first steps. Instead, we see a defensive imitative merging with the primary object, at a purely sensory level, before the formation of representational object constancy, while the primary object, in its objectal not-me dimension separated from the ego, is being foreclosed and excluded from mental representation.

Before the background of the clinic of the conditions in encapsulated autists which keep the psychical circumstances of the beginning of life fixated in a time warp-like fashion, Tustin describes that and in how far the primary psychic functioning is a purely sensory one and proceeds first of all from the unmodulated sensory opposites. I would like to stress that this emphasis on the sensory system also corresponds to my own starting point, when I speak about the fact that after the unfolding of the poles of perception (see there), the primary object consists solely and exclusively in the sensory afferences which are bound together in a unified representation only through temporal contiguity. I have described that, in this psychic state that is tied to two-dimensionality, there are no phantasies in the actual sense, or mental content, as they require object constancy on the one hand, and an inner space (see there) on the other, and thus lead away from immediate sensory perception. In that respect experiencing in the pre-schizoid phase is necessarily bound to the immediate sensory perception.

If one tries to answer the question in which manner the basal sensory integration tasks constitutive for the further development of the psyche normally come about, one is directed back to the theme of the primary object in the pre-schizoid phase before representational object constancy is reached. In this first constitution of the psyche the (non-split) primary object is the only thing that is given and is being positively posited. It is the pre-ambivalent primary object, the basic affirmation of life in its psychic dimension.

As under the condition of globality and totality of the pre-schizoid phase, the representation of a bad presence is not possible as this would deny life itself, the pre-ambivalent primary object of this phase is the precursor model of what will later become the good breast. I assume that it is the central task of this pre-ambivalent primary object to serve as a catalyst and container for this sensory integration. Thus we are dealing here with a basal, early form of the containing function: containment and an archaic, sensorily defined alpha function are being exercised solely intra-psychically by the inner primary object. In any case, it is precisely this task which fails when the primary object of this developmental stage falls under the autistic foreclosure.

A very important concept in the context of encapsulated psychogenic autism is, finally, that of primary envy (*see there*) which Melanie Klein described in 1957. This envy which Klein regards as the elementary destructive force per se, in her description is directed against the good of the good object, if and insofar as this object evades the omnipotent control of the subject. It is obvious that this envy is the complementary piece to the fusional impulse of the death drive as I describe it, which becomes effective as soon as this impulse meets with resistance with respect to its imagination of fulfillment.

Primary envy arises out of the position of an ego that no longer sees the possibility to incorporate the object into its ego-cosmic primary narcissistic omnipotence and which therefore engages in a furious campaign of destruction against this object which is eluding the ego's grasp. I have described that the prohibition of fusion and thus the life drive in the pre-schizoid phase—that is, in the phase before representational object constancy is reached and thus before the good-bad split of the object—can only articulate itself by the primary object itself refusing to fuse, in other words, by withdrawing from the ego when a fusional realization is attempted by the ego. In its traumatic maximal effect, this is the experience of the not-me object, which Frances Tustin defined as the cause and origin of the psychogenic encapsulation autism. Against this primary object that refuses fusion and withdraws from the ego, and that simultaneously is the sum of all that which the ego lacks, primary envy in its pure and early form is directed. Thus, it is primary envy that is behind the foreclosure of the primary object in the case of the psychogenic encapsulated autism. This is indeed the primary form of manifestation of aggression, inasfar as it relates to the object's withdrawing as the primary form of expression of the antifusional principle of the life drive and reacts to it.

In this way it becomes clear that the early development is indeed a trip between Scylla and Charybdis: on the one hand, the fusion between the primary ego and the primary object must be prevented at all cost, in order to prevent the collapse of the poles of perception and thus the self-annulment of the dimension of the psychical. On the other hand, the equally elementary danger of primary envy threatens, by which the primary ego attempts to destroy its object, inasfar as the object withdraws from the ego and refuses itself.

What we in the clinic recognize and dread as manifestations of primary envy in adults and children alike, draws its impact and dangerousness from its provenance out of the pre-schizoid phase, that is, from the phase of primary narcissism with its characteristics of globality and totality. It is evident that this envy is in a complementary relationship to the vision of fulfillment of the fusional death drive: it becomes effective to the degree that the death drive—or, respectively, the ego that is its ally—always and ever finds itself barred from establishing the primary narcissistic union with the object.

Christ

The basic tenet of the New Testament is about a theology of the relationship of Jesus Christ to the God of the Old Testament: Jesus is the son of God, the logos that became flesh, God himself who incarnated in him in human form and who in this human form has defined his relationship to the God who simultaneously remains outside this incarnation, as that of the Son to the Father. Within a perspective which understands the mythos as a representation of the inner world, the Christ thus declares himself as the ego insofar as the ego is always 'the child of ...'.

The Christian mythos thus reveals itself as a religion which has as its subject the relationship with the father, with the father imago (see there). This relationship of the ego to the father imago is accurately described by the religion mythologem when it refers to Christ as both wholly God and wholly human at the same time. The meaning of this dogmatic definition is clearly exemplified in the temptations of the devil, but also in the death on the cross itself, inasmuch as Christ, as wholly human, observes the limitations that apply to humans without at the same time invoking his God-nature in order to override the laws of reality. By doing so Christ declares that his relationship to the Father is one of an identical non-identity: he is of the same essence as the Father, but as a human, as ego, he must not lay claim to the identity with the Father.

As a structural pattern, the above ties in with my deduction exactly, according to which the father imago in its core—which is the position of the ego outside the drive phantasma (see there)—is a split-off part of the ego, by which the ego protects itself against the only danger threatening it from within, namely its fusional self-annulment (see: Fusion). In the father imago, therefore, the ego's nature so characteristically based on non-fusion, becomes expressed. The father imago is a part of the ego that has become objective and absolute, the task of which is, from this moment on, to carry and represent the ego's own law and to sanction its transgression.

It is true that ego and father imago are of the same essence, but in order to not annul the effect and power of the father imago again, which as we know is based on the distancing of the ego from itself, the ego must not equate itself with it. The paradox expressed in the Christian religious myth is that the Son, by internalizing the necessity of renunciation as conveyed by the father imago, to the degree of this specific internalization becomes identical with the father principle itself, that he indeed represents and possesses the phallus *(see there)*, the phallic potency. This identity with the Father thus contains the deepest knowledge about the necessary and indissoluble non-identity. In other words, the identity with the Father, the father principle consists, by definition, of this integrated non-identity.

Death drive and depressive position

The phantasmatic step in which the ego attempts to suspend the experience of lack by establishing fusional union with the object *(see: fusion)*, harbors an unforeseen danger, insofar as by this act the effected suspension of the differentiation between ego and object would bring the whole dimension of the psychical down again, when it has hardly unfolded through the separation of ego and object, perception and the perceived. It would be a self-suspension of the psychical, so to speak, and this is the basic danger which threatens the psyche and which I equate with the death drive, which in this definition is purely psychically captured, and is no longer, as with Freud, a drive with biological origin. That which is deadly in the psychical sense derives only from the unforeseen consequence of the self-suspension of the ego in the fusional movement. The movement itself, however, is an absolutely understandable and compelling consequence of the first concern of life about itself, on the psychic plane.

It is by all means conceivable—as Freud formulated as his starting point—that tension, or unpleasure, basically result from the work demand, seen from a physical perspective, to maintain a multicellular organism. But it is, in my view, a categorical mistake that disregards the fundamental difference, the leap from the biological to the psychical, to assume immediately also for the psychic life that it contains the aim of dissolution of this organism. The biological tendency which we refer to briefly as 'tension', instead encounters the psychical with its own phantasmatic laws and has a totally different effect there than a phantasy of bringing about death in the sense of disintegration. Even though the death drive, which I conceptualize in a psychical sense, if it was fulfilled, would again effect the resuspension of the dimension of the psychical in the fusional coinciding of ego and object representation, it would do so taking a very specific detour, this detour containing the total psychical fate, the psychical constitution of the human being, and which does not consist, by any means, in the search for death.

In this sense I consider the further structural development of the psychic apparatus as a consequence of the necessity to neutralize these inevitable dynamics of the death drive and to shape them so that their potential which threatens the dimension of the psychical is bound up. This is the task of the Oedipus complex (see there).

In any case, insofar as the ego, with the beginning of its existence, pursuing its very own, legitimate goals, namely, to suspend tension due to unpleasure, runs into a situation of an inevitable, elementary thread of annihilation, one must describe the nature of the ego as <u>primarily traumatic</u>. The push from this traumatic quality and dimension is the motor for all further, directly resulting structural development.

The aim of the death drive which is to suspend the separation from the object, remains the same at all stages of mental development and structure formation. The various forms of psychopathology consist in the various attempts of the death drive and of the ego coalescing with it, to enforce this aim of the drive. The central phantasmatic expression and common denominator of all these attempts is the attack on the Oedipal father as the instance that prohibits and prevents the fusional incest with the mother. I would like to stress in this context, however, that this is always and in every single case about suspending the separation from the object.

The death drive thus is the power that negates the primary object's objectal character which is independent from the ego; it is the deobjectalizing drive. This has immediate consequences for the theory of the depressive position. The classical concept (Klein 1935, 1940) sees the depressive position as the complication according to which the clear and unquestioned object splitting of the paranoid-schizoid position can no longer be maintained within a psychical constitution which, in principle, has not yet overcome the good-bad split of the object, leading to the complication that the ego, under the influence of its own panic, in its attacks on the bad object also damages the good object and—in its phantasmatic experiencing—destroys it. In the positive case when the depressive position is successfully worked through and overcome, this leads to the double movement of, on the one hand, mourning for the apparently damaged and destroyed lost object—the source of the good, of satisfaction, of the suspension of lack, and on the other hand, to phantasmatic efforts towards its reparation.

The process of mourning is thereby thought of (cf. Steiner, 1993, following Freud 1917) as fundamentally occurring in two steps, namely, one, in the immediate reaction to the loss, in the denial of that loss and in the attempt to possess the object internally and to preserve it, to keep it safe. In this context a further category of splitting processes occurs within the framework of the depressive position, in order to accomplish this particular protection of the object, also from one's own destructive attacks. This, too, must fail with the experience that the ego cannot provide this protection. The second step of the mourning process then consists in acknowledging the loss and the existence of the object independent from the ego. That is to say, here a situation arises in which as a result of the conflictuous complication of the depressive position the independence and autonomy of the object is being acknowledged.

If one was to consider this formulation before the backdrop of my thoughts regarding the meaning and the psychodynamics of both psychic drives, it becomes evident that, with this perspective, something far more fundamental is happening than has been outlined in the already heavyweight formulas of the classical concept: the death drive is being forced, namely in and through the process of mourning, for the very first time, to withdraw its aim which is directed towards the absolute, omnipotent possession of the object. Or rather, one must formulate this more exactly, as the drive would be no drive if it desisted from its aim: the ego, for the first time, is being forced to realize that its old pact with the death drive in the attempt to establish the primary narcissistic union with the object, is not self-evident and natural, good and right, but rather, to the contrary, that the life-maintaining object, at the level of the drive phantasies, while pursuing this aim, has become badly damaged and perhaps even destroyed. Thus the ego, in its collaboration with the death drive which as said appeared so natural, for the first time encounters a definite no go, a genuine prohibition, and the crisis of the depressive position, in this sense, is a prefiguration of the later crisis of the Oedipal conflict, the intentional task of the latter being to finally bind the death drive structurally, once and for all.

In the crisis of the depressive position with its theme of injuring and destroying the object, and, in consequence, of the enforced acknowledgement of the separation from it through the process of mourning, two themes are, for the first time, simultaneously addressed

255

and psychically captured: one, implicitly, the theme of deobjectalization (and in this sense destruction) of the object which is the theme of the death drive, and two, and above all, the theme of a necessary separation of ego and object.

The depressive crisis into which the early object splitting leads in consequence of the unavoidable developmentally given insight into the fundamental time-space unity of the object, thus has to be considered a brilliant move of nature in order to divide the ego and the death drive. The success of this move then immediately shows by the ego developing, as a result of working through the successive depressive crises, the 'position outside the drive phantasma' (see there), that is to say, the ego is taking up a reflexive distance towards itself for the first time. This reflexive distance consists in a splitting of the ego within itself, through which object splitting as mode of defense against the fusional danger that results from the death drive is overcome. The position outside becomes the seed and core of the father imago (see there) and thus the origin of the Oedipal constellation, the task of which, as said, is to bind the death drive once and for all. The psychic structuring process may therefore be regarded as one in which the psychic separation of the ego from the object becomes codified. This separation is the basis of mental life, and therefore also the basis of mental health.

Just above, I have formulated it in the way that the crisis of the depressive position serves to divide the ego and the death drive, that is to say, to make clear to the ego that its own interest, namely keeping up the relationship to the life-maintaining object, is not congruent with the fusional and insofar deobjectalizing drive aim of the death drive. My mental conception, in this formulation, is to treat this as if the ego and the death drive until that time, so-to-speak, form a coalition, a pact, as the ego has not yet become aware of the contradiction of its own nature to that of the death drive. One may ask, however, if this is actually so or whether in the earliest constitution this primary ego is not simply identical with the death drive.

The ego, as a separate motivational structure, would thus only detach from the death drive with the crisis of the depressive position. In other words, that which we further on call the death drive, would designate the early form of functioning of the ego, in which the ego confronted the object still totally recklessly without any regard and where the only task was to suspend need-tension and in this sense achieve blissfulness. That which we call drive in the psyche would thus conserve the impetus and momentum of the primary narcissism of the primary narcissistic world, i.e. of the pre-schizoid phase (*see there*).

This means that the ego, as the agency that we know, only begins to develop when it struggles with the question of the preservation of the object; that is to say, the ego having the experience that it, as concerns its structural identity, gets the best protection for itself through an object whose identity in turn is protected. This experience is then being laid down structurally in the position outside, and especially in the father imago developing from it, which embodies and exemplifies the anti-fusional principle. The death drive, the primary form of functioning of the ego, would therefore result immediately out of the system property of the human brain, according to which the direct sensual perception is the first form of functioning of this organ that can build up representations and is thus in principle capable of displaying the quality of being conscious. The whole structure-forming process of the psyche that psychoanalysis describes has, from then on, no further task than to make the ego, the subject of perception, understand that the condition of its structural safety is different from its desire of an instant fusional merging with the other pole of the perceptual function, the object.

We have, therefore, succumbed here to a reification, by designating the force which we call death drive in this very manner, and in this way have blocked our view and now cannot see that the death drive is the surviving form of functioning of the primary ego. The cause for this is to be seen, most certainly, in the enormous dynamic power and as-it-were wildness which nolens volens must be ascribed to the death drive and which, as a result, appears to make this classification as a drive unavoidable. In my opinion this dynamic potential comes from the fact that the death drive has its roots precisely in the primary constitution of the psyche, in which the power of desire has not yet been curbed by any reality conditions, and the primary ego in confrontation with the primary object—which in its turn in this earliest constitution, before representational object constancy, was the all-that-is—was faced with the seeming possibility to enlarge itself to the egocosmic ego. There is no greater power of seduction.

Freud, who for his part saw in the death drive fundamentally the drive towards self-destruction, writes in *The Economic Problem of Masochism*: "The libido has the task of making the destroying instinct innocuous, and it fulfills the task by diverting that instinct to a great extent outwards—soon with the help of a special organic system, the muscular apparatus—towards objects in the external world" (1924, p. 163).

For clarification, the death drive for Freud was in this way connected with the aim of destruction, and its primary and fundamental object for him is the self of the subject in its physical and psychical identity. Life, therefore, is only possible for Freud insofar as this death drive is being deviated from the self and directed "towards objects in the external world". Thus this contains a change of object. Contrary to that, I would maintain that the death drive is directed against or towards the object from the beginning, more exactly, it is directed against the separateness of the ego vis-à-vis the imago of the primary object, against the necessary separation of subject and object of perception. The aim of the death drive is the suspension of the tension of unpleasure by fusing with the object. This aim has nothing to do with a primary aggression either against the self or the object.

This leads to the, in my view, theoretically crucial insight that the direction of the death drive towards the external world is no more than the result of the reality access which comes about through the overcoming of the good-bad split of the object as the primary form of defending against the death drive. Through this new feature the erstwhile purely intrapsychic, subjectively defined imago of the primary object is brought into alignment with the representation of the external real object. Before as after, the death drive is directed towards the object. This object, however, is first the primary, subjective object of the splitting constitution, later with the overcoming of the sole rule of the splitting constitution through the acquisition of the position outside, the outer reality can be recognized and perceived as such, and then—and only then—can the death drive be directed towards the external object.

The quality and the object, the content and the aim of the death drive, do not change in any way or form through its direction to the external world, in particular, there is no change from auto-aggression to hetero-aggression, that is to say no change of object takes place, which incidentally would also imply a change in aim. Underlying this is a theoretical misunderstanding with serious consequences: the equation of the death drive with destruction, for one, could only ever have been made on the faulty assumption of an object change, whereby destruction according to Freud enforces this object change so as to prevent the self-destruction of the subject. In this way it was misunderstood that this drive is basically neither directed against the self nor against the object, but against the moment of separation. The death drive is not per se the "destroying instinct".

Only before the backdrop of the hypostasis of an object change which, so it seems, necessarily results from the empirical, descriptive observation of the direction of the aggression towards the external, was Freud able to link the death drive theoretically with aggression. This object change enabled him to deduce heteroaggression from the outward diversion, necessary for maintaining life, of a destructive tendency derived from the organic that seemingly was originally directed against the subject itself. Without this conclusion of an unavoidable object change Freud's concept of the death drive lacks in its axiomatic deduction, inasfar as then the genesis of aggression can no longer be deduced from the death drive's aim of self-destruction.

Without the object change that Freud assumed as necessary in his theory formulation, the death drive would have to be equated directly with "inborn" aggression—irrespective of whether it is directed against the object or the subject—which in the years after his death, under the, as-it-were, application of it from pragmatic points of view, became the course of things. Freud would never have accepted a reduction of the death drive to a general inborn aggression, as with certainty it would have appeared to him as an intolerable theoretical shortcoming to speak of an aggressive drive without any indication out of which necessity within the subject, within the subjective psyche, such aggression conceptualized as a primary drive might possibly arise.

For him this necessity lay in the demand for work to maintain a multicellular organism, and related with it the unpleasure which leads to the wish to suspend this multicellular organization, whereby this "destroying instinct" then—with the implication of object change—must be diverted to the exterior world in order to guarantee the maintenance of life. With the absence of object change, however, this deduction of the death drive becomes untenable.

The reduction of the death drive to aggression, in my view, does not do justice to the circumstance that the theme of the death drive is the fight against the separation from the object. The external appearances of this fight can be either aggressive or sexual, so that the same applies for aggression as for sexuality, namely that it is the medium of expression for both drives.

That Freud could assume such a qualitative change of the death drive with respect to its direction towards the external—in other words, object change—has to do with the historic moment that the formation of a theory of early psychic development had not yet happened, to be specific, the theory that was subsequently formulated by Melanie Klein and her school about the primary stages of psychic structure formation in the splitting constitution. Only this theory, to summarize again, has made it possible to show that the external direction of aggression does not necessarily imply an object change from self to object, but rather, that the early good-bad split of the object imago prevents the mental conceptualization of the real object. Only the overcoming of this good-bad split makes access to reality possible by having the effect that the now no longer split imago of the object can be brought into alignment with the representation of the real object. With this we have—amongst other things—the external direction of the aggression, which, however, before and after is directed to the psychological object; the primary aim of which is therefore not, as Freud had assumed as necessary, the destructive dissolution of the multicellular subject. In consequence, aggression loses that central meaning which it would have if its diversion to the exterior world was linked with the question of being or not being of the subject. Aggression is not at the center of the death drive.

Depressive position
>   See: *Death drive* and *depressive position*

Drive dynamics
>   See: Primal *attachment, psychosexuality* and *drive dynamics*

The drives

The a priori basic thought from which the complete structure formation of the psyche and its pathological deviations can be inferred in a discipline-specific step-by-step argumentation is the following that with the moment in which the first sensory perceptions become possible, based on the ontogenetic maturation of the central nervous system, these perceptions by definition have a bi-polar structure: they consist of the pole of the perceiving subject and the pole of the perceived itself, that is to say, the representation. I assume that in psychoanalytic terms the perceiving subject is directly the archaic, primordial ego, that which is perceived—the representation—is the archaic, primordial object. The other claim which, like the primary hypothesis would have to be proven deductively through the explanatory capacity of these assumptions, is that this is in fact the starting point of psychic life in its total potential impact if though for that matter still at a level that is very primitive in terms of structure formation.

Such a simple system, with the addition of need-tension, instantly and unavoidably meets with problems which constitute the conflictual nature of human psychic life: prompted by need-tension the primary ego attempts to incorporate the primary sensory object into the sphere of its own identity, as in a world that consists only of the early ego and the first object, the only possibility to suspend the unpleasure—that is the sensation of a lack in the sphere of the ego—is localized in the object, as there is nothing else besides this primary object that could be considered 'outside', and because suspension of the lack in the ego must come from the outside. For the ego cannot suspend the lack from within itself, otherwise the ego would not feel any lack.

This psychic movement is the beginning of mental activity in the sense of an archaic, sensorily determined wish. It leads to a constitutive conflict, as in the intended fusion of the ego with the object the bipolar world of internal perception would again collapse, a world that has only just unfolded and out of which the dimension of the psychical is about to develop. This unavoidable fusional movement is therefore in my definition the core of the death drive, the ontic power that opposes it, the power that wants to maintain and secure the dimension of the psychical which is just yet coming into being, is the life drive. Both drives are, therefore, according to this understanding, purely psychical productions.

This primordial sense-based object initially has nothing to do with a human counterpart. It is the precipitate of not yet assigned co-enaesthetic stimuli, which pêle mêle may stem from the external world and could also be of a proprioceptive, enteroceptive or central nervous system-related nature and are only held together by their contiguity in time. The dimension of space, let alone inner space, does not yet exist, the sensory opposites are not modulated yet. These archaic objects of sensory perception are most likely related to those still inanimate object formations which we know from the autistic cosmos. From them, in the process of primal attachment, the imago of the human object, initially as part object, gradually forms. Via primary identification psychical qualities are ascribed to this human imago that is coming into being, qualities that correspond to those in the subject and by which the expectation is put into this imago, at the level of pre-conceptional assignment, that it is able to contain the psychism of the subject, the child.

In this way, through primary identification, life is, so to speak, breathed into the imago of the human object that is coming into being. Thus it becomes the primary object in the sense of the classical terminology, that is to say, the representation which later, when it is a fully formed image, will be the mother. At the basis of it are, however, inanimate object representations which stem directly from sensory perception and the residues of which we see in the strangeness of the object formations of the autistic perception, which we probably all have gone through.

With the primary identification then projective identification is launched, and with it, the original and archaic mode and mechanism of communication. With this definition of the drives that centers on object constitution and the relationship to the object, clinical manifestations which in recent years have begun to occupy us, like the autistic and autistoid phenomena and in general, pathologies of withdrawal, become major themes in the discussion of psychodynamics. Then again this topic of the psychic drives, insofar as there is proof of their determining organizing activity at every level of psychopathology and at every level of structure formation, is evidence, from my point of view, of the fact that the question of the relationship between ego and object is the central theme of the psyche. The qualification as a drive has a direct bearing on the all-pervading character of this theme.

The <u>dynamic unconscious id</u>
    See: <u>Repression</u>, the <u>dynamic unconscious id</u>

<u>Ego-ideal</u>
    See: <u>Sublimation</u>, <u>ego-ideal</u>

Father imago

> See: _Position_ of the ego outside the drive phantasma ("position outside")
> and the _father imago_; the concept of inner _space_ and _primary identification_;
> the _inner world_

Fusion

The primary ego which experiences the first physiological tensions
as unpleasure, can only interpret this unpleasure as the result of a
lack, that is to say something missing from itself, a deficiency. Because
psychically, apart from the ego there only exists the primary object,
the ego cannot localize the capacity to do away with what is lacking
anywhere else but in this object.

The primary ego must, therefore, pressured by unpleasure and
supported by the mode of orality, necessarily and unavoidably arrive at
the first phantasy, the first wish, to incorporate the primary object into
itself and to become one with it, in order to achieve a state of freedom
from tension. As at this early point in time, as we have to assume, no
mental concept whatsoever of ego boundaries or of an identity of the
ego has been developed, such incorporation of the primary object can
only have the form of a global fusional movement.

Insofar as outside of the primary object nothing exists for the
primary ego, and the object therefore is the all-that-is, the universe
for this ego, this wish for the fusional union is the phantasma of
the ego-cosmic ego which insofar—that is to say precisely as a striving
for the merging of object representation and ego—has been identified
as the motor of the narcissistic striving. Narcissism therefore is not
an imaginary primary state—Freud's pseudopodia model—but the
precipitate of a fundamentally defensive movement, consisting in the
attempt to suspend the separation of ego and object. This defensive
narcissistic movement that comes about under pressure of deficiency

must be differentiated from the primary narcissistic state described above, in which the general feeling, from the point of view of the primary ego and of the primary object, is limitlessness.

Fusion
See: *Psychosis and fusion*

Genital phase
See: *Phallic* vs. *genital phase*

Hysteria

The hysteric uses the alternating projective identifications *(see there)* with both parents of the primal scene (see Britton R, 1999) to combat not only exclusion from the primal scene *(see there)* and thus the threat of castration *(see there)*, but at the same time he uses them to deny the sexual difference, not only on the level of the parents with whom he alternately identifies and thus dissolves the sexual difference but also on the level of his own sexual identity. The phenomenon of hysteria is that of the dissolution of concrete sexuality based on sexual difference in a sexualized cosmos carried by bi-sexual individuals with undefined sexual identity, and which is about the search for the possession of the phallic attribute *(see: imago of the phallus)* that is detached from the concrete person of the father *(see: father-imago)*. The denial and destruction of the sexual difference then leads to the known regressive prevalence of pre—and paragenital interests and activities.

This denial of the sexual difference by alternating projective identification within the primal scene, enforced on the psychic level while simultaneously maintaining reality consciousness about the fact of the difference between the sexes, is the cause for the hysteric tendency towards dissociation. At the same time, however, the alternating excessive projective identifications not only dissolve the differentiation between the sexual genders, but as a side-effect also the boundaries of identity itself, one's own and that of the other. Hence the hysteric's proneness towards identification and projection, and his or her suggestibility.

The phallic capacity, over which the battle of hysteria is waged, comes into being through the position of the ego outside the drive phantasma (the ʹposition outsideʹ) (see there), out of which the father imago constitutes itself. The two central effects of the position outside are, first, reflexive awareness; and secondly, access to reality as the result of the suspension of primary object splitting, the latter being the primary defense against the fusional aim (see: fusion) of the death drive (see there) that becomes obsolete with the reflexive split of the ego within itself. The ability to access reality in turn culminates in the recognition and acknowledgement of the sexual difference which is constitutive for the Oedipal formulation (see: Oedipus complex) of the parental relationship in the formation of the imago of the primal scene.

The growing awareness of the sexual difference is the sign and symbol of the ability to perceive reality; it is what this newly acquired ability brings about in the first place, and how it provides evidence for its truth. The difference between the sexes and reality are therefore psychically speaking synonymical factors. The attack against one is always also directed against the other.

If then it proves impossible to gain possession of the phallic capacity of the father in the primal scene, the hysteric ego turns against the process which led to this experience of castration, consequently turns against reality, the gender difference and sexuality that manifests through it, turns against reflexive awareness. Hence hysteria is characterized by a triad of denial: denial of the threat of castration, of the gender difference, and of reflexive awareness.

267

Amongst these three the denial of reflexive awareness is the central moment, from the point of view of the genetics of structure formation, for it contains the reference back to that developmental step which constitutes entry into the symbolic order in the first place, namely taking up of the position of the ego outside the drive phantasma. Hysteria in fact turns against and opposes the whole process which has been triggered with this crucially important developmental step. The path on which the suspension of the reflexive awareness of the position outside is sought, is precisely the transgression of the threat of castration that results from the position outside and underlines its importance: namely the necessary non-identity of the ego with itself, which is the condition for the suspension of the early object splitting and which has been psychically expressed in the form of the commandment of non-identity with the father; the so to speak operative manifestation of which is the threat of castration.

In hysteria, sexuality in the area of conscious experience and thus of clear perception of reality must be strictly circumvented because otherwise, the denial of the perception of the sexual difference as such—that is to say as perception of a piece of reality—could not be maintained. This is therefore not a repression, but a dissociation.

The hysteric, at the level of the hypnoid state of awareness actually does take back the position outside and thus loses the basic access to reality, so that the differentiation between inside and outside cannot apply any more. This differentiation between inside and outside which is lost implies that, in the experience of the subject, a phantasy can assume the full and complete appearance of an outer event. The theoretical mistake is that of assuming a confusion of self and object differentiation for the earliest phases of development. The actual confusion, however, does not lie in the differentiation of the ego and the object or the object imago, which is there from the beginning,

268

but in the confusion of what belongs to the reality aspect of the ego, on the one hand, and of the object, on the other. For reality as an independent variable has gone missing due to the attack of denial with regard to the position outside. This is the specific hallucinatory quality of hysteria, that makes for its phenomenological closeness to psychosis.

Hence the danger arises to take a subjective memory, which has all the characteristics of clearly delineated ego and object experiencing, for probable reality because of these very characteristics. This is one of the prime examples for the extent to which a wrong theoretical basic assumption relative to the early development may lead to a complete misjudgement of a clinical fact.

In hysteria the typical sexualization of the delay of gratification, of "not now, later", is the result of the constitutive denial both of the difference between the sexes and the threat of castration, for the realization of sexual union would confront the hysteric, female but also male, not only with the denied difference between the sexes but also with the very impossibility to "create access for oneself to the mother's body after all in the identification with the penis of the father who enters into the mother" (Rohde-Dachser 2004, p. 351; transl. P.Z.). This is the phallic threat of castration. The hysteric idealization of the specifically absent or unreachable man (or woman) has the same purpose as the delay of gratification itself, namely that of avoiding the realization of the threat of castration which is being denied.

The hysteric games of confusion, according to which the male or female hysteric, as a rule, can never be found where someone is looking for him or her, are equally an expression of that same denial of the difference between the sexes and the threat of castration, for one must not be found, as this would confront one with the untenability of denial and furthermore affirm reality which is being negated by the hysteric in the same movement of withdrawing one's presence. The

269

simultaneous hysterical sexualization, in so far as it serves the theme of erotic manipulation of the other in the sense of exercising power over him, thereby serves to maintain the phantasy of, in reality, possessing and controlling the fatherly phallus.

The hysteric struggle against the physical body and the physical sexual lust, which is being waged based on the connotation with the sexual difference, can further lead to the ascetic and anorectic forms of expression of hysteria on the one hand, and on the other to the transformation of sexual excitement into suffering and pain, in the conversion symptoms and equally in the hysterical functional disorders and the hysteric pain syndromes.

The critical train of thought for understanding the importance of the primal scene imagination in the inner theatre of hysteria, in any case, is that the position outside is based on the ability of the child to maintain the memory of the good object also in its factual absence, that is to say, to endure the fear of its destruction, implying the child's belief, acquired during the conflict of the depressive position, in its own reparation ability. This leads to the establishment of what Britton (1995, p. 120-127) calls "the other room", that of the imagination. "I suggested (...) that the 'other room' of the imagination comes into existence developmentally when the primary object is believed to continue existing in its perceptual absence. It is the place where the object spends its invisible existence. I think it is conceived inevitably as in relationship with another object that is a condition of existence. The 'other room' is, in other words, the location of the invisible *primal scene*" (1999, pp. 7, italics R.B.).

This other room, the room of the imagination, thus becomes the room of the primal scene, whereby Britton's formulation remains somewhat vague as to how the father comes into play here. The understanding that I propose, however, makes this totally clear, for the father is the very personalization of the dynamic effect of the position outside, namely to overcome the splitting of the object. And the core of the 'position of the ego outside the drive phantasma' consists in the ability, suddenly available at a certain moment in time, of the child to place itself next to its direct experiencing of the immediate present, and, with a reflexive distance towards its depressive fears, to maintain the inner representation of the good object also in the object's absence.

It is important to note that in this view the primal scene is first of all the mental version and imaginative formulation of two immensely positive events, namely one, of the child's ability to maintain the idea of the good split-object also in its absence, and two, of the effect which arises from the related ability of the child to step outside its own experiencing and take a reflexive position, namely of the effect of the suspension of the primary object splitting, and thus of access to reality. The primal scene captures this dynamic development into a picture, in which the effect on the imago of the primary object (see there), namely to achieve the suspension of its splitting, is being ascribed to a personalized force, step by step with the identification of this imago and this force with the real persons—mother and father—and their investiture with the insignia of sexuality.

That way the primal scene is and remains the most important image, the most important phantasma of the psyche, for in it lies the key to overcoming the terrors of splitting, and access to reality.

It is important for one thing to realize this, because, if considered in this way, it is incorrect to understand the primal scene primarily and basically as the cause and sign for the separation of the child from the mother (see: mother imago), as it is being reflected for instance when Christa Rohde-Dachser speaks of the "phantasma of the invisible primal scene", "which from the viewpoint of the child is the cause for the absence of the mother" (op. cit. p. 333; transl. P.Z.). The primal scene is first of all the image of a colossal presence, namely of the ability to maintain a psychical presence of the absent object and to build up a reflexive frustration tolerance against the depressive anxieties connected with the absence.

The moment of separation only comes into play when the child fails in the attempt to put itself in the place of the father in the primal scene, and to establish the unity with the primary object via the father, via his dynamic potential; in other words, when the child is being confronted with the phallic threat of castration. Only then does it experience the exclusion from the primal scene and experiences the primal scene as the separation from the object. When looked at in this way, this experience of separation is synonymous with the threat of castration, here we have the two sides of the same coin. However, the primal scene is principally never simply the sign for separation, this is a crass reduction and one-sided view of its meaning, it already is the reduction which is the effect of pathology. The child, from the beginning, has an intense relationship with the primary object, and the project of Oedipal development consists solely and exclusively in linking this representation of the internal object with reality, opening the path for it.

Christa Rohde-Dachser references Lacan, saying that the symbolic castration, or the law of the father, respectively, "puts a stop to the child´s unlimited enjoyment of the mother" (op. cit. p. 334; transl. P.Z.). We must ask, though, what unlimited enjoyment this might refer to? In my opinion this is about a shared phantasy between analysts and patients, that such unlimited enjoyment might have taken place at all. This expresses a theoretical idealization of the earliest childhood which has its precipitate also in the typical formulations of 'mother-child-union' and the 'originally symbiotic universe'. From the beginning, and certainly also in utero the child has to cope with the unavoidable physiological tensions of unpleasure, even if all further accidental causes of unpleasure were excluded by optimal mothering, which in this manner is not possible at all.

All this is, however, not really about the quantification of unpleasure. The problem is that already by a relative minimum of factual unpleasure the process of the drive dynamics is being triggered which consists in the early ego's development of the phantasy of fusional merging with the object representation, in order to absorb the source for the abolishment of unpleasure into one's own omnipotence. But this attracts the counterreaction of the life drive in the shape of the formation of the deterring split imago.

From this dynamic interplay the ego development and the structuring of the psychic organism is generated, and one would do best to assume that already relatively minor amounts of unpleasure are sufficient to trigger this process, and that it builds itself up and escalates to its full impetus, simply and purely because this is necessary and intended by the course of development, that is to say in other words, results from the system properties of the dimension of the human psyche.

If it is important that mothers do not expose their babies to traumatic stress. If mothers are endowed with a special sensorium in order to feel the needs of their children, then this is not in order to afford them unlimited enjoyment, but rather to avoid inciting the, as it is, dramatic confrontation of the drives in the early splitting world to a degree which could not be dealt with by the instruments of the ego that are only about to take shape. The goal to basically spare suffering and enable unlimited enjoyment is an illusion, a precipitate of the objective of the death drive.

Inner world

*See: <u>Position</u> of the ego outside the drive phantasma ("position outside")
and the <u>father imago</u>; the concept of inner <u>space</u> and <u>primary identification</u>;
the <u>inner world</u>*

Latency

Oedipal phantasmatization *(see: Oedipus complex)*, according to its own
inner laws, by necessity leads to its dissolution by repression in the
confrontation with the phallic threat of castration *(see there)*. In this way
the particularly human phenomenon of psychosexual latency comes
about, in agreement with Freud's respective formulations in the third of
the *Essays on the Theory of Sexuality* of 1905. Like Freud, I also consider it
the task of latency to have the defensive boundaries established against
the oedipal objects to the degree that, when genital sexual development
sets in in puberty, the sexual interest is no longer directed towards
the oedipal but the displaced objects. From my theory formation it
can therefore be inferred that this dissolution by repression—and thus
latency—is a logically inescapable structural consequence, provided that
the oedipal conflict constellation has been correctly established.

Latency, therefore, is no biological fact, but one purely contingent
on phantasma. This fact entails that derailments of development in
the infantile working through of oedipality may lead to latency not
or not sufficiently being established, or, to the contrary, may develop
such repressive impact that it also withstands the hormonal and
maturational push of puberty and may even continue into adult life,
as-it-were, unbroken. Both are known clinical phenomena of child and
adolescent psychoanalysis which have a high diagnostic significance.
In latency the power and impact of the phantasmatic side of human
existence shows itself, and especially the power of the oedipal conflict

constellation, to the degree that this central crisis of the ontogenesis of the psyche directly affects psychosexuality *(see there)* which in its course appears totally caused by biology, but is not, in this, therefore, so very important place. In this sense, latency separates the infantile phallic phase *(see there)* of psychosexual development from the genital one *(see there)* that sets in with puberty.

Life drive

Starting from the basic situation of the wish of the ego for union with the primary object, which I identify with the death drive, the question results how and with what means this fusional phantasmatisation could be countered in order to prevent a self-suspension of the psyche. This happens in principle through a complementary string of phantasmatisation, which has its core in the imago of the devouring object. Through this imago of the devouring object the self-preservation effort of mental life expresses the danger of self-annihilation inherent in the fusional tendency. This counterreaction, in my understanding, is the core of the psychic life drive, and we basically end up here in the split world of Melanie Klein's paranoid-schizoid position, whereby quite remarkably, the apparently bad, devouring object as a countervailing force to the idealized fusional union, is in reality the imagination of the life drive. It should be stressed, however, that this danger of self-suspension is an objective, actually existing danger and not a production of the life drive. The life drive only stands in for this danger; in other words, this danger is the cause, the raison d´être of the life drive.

As it is the interest of the life drive to preserve the objectal character of the object with respect to the fusional tendency of the death drive, the life drive is the objectalising tendency and force in the psyche.

This interpretation thus sees the origin of the bad object of the early paranoid splitting dimension in the dynamic of the drives, more exactly in the counter reaction of the Eros to the death drive's vision of fulfillment, and specifies the bad as the devouring object. The devouring quality is hereby the psychic representation of the annihilation of the ego in the fusional self-suspension and simultaneously the projection onto the object of the devouring tendency of the ego suffering an experience of lack.

Thus in my opinion, the <u>primary</u> and fundamental good-bad split of the object is therefore no defense mechanism of the ego as it is for Melanie Klein, but an effect of the immediate drive antagonism. Secondarily, this situation is intensified and exacerbated, however, by further active splittings of the object which retroactively lead to respective splitting of the ego, and also by projections and introjections, which stem from the actual frustration experiences during the time of the infantile paranoid-schizoid position. These now are actually active defense processes of the ego in the struggle with the bad object, which produce the full clinical picture of the paranoid-schizoid position.

It will also be true that the imago of the devouring object when it passes through the paranoid-schizoid and depressive positions is progressively taking in sensory moments arising out of the actual frustration situations. This does not change the fact that the basic phantasmatisation in the described sense is of a purely psychogenic nature. The imagination of the devouring object sets the scene within which the aversive stimulation organizes itself.

The life drive would have to be regarded as the force, which represents the natural law based system property of this newly arisen dimension of the psychical. This means it must be assumed that when this new dimension comes into being through the poles of perception (*see there*) separating out, that is to say with the constitution of the primary ego (*see there*) and the primary object (*see there*), that there exists a system consciousness of the fact that the realization of the aim of the death drive of fusing the primary ego with the primary object would lead to the reannulment of this newly arisen dimension. This tendency of the psychical to preserve itself would oppose the realization of the death drive and lead to the development of the mental apparatus, by which the death drive—we should rather say: the primary narcissistic ego of the fusion phantasy (*see both there*)—is being bound. The life drive is the dynamically effective principle that from the very beginning represents the fact that the ego and the representation of the primary object must be kept separated, to prevent the ego from getting lost in the fusion. I have therefore referred to Eros or the life drive as the drive of ego protection. The theme of the life drive is that the safety of the object from the fusional attacks of the death drive simultaneously means, and is in fact, the safety of the ego. Insofar as the life drive represents and protects the object and is about this secret relationship of mutual safety between ego and object, it is not inappropriate to designate it with the alternative term Eros.

The energetic potential of the Eros or life drive captured in this way, if one was to follow this thought, paradoxically ensues directly from that of the death drive, that is to say, from the existential necessity to hold up against the death drive's primary-narcissistic impact. One could say that without the death drive, there would be no life drive, either; that the life drive has its raison d'être in the death drive. Without death drive there would therefore be no psychic structure formation and thus no formation of the specifically human quality of a self-reflexive consciousness in the sense of the position outside (*see there*). Sexuality, the physical sexual drive, is only later linked to these drive dynamics of the psyche via the primal attachment (*see there*) to the human object, and then becomes the arena for the manifestation of both psychical drives that finally leads to the fully developed Oedipal conflict constellation (*see there*), the aim and objective of which is to structurally bind the death drive once and for all. That this attachment to physical sexuality, to the human object, is reversible or may not happen, respectively, is known from cases of the most severe psychopathology.

In the primary, pre-schizoid constitution (*see there*) of the psyche there is no cognitive object constancy (*see there*) as yet. This means, experience is always experience of the present to begin with, there is no maintaining of representations over time yet, and therefore they also cannot be compared with each other. There is no experience of time, of temporal continuity.

If these claims about the primary functional level of the mental apparatus and thus of the psyche are true, then it follows in logical consequence that there cannot be, in this primary constitution, a direct objectally bound representation of a bad present, of a frustration experience as a, in this sense, bad, that is to say, frustrating object. For if an experience of unpleasure would translate so directly into a representation of a bad object, then the ego, on this level of functioning in which the primary object is the all-that-is outside of which nothing exists, would be confronted with a bad cosmos. This is not imaginable, as the ego then would have to negate the only object available to it, which would equal the ego denying itself the fundamental basis of life. This also means that the splitting of the object—that is to say the parallel representation of a good and bad split object—is only conceivable once representational object constancy is reached, insofar as then, in the background, the life-sustaining memory of the good object enables the manifestation of the bad object.

In consequence, the lack, the disturbance of the physiological homoeostasis and thus the psychical experience of unpleasure on the level of the most basic mental units, that is to say before object constancy, cannot have an objectal or object related representation, but is only present as an energetic phenomenon in the sense of an inescapable pressure to change the existing overall situation in psychic space. It is evident that this refers to the basic energetic quality of drive, to that which is related to the drives.

We can therefore say that the bad, devouring split object of the paranoid-schizoid position, as the, then, manifestation of the life drive, would have to be, paradoxically, energetically carried by this pressure stemming from the phase before object constancy is acquired, i.e. from the energetic source of the life drive within the pre-schizoid constitution of the mind that, as ontogenetic layer of the psyche, continues to exist and proliferate throughout life. The drive moment of the death drive, in contrast, always consists of the unconditional and direct wish to establish ego-cosmic, fusional union with the object, which is seen as the condition where lack is annulled.

Thus the drive concept as I posit it defines itself in the sense of a general theme running through the total unconscious constitution of man, and is the basis as well as the cause, the impetus for psychic structure formation.

I consider the encapsulated psychogenic autism as the clinical evidence for the actual existence of that psychical power, given from the beginning of mental life, which I call the life drive, and as evidence that the psychic struggle which the antagonism of the drives is about centers on the subject of the fusion with the primary object: this is, in this sense, a compelling result from the double aspect of the pathognomonic symptomatology of encapsulated autism, that on the one hand the traumatizing event consists in the manifestation of the not-me object refusing to fuse, and that on the other hand, the circumstance that this not-me object is in fact about the fusion theme, is evidenced by the autist's development of the symptoms of the imitatory merging in a compensatory way, the only meaning of which is to deny and annul the traumatic refusal to fuse through the imitative and repetitive mechanisms.

Mother imago

The early psychic development, on the one hand, consists in the attachment *(see there)* of the representation of the primary object *(see there)* to psychosexuality, which during orality leads to the development of the part-object *(see there)* of the breast; on the other hand, in the overcoming of the split conceptualization of the object in the depressive position *(see there)* and the breakthrough to the position outside *(see there)*. Following this, the relationship with the part-object is expanded in the involvement with reality to encompass the relationship with the whole, time-space identical object of the mother, and psychosexuality develops through negotiating the psychosexual phases, the gender difference is recognized and sexually cathected.

However, at the basis of this whole development is the attachment of the primary object, which initially had only consisted in the representation of a temporally contingent sensory stimulation, to psychosexuality during the breast-feeding experience. I understand the experience of breast-feeding which as such may not always be a factual experience, in the sense of a symbolic pre-conceptional proxy for all pleasurable contacts with the real mother, or the caregiver, respectively, whereby the latter, on its part and depending on circumstances, does not have to be the real mother. The internal image, the imago of the mother is, in this sense, the condensation of all objectal experiences which are connected with the original representation of the primary object, develop from it, and more closely determine and differentiate this representation. The direct descent of the mother imago from this primal attachment makes it the centrally important mental object; makes it the imago from which, after access to reality is gained, the relationship to all other real objects is originating, thus, so to speak, the sum imago of the world.

The imago of the oedipal mother, before this background, must therefore be thought of as the central successor representation of the primary object, which in the confrontation with reality as well as with the biologically determined pre-conceptions, has taken on the form of the mother as the giver of birth. What is symbolised in her, in the world of real objects, most fittingly is the relationship to the primary object, in reference to which no outside is conceivable as yet, and which in this sense also contains the primary ego itself.

Object constancy (more exactly: representational object constancy)

For the purposes of my present investigation in which I want to clarify the basic conditions in the relationship with the imago of the primary object, I use the term object constancy as the mental maintenance—that is to say the keeping constant—of a representation that goes beyond the timeframe of the immediate stimulus situation which the representation depicts. The descriptive aspect, observable from the outside, shall remain unconsidered in this definition. As the term object constancy is the one that does best justice to the content of this definition and as the classical ego psychological use of the term leads to problems I discuss in chapter 2, I draw from this the legitimisation to rephrase this definition.

It is obvious that making the leap to representational object constancy contains as elemental a change in the mode of functioning of the ego as does its later change to the position outside (*see there*). With the introduction of object constancy the functional level of the good-bad split of the object imago becomes possible; as for the splitting of the imago of the object, it is necessary to keep up previous states of experience of the object over time. This enables the child to enter the world of the splitting-mode of the paranoid-schizoid and the depressive positions. With the position outside, on the other hand, this splitting mode is overcome and the child gains access to reality.

With the breakthrough to object constancy the infantile ego leaves the level of unconditional binding to immediate sensual experiencing, as it is preserved in the encapsulated autism, for it is the decisive moment concerning the level of functioning of the ego that the ego is then able to create phantasies. Phantasies are tied to the maintenance of an object representation over time, successive object representations are linked to each other through the phantasy.

Oedipus complex

See: *Primal scene*, imago of the *phallus*, *Oedipus complex*

Part object, split object, primal attachment

For reasons of theoretical clarity when speaking about the onset of the structural development of the psyche, I speak of the necessity to split the object representation—and consequently of good and bad split objects—in order to build up a defence system against the danger of fusion with the object. After a certain very early point in time these representations of the good and bad split object become organised as partial objects in the imagos of the good and bad breast. In the formation of this part object, the imagination of the primary object attaches itself to the oral mode of a biologically determined psychosexuality. Put differently, the general lust and satisfaction quality which comes with orality as well as its specific orgasmic quality leads to the organisation of the representation of the primary object around the central nucleus of the imago of the breast as the subjective experience of something hard (nipple/tongue) enclosed by something soft. This central sensory experience of orality is highly pre-conceptionally preformed and is largely independent of the fact of whether the child is being breastfed or bottle fed.

In this sense, therefore, the formation of the partial object of the breast follows Freud's (1905) description of object choice according to the anaclitic type. With this step, the primary object's early representation which consisted in the mere temporal contiguity of a complex sensory stimulation co-occurring at the same time moment in the central nervous system, has thus bound itself to the manifestation of bodily sexuality. With this event, the central force which will carry forward the development of the psyche is locking into place. In particular, this means that the imago of the primary object, in fusion with which the primary ego wanted to merge with the source of the suspension of all unpleasure, is now being equated and identified with the object of experience of sexual pleasure.

This is the metapsychological formulation of primal attachment. Only in the most severe form of psychopathology, namely in the encapsulated form of childhood autism (see there), does this equation and attachment which is constitutive for the human situation, not occur; then again, the annihilatory aggression directed at the destruction of the real object has the dissolution of this same attachment to sexuality as its aim.

By acquiring the position outside of the drive phantasma and with it access to reality, this central partial object of the good and consequently the bad breast undergoes a suspension of its internal splitting and is clearly identified as existing in objective reality. I assume that it is this process which is behind the "recognition of the breast as a supremely good object", which Money-Kyrle names as one of the three "facts of life" (1971, p. 443).

Hence, behind this interpretation of the breast "as a supremely good object" one would already have to assume the suspension of splitting through the position outside of the drive phantasma, that is to say through the position of the third, and thus a prefiguration of oedipality. Its precondition is the working through and the overcoming of the conflict of the depressive position. I think that it is this meaning as the encoding of this central task of early development which lends the phantasma of the breast as the supremely good object the position, that causes Roger Money-Kyrle to name it one of the three facts of life.

The good breast in this meaning—perhaps one should say: the good reality breast—thus is not identical with the unilaterally idealised good breast of the splitting constitution. It still is a part-object but no longer a split object. Its quality as the "supremely good object" is defined by it containing and expressing the solution of the conflict of the depressive position and by this it becomes the life-sustaining source of the good existing in reality.

The "recognition of the breast as a supremely good object" thus refers to the 'reality breast', that is to say, to that concept of the breast which is being suspended in its original good-bad dichotomy by the self-reflexive splitting of the ego. The position of the ego outside the drive phantasma—that is to say the self-reflexive splitting of the ego—constitutively implies the recognition of the separation from the object, by the very fact that the triangulation that comes with this splitting excludes the fusional merging with the object. The splitting of the object as the early form of the defence against the danger originating from the attack on the separateness of the object, is then no longer necessary. Through this the breast becomes the object existing in reality and thus the supremely good object in the sense of Roger Money-

Kyrle's "fact of life". John Steiner formulates this interconnection with the recognition of the separation from the object as follows: "The first fact, 'the recognition of the breast as the supremely good object', is a poetic way of expressing the fundamental truth that the chief source of goodness required for the infant's survival resides outside him in the external world." (1993, p. 95)

Phallic vs. genital phase

According to Freud, in the phallic phase, which in his opinion lasts from the third to the fifth year of life and temporally coincides with the Oedipus complex (*see there*), "...only <u>one genital</u>, namely the male one, comes into account. What is present, therefore, is not a primacy of the genitals but a primacy of the phallus" (1923e, p. 142; emphasis S.F.). Melanie Klein in turn writes: "In my view, infants of both sexes experience genital desires directed towards their mother and father, and they have an unconscious knowledge of the vagina as well as of the penis. For these reasons Freud's earlier term 'genital phase' seems to me more adequate than his later concept of the 'phallic phase'" (1945, Writings p. 414).

In my opinion the genealogy of the meaning of the imago of the phallus (*see there*) as the condensed representation of the position of the ego outside the drive phantasma (*see there*)—and thus of the father imago (*see there*)—can create the theoretical connection between these two positions by furnishing a reason for the "primacy" of the imagination of the phallus, but without containing an, as it were, genital monism, in the sense of the thesis about the representational accessibility of only one genital organ. The contrary is true, as the background phantasy is that of the fusional (*see there*) incest with the mother.

Like this, it is my contention that Freud's 1926 and up to this day still very controversial distinction made in *Some Psychical Consequences of the Anatomical Distinction between the Sexes* into an infantile phallic and, starting with puberty, a genital phase of sexual development, is correct in my view, only that—speaking for the boy—I would not link the overvaluation of the phallus during the infantile oedipal phase (*see there*) to the boy's own genitals, but to the father's, and that I deduce the overestimation of one's own genitals from the death-drive related oedipal phantasy of the identificatory appropriation of the phallus of the father. Thus what we are dealing with here in this identificatory appropriation is a manifestation of the death drive.

For the girl the same applies mutatis mutandis, insofar as for her, too, the phallus of the father, under the influence of the death drive, represents the central means for the realization of the fusion with the mother. The formulation of an infantile phallic phase in this sense applies for both sexes, and this had also been Freud's position.

The dissolution of the Oedipus complex by repression includes the receding of the phallic theme and opens up the way for the genital cathexis of puberty, inasfar as this development is not blocked or changed by irregularities in the oedipal working through.

In other words, I consider the clinical facts which Freud had referred to as givens, despite the critique that has meanwhile been expressed about Freud's phallic monism. I think that this criticism, as well as Freud's formulation itself, is based on the error that the phallic primacy is about the genitals of the boy, that is to say, the (male) ego. In truth, however, it is about the phallus of the father which has the same meaning for both sexes. Even the male child never fails to recognize the female genitals. What is more, they are in fact the goal of the oedipal, incestuous wishes. Where the existence of the female, penis-less genitals is being disavowed, this is already a consequence of the phallic threat of castration (*see there*) and the expression of the disavowal of this threat. But the phallic primacy of the oedipal phase exists, it is a clinical reality. The phallic theme is the pivotal point of oedipality.

<u>Phallus</u>, imago of
  See: <u>Primal scene</u>, imago of the <u>phallus</u>, <u>Oedipus complex</u>

<u>Position</u> of the ego outside the drive phantasma ("position outside") and the <u>father imago</u>; the concept of inner <u>space</u> and <u>primary identification</u>; the <u>inner world</u>

Within the description of my model of the course of structure formation, we can say that the transition to the depressive infantile position happens in the classic way described by Melanie Klein, by the child, before the background of its ongoing cortical maturation and its ongoing formation of experience, beginning to question its paranoid splitting reality and traumatically experiencing that its aggression directed against the bad object also damages the good object. Cortical maturation and the formation of experience contribute to the constellation of this depressive conflict to the degree that the child, in a balanced mental constitution, begins to experience and acknowledge the perceptual unity of the object, while under the pressure of deprivation it must resort to object splitting as the only available mode of defense.

The child then escapes from this dilemma not only through his reparative effort, but also, before the background of the dualistic drive dynamics, through a specific developmental leap: what develops under the pressure of repeated depressive crises, and more or less suddenly at that, is the ability of the ego to stand beside itself as an observer and

287

to calm itself down in the actual crisis. This ability comes about out of the growing trust in his own reparative powers, as well as from the experience of the indestructibility of the good object resulting from all previous depressive crises which the child survived.

I call this the 'position of the ego outside the drive phantasma', or in short the 'position outside'. It is the position of the third which adds to the juxtaposition of ego and primary object. From it develops subsequently, in my view, the father imago in its meaning as the exemplary not-mother-object, that is to say, the imago of an experience, or better of a dynamic effect that is not in the direct genealogy of the primary object. Its meaning in view of the antagonism of the drives is that now the splitting of the object is not the only means any more to protect the ego from the danger of fusion. Rather, this protection is warranted in the future by the splitting of the ego within itself, out of which the ego, as long as it confronts itself in an observing position, cannot be lost any more in a fusional movement, because the observing part always remains outside of the fusion which, by its own logic, obeys the law of 'all-or-nothing'. The splitting of the object as the way of defense against the death drive is therefore being replaced by a splitting of the ego and thus becomes obsolete.

This is, and I wish to emphasize this, a psychologically simple procedure with, however, far-reaching dynamic and structural conse-quences. It is about the formation of experience, that is, about the growing overview of the ego over its states across time, from which results the ability of the ego, given a certain degree of saturation—and, as said, under pressure from the crisis of the depressive infantile position—to extract itself from whatever current state it is in, in the sense and to the degree that it is able to put itself beside itself and simultaneously observe and comment on itself. This simple act implies a splitting of the ego within itself and consists of this split.

I therefore propose to consider this split in the ego as the actual central gain, as the structural result of the depressive position, in as far as it is linked with the suspension, with the overcoming of object splitting. As said, it is the core of the father imago.

The acknowledgement of the separateness from the object is the central constitutive, intrinsic, essential characteristic of the position of the ego outside of the drive phantasma, in as far as through it the striving for fusional union with the object becomes suspended, i.e. made impossible. In this way the split within the ego also contains the mourning, the depressive working through of separation and is not possible without this work of mourning which is part of overcoming of the depressive position. Said the other way around, the fight against acknowledging separateness—which in its essence is narcissistic (see Rosenfeld 1964)—and which expresses the intention of the death drive, will always imply the fight against the self-reflexive position of the ego.

With the suspension of object splitting through the self-reflective split within itself, the ego acquires access to reality, as the latter presupposes not a split but a unified object conception. Therefore access to reality under a constitution of mental functioning based on the good-bad split of the object representation as the mode of drive regulation was structurally not possible as yet. Strictly speaking one would have to say that the depressive position is about gaining access to reality in a structurally guaranteed manner and in a way that it will remain stable and upheld even under states of need-tension and the pressure of gaining satisfaction. We are thus dealing with an alternative to the splitting constitution as a mode of defence, and this exactly is the position of the ego outside the drive phantasma, i.e. the self-reflective splitting of the ego within itself.

Subsequently it is then the massive impact of reality—in the sense of the enormous importance that access to reality has for the ego concerning the reliable option of access to the world—which secures the transition to the position of the ego outside the drive phantasma. This means that the father imago and access to reality are intimately related as to their psychic background.

The concept of the inner space is lastly a consequence of the break-through to the position outside in the depressive position, which, via the taking up of the reflexive distance of the ego towards itself opens up the third dimension and, via the process of projection and re-identification, of the primary identification, makes the idea of an inner space possible.

The pre-ambivalent object

An outside of the primary object, an alternative to it, does not exist in the earliest constitution before object constancy (see there), where the primary object (see there) is the totality of the activated perceptual situation(see: Perception) and insofar the all-that-is. If then the suspension of the lack by necessity has to be located in the primary object of the still unmodulated primary narcissistic constitution (see: primary narcissism), this primary object must then represent the plenitude of possible gratification, and the ego, under pressure of unpleasure, must seek the fusional identity (see: fusion) with it. This is the pre-ambivalent object.

As under the condition of globality and totality of the pre-schizoid phase (see there) the representation of a bad presence is not possible as this would deny life itself, the pre-ambivalent primary object of this phase is the precursor model of what will later become the good breast. I assume that it is the central task of this pre-ambivalent primary object to serve as a catalyst and container for the integration of the sensory, sensual opposites, which is the first task to be performed by the psyche.

Thus we are dealing here with a basal, early form of the containing function: containment and an archaic, sensorily defined alpha function are being exercised solely intra-psychically by the inner primary object, by the pre-ambivalent object. In any case it is precisely this task which fails when the primary object of this developmental stage falls under the autistic foreclosure (see: Encapsulated autism).

Pre-schizoid phase

In the primary constitution of the psyche there is no cognitive object constancy (see there) as yet, that means, experience is always experience of the present to begin with, there is no maintaining of representations over time yet, and therefore they also cannot be compared with each other. There is no experience of time, of temporal continuity.

If these claims about the primary functional level of the mental apparatus and thus of the psyche are true, then it follows in logical consequence that there cannot be, in this primary constitution, a direct objectally bound representation of a bad present, of a frustration experience as a, in this sense, bad, that is to say, frustrating object. For if an experience of unpleasure would translate so directly into a representation of a bad object, then the ego, on this level of functioning in which the primary object is the all-that-is outside of which nothing exists, would be confronted with a bad cosmos. This is not imaginable as the ego then would have to negate the only object available to it, which would equal the ego denying itself the fundamental basis of life. This also means, in principle, that the splitting of the object—that is to say the parallel representation of a good and bad split object—is only conceivable once representational object constancy is reached, insofar as then, in the background, the life-sustaining memory of the good object enables the manifestation of the bad object.

291

A further still more fundamental argumentation which leads to the same result is the following: According to our primary hypothesis the initial situation out of which the dynamics of psychical life unfold, is one where the primary ego, confronted with the cosmos of the primary object in its globality and totality, can only deal with the experience of need-tension—in other words an experience of lack—by locating the means to suspend this lack in the primary object, and it could not do otherwise. For outside of the primary object there is nothing, and the lack, by definition, cannot be remedied out of the ego itself, or it would be no lack. Before this backdrop the ego attempts, by creating the ego-cosmic, primary narcissistic fusion with the primary object, to incorporate the source that can suspend the lack, and thus to compensate the lack.

But if this is so—then the primary object can only be the representation of abundance. A primary object as the representation of lack is not conceivable. The object, therefore, in both lines of argument, is always to be assumed on the primary and thus fundamental level as that which is positively given and the connection of the experience of lack with the mental representation of a sensory stimulation is already a complicated operation with many requirements, which therefore belongs to a later stage of development of the ego – i.e. the paranoid-schizoid position.

One could define this primary conditionality of the object as that which is positively given as the fundamental affirmation of life in its psychic dimension.

This means that the lack, the disturbance of the physiological homoeostasis and thus the psychical experience of unpleasure on the level of the most basic mental units, that is to say before object constancy, cannot have an objectal or object-related representation, but is only present as an energetic phenomenon in the sense of an

292

inescapable pressure to change the existing overall situation in psychic space. It is evident that this refers to the quality of the drives, to that which is related to the drives.

A consequence from the above considerations is that they would suggest the existence of a phase before the paranoid-schizoid object splitting—that is to say a pre-schizoid phase—for object splitting, for the above reasons, is tied to representational object constancy. In other words, the good-bad split of the object would not be regarded as the primary form of mental functioning. Conversely this means that the beginning of the infantile paranoid-schizoid position has to be set at the point in time when object constancy is reached. Thus a psychic organization built on the good-bad split of the object is only possible with object constancy.

As I show within the context of a detailed clinical study, the encapsulated form of infantile autism (see there) can be regarded as clinical evidence for the existence of a pre-schizoid phase. Tustin traces the basic problems of infantile psychogenic autism back to a premature and traumatic experience of separation from the primary object, more exactly to a traumatic experience of the not-me character of the primary object. In this not-me experience the child is experiencing in a traumatic manner the failure of the project to suspend the lack through fusion with the object. This failure, however, is not experienced in a way that the primary object as such turns into a representation of lack, but into an object that resists the fusional claim of the ego-cosmic primary ego and in this specific sense becomes a frustrating object. The frustration thus is not an expression of lack but of the rejection of fusion. Hence this traumatic primary object becomes a not-me object and leads to a traumatic experience of separation, to which the ego of the autistic child reacts by rejecting the not-me object.

In this way the primary narcissistic illusion of omnipotent control over the object necessary for healthy development is being traumatically broken. This leads, as far as concerns the encapsulated type, to a complete withdrawal from the primary object, the ego encapsulates itself and the object separated from the ego is being excluded from mental perception, an attachment is not being formed. Such foreclosure of the primary object can only be conceived as a global and total one. But this also means that such a global and total foreclosure is only possible in a phase prior to the beginning of object splitting. After splitting of the object begins, there would always be an aspect of the object that would remain outside of the foreclosure. We must, therefore, in fact be dealing with a foreclosure before object constancy is reached, that is to say, in the pre-schizoid phase. It is for this reason that the encapsulated form of infantile autism, in my opinion, can be regarded as clinical evidence for the existence of a pre-schizoid phase.

The continued existence of the good-bad split of the object in that part of the psyche that, also after the resolution of the crisis of the depressive position (*see there*) by establishment of the position outside (*see there*), keeps functioning in the mode of the identity of the ego with the drive phantasma (*see: position outside*) thus also means the parallel keeping up of two different and mutually incompatible object conceptualizations, namely one, the splitting concept of the object, and two, the concept of time-space identity of the object, with which access to reality is given. This, in my definition, is the reason for which the structural unconscious and therefore the core of the id come into being (*see: structural id*).

One can ask if something similar is also the case with respect to the object conceptualization of the pre-schizoid position, in which, before the establishment of representational object constancy, the experiencing of the object is still exclusively bound to immediate sensory

294

stimulation, as I have set out in detail in the context of the infantile encapsulation autism. Following Tustin, I have discussed the hypothesis that there is possibly a close link between the continued unconscious existence of this form of experiencing and the psychosomatic illnesses. If my above deduction of the death drive (*see there*) from the dynamic circumstances of this earliest constitution is correct, the death drive in its characteristics has a lot to do with its being bound to the immediate sensory experience. This, too, is a hypothesis which unquestionably has a lot going for it.

Unlike the object conceptualization of the splitting world and that of the (post-depressive positional) time-space identity of the object, which show a radical and unreconcilable rift between them, the object conceptualization of the pre-schizoid phase or position and that of the representational constancy of the object are not quite so different as to their essence. What is being added with object constancy is first of all 'only' the ability to split, that is to say, the ability resulting from the new capacity to maintain the representation over time—in plain language: resulting from the new capacity to remember—to counter the representation of the good, need-satisfying object with that of a bad, persecuting object. Consequently one can assume that the transition from the object conceptualization of the pre-schizoid phase to that of the level of splitting is a fluid one.

The central difference here consists in the form of function of the ego: in the pre-schizoid phase, which is that of primary narcissism, the ego, on the affirmative side of experiencing, is able to experience itself as completely unrestricted. It is under the absolute omnipotence of thought and under the illusion that it possesses the ability to aggrandize itself into an ego-cosmic ego through omnipotent control over the object and fusion with it. This illusion comes to an abrupt end through the appearance of the bad, persecuting splitting object. I assume that this primary narcissistic form of how the ego experiences and of its motivation remains in existence and conserves what we subsequently call the death drive. If, therefore, in the transition from the splitting constitution to the position outside the conceptualization of the object undergoes dramatic changes, when time-space identity develops out of the split object, then, in the transition from the pre-schizoid to the splitting constitution, the conceptualization of the ego changes: the ego of the primary narcissism which posits itself as absolute turns into the attacked ego of the paranoid-schizoid position which fights for its existence, and, although it tries to maintain the old megalomania, goes more and more on the defensive until it eventually fails in the depressive position.

To summarize: I have pointed out that the splitting of the imago of the primary object is only conceivable as of the time when a rudimentary memory function—in other words a rudimentary representational object constancy—is present, where the ego simultaneously with calling up a negative, bad split image, can *in principle* maintain the memory of the good object. The splitting presupposes the parallel maintaining of the representation of the good and bad objects in time, and consists in it. Only when the condition of object constancy is met, is the splitting of the object representation possible. The breakthrough to the perception of time via the maintenance of a past experience of the object in memory constitutes the definitional content of representational object constancy.

Said the other way around, an outside of the primary object, an alternative to it, does not exist in this earliest constitution before object constancy, where, as said, the primary object is the totality of the activated perceptual situation and insofar the all-that-is. If then the suspension of the lack by necessity has to be located in the primary object of the still unmodulated primary narcissistic constitution,

296

this primary object must then represent the plenitude of possible gratification, and the ego, under pressure of unpleasure, must seek the fusional identity with it. In this first constitution of the psyche the primary object is that which is being positively posited, positively given. It is the <u>pre-ambivalent object</u>, the basic affirmation of life in its psychic dimension.

In the situation of the psychogenic encapsulation autism, the case now seems to arise that based on accidental circumstances the felt pressure of the unpleasure of lack and thus the pressure towards fusion become so enormous that, as a drive dynamical emergency reaction, a refusal to fuse manifests out of the imago of the primary object itself in order to counter the threat of ego dissolution in a fusional realization. Thus the primary object becomes a traumatic not-me object in Frances Tustin's sense. This means that the phantasy to compensate the experience of lack via the fusion of ego and primary object collapses, and in this way the traumatically premature experience of separation from the primary object occurs which Tustin named as cause for the infantile psychogenic autism, expressed in her formula of the "not-me object": The primary object can no longer be incorporated into the ego by way of the ego-cosmic, primary narcissistic fulfillment phantasy. Thus also the experience of dependency from this not-me object becomes, as Tustin emphasizes, a premature, and insofar traumatic, experience. For as long as the ego entertains the phantasy of fusional, ego-cosmic control over a primary object that represents fulfillment of satisfaction, dependency is clearly no issue.

The triggering of the infantile psychogenic autism therefore is not about a primary object as a representation of lack, but about a primary object that rejects fusion. The prohibition of fusion confronts the primary ego here in the primary object itself and out of it, as this primary object cannot yet be split because the stage of representational

297

object constancy has not yet been reached so that the prohibition of fusion cannot be expressed via the split. The consequence of this traumatic disillusion, in the psychogenic autism of the encapsulation type, is the foreclosure of the not-me object. The not-me object is thus a traumatic manifestation of the anti-fusional principle on which the maintenance of the dimension of psychic life rests.

From these considerations follows that the specific psychogenic anxiety of the pre-schizoid phase of psychic development must be that of the manifestation of this traumatic not-me object. That this anxiety has a factual basis is evidenced in the clinical picture of the psychogenic encapsulation autism. One might conclude here that the dynamic reason for establishing the paranoid-schizoid object splitting after reaching the developmental phase of representational object constancy is to counter, in this way, the danger of foreclosure of the imago of the primary object which results from the dynamic antagonism of the two drives. The reality of this danger is evidenced by the encapsulation autism in which mental development is arrested immediately after the start.

It is important to note that in the psychodynamics of primary psychogenic encapsulated autism, there are no splitting mechanisms in the sense of the good-bad split of the paranoid-schizoid position involved. Instead there is a succession, and later a side-by-side of mutually contradictory, or somehow exclusive, global states as, on the one hand, the autistic foreclosure of the traumatic primary object (the not-me object) that leaves a hole which is filled by the autistic object; and, on the other hand, the imitative fusional practices and manoeuvres that serve to deny the trauma of the manifestation of the antifusional not-me object. Both states of mind are, as said, running counter to each other but don't imply a split neither of the ego nor of the primary object. The possibility of their coexistence signifies a psychical constitution before representational object constancy is attained, that is a constitution in which time and comparison of different states of mind in time are not yet experienced, and, therefore, the respective activated representation of the primary object on the level of subjective experiencing is the all-that-is outside of which nothing exists. Under this condition, these two states of mind are pulled together and consolidated into one uniform experience by the common traumatic context, within which the primary object is at the same time foreclosed in its totality and the ego enters—also in totality—into the pathognomonic imitative fusion with it. This constitutes the clinical picture of the psychogenic infantile autism of the encapsulation type. There is no splitting mechanism underlying it.

The character of totality and globality of the inner perception of the primary object in this primary constitution of the psyche leads to these two psychic movements that actually contradict each other—foreclosure and imitative fusion—to paradoxically co-exist peacefully and undisturbedly side by side due to the totality claim of both, because this unconditional experience of absoluteness leads to a situation where contradiction and mutual exclusion are not finding a representation. The resulting quality of totality of the symptomatology spans the whole spectrum of experience, with its character definitely blocking development as a whole.

Through this constellation two things become evident:

1. Primary experiencing in fact takes place in timelessness.
2. The primary object, in this first phase of mental life, has in fact this character of totality and globality which I have summarized in the formulation of the "all-that-is" outside of which nothing exists.

This is the metapsychologically stringent explanation of this first form of psychical illness, and in reverse, I consider this very succession or, later, side-by-side of the foreclosure of the traumatic not-me version of the primary object and the reactive imitative fusion with its non-traumatic form of manifestation as clinical evidence for the correctness of my reflections on the existence of a pre-schizoid phase, for such parallelity of contradictory relations with the object is only possible before the background of a not yet established object constancy, so that successive states of the relationship to the primary object cannot be compared yet with each other and thus be recognized as incompatible.

In terms of theory, this is a metapsychological conclusion of prime importance. It is the gain we can draw out of our understanding of this earliest form of psychic pathology, proving that our inferences about mental functioning at the primordial level are correct.

The open question of the genesis of the primary psychogenic autism has thus become clarified to the extent that the traumatic manifestation of the not-me object is not the direct consequence of an external influence, but that of a psychic materialization of the anti-fusional principle of the life drive within the imago of the primary object itself, which results from the dynamic opposition of the drives and which represents an extreme emergency reaction in order to prevent the imminent collapse of the dimension of the psychical in a concrete fusional realization.

In this sense I consider, further, the encapsulated psychogenic autism as the clinical evidence for the actual existence of that psychical power, given from the beginning of mental life, which I call the life drive, and as evidence that the psychic struggle which the antagonism of the drives is about centers on the subject of the fusion with the primary object: this is, in this sense, a compelling result from the double aspect of the pathognomonic symptomatology of encapsulated autism, that on the one hand the traumatizing event consists in the manifestation of the not-me object refusing to fuse, and that on the other hand, the circumstance that this not-me object is in fact about the fusion theme, is evidenced by the autist's development of the symptoms of the imitatory merging in a compensatory way, the only meaning of which is to deny and annul the traumatic refusal to fuse through the imitative and repetitive mechanisms.

Before the background of the clinic of the conditions in encapsulated autists which keep the psychical circumstances of the beginning of life fixated in a time warp-like fashion, Tustin describes that and in how far the primary psychic functioning is a purely sensory one and proceeds first of all from the unmodulated sensory opposites. I would like to stress that this emphasis on the sensory system also corresponds to my own starting point, when I speak about the fact that after the unfolding of the poles of perception (*see there*), the primary object consists solely and exclusively in the sensory afferences which are bound together in a unified representation only through temporal contiguity. I have described that, in this psychic state that is tied to two-dimensionality, there are no phantasies in the actual sense, or mental content, as they require object constancy on the one hand, and an inner space (*see there*) on the other, and thus lead away from immediate sensory perception. In that respect, experiencing in the pre-schizoid phase is necessarily bound to the immediate sensory perception.

If one tries to answer the question in which manner the basal sensory integration tasks constitutive for the further development of the psyche normally come about, one is directed back to the theme of the primary object in the pre-schizoid phase before representational object constancy is reached. In this first constitution of the psyche the (non-split) primary object is the only thing that is given and is being positively posited. It is the pre-ambivalent primary object as the basic affirmation of life.

As under the condition of globality and totality of the pre-schizoid phase the representation of a bad presence is not possible as this would deny life itself, the pre-ambivalent primary object of this phase is the precursor model of what will later become the good breast. I assume that it is the central task of this pre-ambivalent primary object to serve as a catalyst and container for this sensory integration. Thus we are dealing here with a basal, early form of the containing function: containment and an archaic, sensorily defined alpha function are being exercised solely intra-psychically by the inner primary object. In any case, it is precisely this task which fails when the primary object of this developmental stage falls under the autistic foreclosure.

Primal repression

See: The structural unconscious and the two parallel worlds of psychical functioning; primal repression

Primal scene, imago of the phallus, Oedipus complex

The primal scene is bestowed its central significance for the psyche inasmuch as, from the concretistic perspective of the death drive, it represents the—seeming—opportunity presented by the example of the father (see there), to carry out fusion (see there) with the mother (see there) without the danger of ego dissolution. From the point of view of the life drive (see there)—which contains the symbolic function—that same image of the primal scene represents the suspension of the fusional danger and thus in fact of the death drive (see there), in so far as the core of the father imago is the distancing of the ego from itself which impedes the fusion.

In this latter sense, the image of the primal scene, as seen before the psychical background of the meaning of the father imago, already implicitly contains the motive of the renunciation of the ego with regard to the fusional wish, and the incestuous misinterpretation and corruption by the death drive contain a purposeful denial with reference to the significance of the father imago, which of course is not unfamiliar to endopsychic perception.

Under both perspectives, however, the power of the father condenses in the imago of the phallus as the means that links the father in the primal scene to the mother. Thus the phallus, by definition, is the penis of the father.

In this manner, in any case, the primal scene becomes the central imago of the psyche, in as far as in it both drives simultaneously find their imaginative realization: the life drive in the sense of the ego's self-imposed abstinence with respect to the fusional implication of the incest, whereby this self-imposed abstinence—because of and via the anti-fusional meaning of the father imago—is referenced and expressed under the aspect of the Eros in the coupling of the father with the mother. In this sense the imago of the primal scene is <u>the phantasmatic definition of the life drive</u>. The death drive, as said, perverts this meaning of the primal scene concretistically, in the sense of the seeming possibility of the realization of the fusional incest, insofar as the father, in the sexual union with the mother, seems to be protected by the power of the phallus from the danger of annihilation contained in the fusion.

As the appropriation of this apotropaic phallus, however, is being thwarted by the threat of castration (see there), or rather and more exactly, by the event of castration which consists in the catastrophic loss of the protective effect and power of the phallus in the incestuous approach towards fusion, the Oedipus complex in this way becomes

303

the complex which bonds and neutralizes the death drive. This, in my opinion, is its psychobiological meaning, which not only makes it the "the central core of all neuroses" (Freud, 1931), but also the central core of the psyche in general.

In any case, in this consideration it becomes clear that genital sexuality is the field within which <u>both</u> drives articulate themselves. It cannot, therefore, be attributed unilaterally to one of the two drives only.

In this sense the primal scene imago represents, so to speak, a time shaft which, with respect to the psychological meaning of the parental images, refers directly to the earliest structural constellations and problems. I therefore regard the primal scene as that psychical imagination in which the natural law conditions are expressed which constitute and maintain the dimension of the psychical. This affirms also under this aspect the central meaning of the Oedipal constellation.

Furthermore it is necessary to bear in mind a fundamental complication in the relationship with the parental images. To 'be a mother' and 'be a father' belongs to the everyday topics of our lives. We easily fail to see that from the point of view of the inner perspective of our Oedipal constitution we are all egos, and that within ourselves we find ourselves opposite our motherly and fatherly imagos. Each flesh-and-blood man and each flesh-and-blood woman can take up the position of the father or mother only within the inner world of his or her children, but can never be it in his or her psychic reality. As concerns oneself, one is always the ego which finds itself opposite its own father and mother imagos, and which, as it were, declares itself ready and willing to play this role for the child, to take it on, to represent it.

Looked at it this way one could say that 'mother' and 'father' are the most monumental abstractions we have to deal with in our lives.

That there are only ever father and mother <u>places</u> so to speak, but that no one single living individual can ever be identical with these places.

The father himself is extramundane—in the sense of the impossible identity of ego and father place, he does not exist on this earth. For while the ego is being defined by the father imago, it cannot, however, become identical with it, as the father imago arises from the position outside and as the latter would be annulled again by establishing an identity between ego and father imago.

In the same vein, the mother in her ontogenetic background is the imago of the primary object (*see there*), from which in the course of the individual developmental history—via the entry of the father imago, which is truly generative in this psychic sense—the whole world of real objects differentiates out, so that the oedipal mother in the unconscious background is the sum-total imago of the world. Ego and mother, therefore, cannot be identical either: the mother is the object, the perceived, which is opposite the ego as the subject of perception (*see there*). The ego can only take up the mother place for its own child.

The conceptualization of the primal scene is the phantasmatic definition of overcoming the early good-bad split of the object through the position outside (*see there*) which does open up access to reality and which finds its phantasmatic formulation in the imago of the father. Only then can the external parents be perceived at all in their reality and be brought into congruence with the primal scene imago that is being formed, only then can the difference between the sexes be recognized and used for defining the parental relationship, and last but not least, only then can the "other" in the perceptual external world be localized and purposefully entered into contact with, one's own body really be recognized as "ego" and cathected.

In summary, it can be said that the Oedipus complex, in my perspective, is a primarily intrapsychic, that is to say, interstructural matter and necessity, which inevitably results from the activity of the death drive. In this view the motive of the Oedipus complex in both sexes basically consists in the effort to circumvent the father imago, to lever it off and lastly to annul it, inasfar as the core of the father imago consists of the position of the third, i.e. the position outside the drive phantasma which opposes the fusional merging with the mother, with the primary object. The father imago comes into being as a bastion against the death drive, and the death drive therefore, for its realization must strive for the reannulment of the father imago.

Said the other way round, the striving for fusion with the primary object—oedipally formulated for the fusional incest with the mother—would have to be deemed the fundamental unconscious motive for both sexes. It is true also for female sexuality that the wish for the fusion of the ego with the primary object which satisfies all needs is the governing basic phantasy. With the help of the child, who, on the unconscious transference plane represents the penis of the father, that is to say the phallus, the girl, the woman, desires to carry out the actual fusional incest with the mother at the unconscious-phantasmatic level, by equating her body with the mother of the primal scene, and by identifying her ego with the phallus-child. Insofar as this identification with the phallus in fact signifies that with the father of the primal scene, we are dealing with an enactment of the oedipal situation within one's own person.

The specific threat of castration of the female death drive then would be that the child which cannot carry this attribution and use of itself as the phallus of the father because of its own prohibition of fusion which in turn is interlocked with that of the mother, collapses under the weight of this attribution, or would collapse, respectively, if this attribution was realized.

So, biologically speaking, in justification of the purpose of this detour via the child, one could adduce that the relationship to the child is, in any case, part of the fundamental structural demands of the female psyche. One could further conclude that the woman as a mother through her own sublimative renunciation with respect to the child—that is to say with respect to the use of the phallus-child within a phantasmatization of the realization of the fusional incest—is at the same time protecting the child itself from its own incestuous striving by not seductively inviting such striving and in this way opening the path to the basic work demand for the ego of the child, namely to renounce the fusional incest.

In this sense one must say, therefore, that the birth of the father imago and the stabilization of its function, on the plane of the psychic reality of the child, depends on the state of the Oedipal working through by the mother. The mother allows and enables the child to construct the phantasmatization concerning the father, or she prohibits it.

Oedipal phantasmatization, according to its own inner laws, by necessity leads to its dissolution by repression in the confrontation with the phallic threat of castration. In this way the particularly human phenomenon of psychosexual latency comes about, in agreement with Freud's respective formulations in the third of the *Essays on the Theory of Sexuality* of 1905. Like Freud, I also consider it the task of latency to have the defensive boundaries established against the oedipal objects to the degree that, when genital sexual development sets in in puberty, the sexual interest is no longer directed towards the oedipal but the displaced objects. From my theory formation it can therefore be inferred that this dissolution by repression—and thus latency—is a logically inescapable structural consequence, provided that the oedipal conflict constellation has been correctly established.

307

Latency, therefore, is no biological fact, but one purely contingent on phantasma. This fact entails that derailments of development in the infantile working through of oedipality may lead to latency not or not sufficiently being established, or, to the contrary, may develop such repressive impact that it also withstands the hormonal and maturational push of puberty and may even continue into adult life, as-it-were, unbroken. Both are known clinical phenomena of child and adolescent psychoanalysis which have a high diagnostic significance. In latency the power and impact of the phantasmatic side of human existence shows itself, and especially the power of the oedipal conflict constellation, to the degree that this central crisis of the ontogenesis of the psyche directly affects psychosexuality which in its course appears totally caused by biology, but is not, in this, therefore, so very important place.

Primary ego

I proceed from the basic assumption or axiom of an ontogenetic initial situation, in which based on a certain neuronal stage of maturity of the cortical and subcortical CNS, perception sets in and with it an experiencing which is still directly identical to perception to begin with, and thus, as I would argue, the ego is also immediately given, in as far as agreement can be reached that the ego must be centrally and fundamentally regarded as the instance, as the subjective agent of perception and the formation of experience which derives from it. By perception I here understand the ability to create a central representation of an afferent stimulus. Presupposition for this axiom is solely the system properties of the human brain, i.e. the fact that neuronal activity patterns are expressed as perception and as experiencing tied to perception.

This opens the dimension of the psychical, and what follows next from this train of thought is that it is not the id which must be regarded as the first instance of the psychic apparatus, but the ego.

Under the condition of the as yet undeveloped time perception in a primary ego constitution making no structural presuppositions as yet the ego is also unable to perceive its possible factual disintegration into various ego nuclei. The experience of an incoherence of the ego paradoxically presupposes a rudimentary ego constancy, that is to say, the possibility to compare an ego state A with an ego state B within the time axis. In other words, an ego which experiences itself as split and disintegrated into bits and thus weakened, presupposes a beginning ego coherence or ego constancy.

This means that the indication that there is a probable primary disintegration of the ego into various ego nuclei—important as this may be under the developmental-descriptive aspect—plays no role, psychoanalytically, that is to say, with reference to subjective experiencing, in the same sense as the indication that the primary object, under the point of view of reality, has a completely illusory character. It follows from these considerations that the ego as the subject of perception, precisely on the conceivably simplest level of its functioning, from a perspective of subjective experiencing, acts in every single time moment in its full potential identity and energetic wholeness and completeness, even if, seen from the outside, it may appear ever so deficient and fragmented. The primary ego does not yet, have a reflexive distance to itself, there is no relativisation of the ego by comparing its states; just as there is no concept of an outside of the object as yet and thus no relativisation of the object.

This, in my definition, is what is meant by primary narcissism. The primary ego which is not yet relativizing itself is confronted in the primary object with the full implication which we psychoanalytically connect with the term of the object; in a more comprehensive sense than at any later time, for the relationship with this primary object knows neither an alternative nor an outside. This defines the power of the object and allows a glimpse, gives an idea of the elementary dynamics of the emotional conditions which are involved here. Perhaps it is due to this circumstance that this basic experience seems to have such formative power to determine the fundamental conditions in the psyche.

If ego and object constitute themselves in the same moment ex nihilo and if their relationship with each other is that of perceiving subject and the perceived, this means on the energetic plane that the cathexis of the object by the ego is primary and spontaneous, the event with which the psychic life begins, the immediate given. There is therefore no primary cathexis of the ego alone—Freud's pseudopodia model—and the object is not being invested only by the withdrawal of cathexes from the ego.

Primary envy

See: Annihilatory aggression, primary envy

Primary identification

See: Position of the ego outside the drive phantasma ("position outside") and the father imago; the concept of inner space and primary identification; the inner world

Primary narcissism

See, first, the entries under primary ego and primary object.

The level of functioning before representational object constancy
(see: object constancy) is reached is tied to an ego experience and an
experiencing of the primary object which is unconditional, all-
comprehensive, and in this sense absolute, and it takes place in
timelessness. In my opinion, it is the complete package of these
characteristics which gives a continuing, dynamic, radiating potential
to this earliest layer of the ontogenesis of mental life, for mental life
preserves all ontogenetic layers of its functioning and keeps them
simultaneously active.

The above-named characteristics of this pre-schizoid constitution
(see: pre-schizoid phase)—comprehensive, absolute, timeless—are those
that were traditionally linked to primary narcissism and deduced
from the supposed absence of an object in this constitution. The train
of thought I propose is in reference to showing that the object, based
on the ego's infantile omnipotence, is included in this constitution
without it leading to a limitation of the ego and that this object of the
pre-schizoid phase cannot be negated yet as there is nothing outside
this primary object, and the primary ego cannot negate the only
object it has. This is therefore the pre-ambivalent object. The negative
is as yet unrepresentable. The constitution of the pre-schizoid phase
thus posits a powerful experience of wholeness, completeness, and
omnipotence, which, as is easily conceivable, may become the basis
and reference point of a mystical yearning back to the past, and,
on the psychopathological plane, the fixation point and point of
attraction of a correspondingly powerful regressive tendency. In any
case, primary narcissism thus conceived could not be regarded as an
objectless phase.

Primary object

I define the primary object as the objective pole of the basic act of perception (*see there*). By perception I here understand the ability to create a central representation of an afferent stimulus. With this moment the object as an achaic representation is also given, for perception is logically impossible without that which is perceived, and this exactly is the first, the primary object.

It is important to note that the primary object, which is perceived by the primary ego, must be thought of as the sum of those sensory data mediated by the senses which hit the central nervous system at a certain point in time and by this contiguity of time are experienced as a uniform representation. From a descriptive point of view, most variously generated data enter into this representation: external world stimuli, proprioception, stimulation from human contact, etc. mingle completely undifferentiated, as the respective categorisations cannot be made yet, that is to say, a differentiation between an inside and an outside cannot be made yet, and a concept of reality does not exist. What we are dealing with here is the level of the very first objectal representations in the sense of the precipitate of sensory stimuli, organized, that is to say bound together, only by their simultaneity within a primordial constitution, which, apart from the sensory stimulation, does not know differentiated psychic content like phantasies, thoughts, or symbols, as the necessary mental space for it has not yet been built. We are, therefore, far before the level of part-objects, which represent a far more highly developed objectal formulation. The primary object on its pertaining level of the structurally most basic organisation of the mental state is the only thing that exists at all. An outside of the primary object cannot yet be conceptualised.

As long as the primary object of the time moment A, because of the not yet developed rudimentary constancy (see: object constancy) cannot be compared yet with the primary object of the time moment B, firstly, object A and object B cannot be moderated yet with each other, and secondly, there is no outside of the primary object, as this mental concept presupposes time and the comparison between the different object conceptions in time. For the primary ego therefore, the primary object in this primordial condition, before representational object constancy (in my definition of the term; see there) is reached, is, so to speak, the universe, the all-that-is, outside of which nothing exists.

The psychic dimension thus constitutes itself in the perception of the primary object and outside of the perception of this primary object there is nothing. There is no outside as yet, and also pertaining to this primary level of functioning is the quality of timelessness. Conversely this line of argumentation means that this primary condition of the psyche ends as soon as object constancy and thus the concept of time is being established.

Projective identification

It should be pointed out that projective identification which, for the purpose of controlling the object, but also for the purpose of an archaic form of mental communication (Bion), consists in injecting parts of the self into the object, must be regarded, in its pathological sense, as the operative mechanism for the production of a fusional (*see there*) state insofar as through it the boundary between the self and the object is dissolved, which is its central intention. It is, therefore, the principal mechanism of the death drive (*see there*), and its structural closeness to incestuous phantasy, namely via the insertion of parts of the self into the object, must not be overlooked. I point out in this context that Rosenfeld (1964) has described it in this sense as the mechanism of

313

denial of the separation and separateness from the object. Beyond this, in 1983, he depicted a global kind of projective identification in which the self as a whole, in the context of a symbiotic kind of object relation, is projected into the object and seems to live like it was inside the object. Betty Joseph (1987, p. 178) formulates the issue poignantly: "At the very primitive end of projective identification is the attempt to get back into an object—to become, as it were, undifferentiated and mindless and thus avoid all pain." At the level of the not per-se pathological meaning in the framework of primal mental communication processes, Bion (1962) places projective identification within the context of his container-contained model, in as far as the child here with the help of projective identification injects content or sensory qualities, respectively, which are indigestible, incomprehensible for it, into the mental organism of the mother and which it obtains back from the mother on the same path in a mentally representable form (alpha process). In any case, it is here where we find the prefigurations which turn the incest with the mother into an unconscious representation of the fusional phantasma at the level of whole objects and genitality.

John Steiner (1993) worked out that what has to be taken back in mourning, chiefly and all in all—in the depressive position and elsewhere—are the projective identifications which the subject has put into the lost object and through which it is connected to it. The projective identifications, also in Steiner´s view, can be regarded as particular fusional movements via which the ego attempts to force a fusional connection with the object. In Steiner's words: "One of the consequences of projective identification is that the subject relates to the object not as a separate person with his own characteristics but as if he is relating to himself. He may ignore aspects of the object which do not fit the projection or he may control and force or persuade the object to enact the role required of him." (1993, p. 42). And: "We can see that projective identification gives rise to a state in which true separateness is not experienced. This state of mind provides relief from anxiety and from frustration as well as from envy, and is idealized." (op. cit. p. 44). Sohn (1985) describes, as an extreme, narcissistic organizations in which the massive use of projective identifications leads to the subject having the feeling to become the object and to possess all that is good and the properties of the object, so that the object is very concretely being taken into possession.

This so to speak narcissisalizing trait of projective identification applies irrespective of the fact that the projective identifications largely serve defensive purposes, that is to say, are there to enable the evacuation of unloved parts of the personality. If one takes into account that through the fusion with the primary object (see there), wholly and largely, relief is to be provided for the experience of lack by equating the object, as the source of complemental plenitude, as the source of suspension of the lack, with the ego, it would be completely along these lines if these parts of the ego that are in one way or other tainted by the experience of deficiency or lack, were evacuated into the object. At the same time, the connection with these parts is maintained, since with the same movement the aim of fusion is to be reached. If one cannot equate the good, the object, in a global fusional movement with the ego, so as to suspend the lack, one can at least try to relocate the lack, the negative in parts into the object and thus simultaneously bind the object to the ego. This also clarifies the theoretical question of why the ego may want to get rid of an aversive content, on the one hand, by evacuating it into the object, and on the other, may not want to give up the connection with it.

Projective identification in the sense of the above evacuation and defense, which simultaneously establishes a fusional connection with the object, and thus undercuts the separation between ego/subject

315

and object, is, therefore, the main mode of operating of a death drive which sees itself barred from fulfillment via the large-format primary narcissistic fusion between the primary ego and the primary object (*see there*). In a similar sense, John Steiner (1993, p. 61) writes: "Today, as we recognize the central role of projective identification in the creation of pathological object relations (....)", thus designating the striving for suspension of the separation from the object as the motor of psychopathology.

Psychopathology

Under the perspective of the drive concept presented in this work, what would have to be said as the sum of all my reflections, is that any form of psychopathology must be regarded as a form of activity of the death drive (*see there*). Under the definition which I have given the death drive this means, however, that psychopathology, in whichever form, goes back to the attempt to suspend the separation between the ego and the object—the object imago or the representation of the object, respectively. This, too, the question of separation or non-separation of ego and object as a determining factor of mental illness is by itself no new theme. It is new, however, to regard this theme as the sole and exclusive axis around which psychic structure formation revolves and from the systemic error susceptibilities of which the individual forms of psychopathology systematically and describably develop. I have endeavored to give examples for this in the individual clinical investigations of this work (hysteria, psychogenic encapsulated autism, annihilatory aggression).

John Steiner (1993) has formulated a theory of 'psychic retreats', which in its turn already covers a very wide field of psychopathology. He conceptualizes these psychic retreats as fallback positions, be it in the form of concretely thought of inner places or as special forms of organization of defensive processes or as a special construct of internal object relations or as a combination of all of these. As to their content, they are characterized, for one thing, by a denial of the separation from the object, and for another, by a simultaneous acknowledgement and non-acknowledgement of reality, which is what carries this denial. He calls this simultaneous acknowledgement and non-acknowledgement the 'narcissistic perversion', following Freud's work on fetishism of 1927. The points in common with my view are obvious here.

The theme is too broad for me to even attempt to comprehensively deal with it, not even in approximation. But I would like to raise the question of whether or not each form of psychic illness can be regarded as a specific psychic retreat; as a form of resistance and defense which attempts to enforce the aim of the death drive after all, or at least to not give up the claim to its realization (as in grudge, resentment and remorse—all of them retreats described by Steiner). Each and every psychic illness would then be a retreat, a place of mentally withdrawing in the sense of a, in each case, specific evasion from the necessity of acknowledging the separation from the object. With every form of such an evasion from separation comes with necessity, as I have described, both a simultaneous acknowledgement and non-acknowledgement of reality, in the sense of a simultaneous evasion and non-evasion from the position outside *(see there)*; in any case above the psychotic level of functioning *(see: Psychosis)*.

I think, however, that the withdrawal or retreat characteristic of psychopathology under the precondition of my death drive model can be described even more exactly: at the basis of it is, in each single case, the maintenance of an absolutely posited and as-it-were relentless egocentric satisfaction claim of the ego with respect to the object, which in its core is an attack against the object and actually an attack against the primal scene *(see there)*, against the excludedness from the primal scene. The retreat theme—narcissistic in this sense—consists in

317

the fact that the ego, under the fiction of deprivation, of lack, feels that it is being attacked and thinks it has to secure its survival by attacking the object and, in the phantasmatic background, by pursuing its incorporation into the ego. The ego is thereby not courageous enough to allow the insight that the psychical condition of its secured existence lies in the intangibility of the object; that the ego by withdrawing from the primal scene defines its own structural safety.

The deprivations and needs, imagined or real, hereby support the fiction of entitlement of the death drive to face the object with the mentality of an animal of prey, in order to counter the fear. What is misunderstood here is that the psychic, structural condition, that is to say cause of fear lies in the attack on the object imago because through it the structural delimitation between ego and object imago is attacked and threatens to collapse. Through this attack the ego wants to enforce fusion (*see there*) and ignores the fact that it would itself be suspended in fusion. Therefore, the delimitation between ego and object is being secured through the—in this sense—psychogenic fear. For this reason the acknowledgement of this delimitation is the condition for freedom from fear; in any case as far as the latter has intrinsically psychic reasons.

One more theme I would like to touch on in the context of these general considerations, as it is of importance for our psychotherapeutic-psychoanalytic conception of man, for the image we have of our own science and profession, and thus for the consideration of our own existence. We are used to seeing the psyche as an infinity, as a field that is inexhaustible. Not much will change here, on one side, for the occurring cases of combinatory possibility of circumstances and personalities continue to be unfathomable. On the other side the basal structure of the human psyche, before the background of my reflections, is given a comprehensible and describable framework. This means a change of our view of the human being and frees up capacities, as a certain problem—that of this basal structure—can be deemed as solved.

Psychosexuality

See: Primal *attachment, psychosexuality* and *drive dynamics*

Psychosis and fusion

The psychotic phenomena are not the result of an actual fusion, for the fusion as a factual realization is psychically not possible as in it the juxtaposition of ego and object, perception *(see there)* and that which is perceived would be abolished, out of which the mental space, the dimension of the psychical originates in the first place and which constitutes it. Fusion therefore would annul the dimension of the psychical. The process geared towards it which is carried by the death drive *(see there)* leads, however, to the collapse of the position of the ego outside the drive phantasma *(see there)*, thus to the collapse of access to reality, and brings back the good-bad split of the object imago, and this in turn gives rise to the phenomenology of the psychotic constitution. When Hanna Segal, for example, speaks of the fusional identification of ego and object in the psychoses, this is more precisely about an identification which works towards fusion under the influence of the death drive, but which can never actually bring it about.

Reality breast

See: *Part object, split object,* primal *attachment;* the *reality breast*

Representation

The system psyche rests on representation. The representations are the screen, the membrane that separates the psyche from the soma. The central danger for this system lies in the suspension through fusion *(see there)* of the perceptual distance between the ego and the representation—i.e. the distance of non-identity between perceiver and perceived that belongs to the logical system properties of the act of perception *(see there)*-, as this fusion would mean the collapse, the self-suspension, of the system. We are here dealing with the internal perception in the sense in which Freud, in *The Interpretation of Dreams*, spoke of consciousness as the sense-organ for the perception of psychical qualities. The ego is under the illusion to be able to escape unpleasure and suffering, to find salvation, by suspending this separation from the representation of the object. This conflict is reflected in the antagonism of the psychical drives. It is the biological task of the Oedipus complex *(see there)* to bind this system danger inherent in the psyche.

We do not know the information deposited in the system properties of the brain with which the individual is born. What can be said, however, is that the structures described by psychoanalysis are building up starting with the formation of the first representation with which a sensory event is registered, encoded, in the central nervous system. More is not needed. The psyche, therefore, as a system, is bound to the representations. Only that which passes through this process of encoding in the course of representation formation, or has such a representation process as its base, is psychic content. Also, all information which, as the case may be, is stored in the system properties of the brain, must, for its psychic activation, first elicit a process of representation formation. This is the reason why, for example, the pre-conceptions that Bion describes, need events for their activation through which they can then express themselves. It may well be, however, that these pre-conceptions (and other inborn information) have an attracting effect for the constellation of such events. The representations are originally purely sensory, or hallucinatory-sensory, see also the world of psychogenic autism (see there). They only gain a symbolic, that is, symbolising dimension through the position outside (see there), in the course of the depressive position (see there).

Repression, the dynamic unconscious id

Because of both its dynamic and its structural importance, the threat of castration (see there) and behind it the threat of loss of the father imago (see there) becomes the agent of repression and in this way the agent of the creation of the dynamic unconscious part of the id. Repression here uses the dimension of the structurally unconscious which arises in the transition from the splitting conceptualization to a realistic identity conceptualization of the object by using the quality that comes with it, namely the categorially unconscious quality of contents that are psychically active nevertheless, in order to achieve a structurally secured non-identity of the repressed contents with respect to the ego of the position outside (see there).

I have described that the dimension of the psychogenic unconscious results from the incompatibility of the splitting conceptualization of the object with the suspension of this split through the position outside. Seen under this perspective, the functional mechanism of repression can also be formulated differently: that in the case of an interpretation of the relationship to the object that stands under the reign of the death drive (see there), the good-bad split of the representation of this object reappears in the background, and that therefore, this representation falls into the catchment area of that dimension of the psyche that is incompatible with regard to the position outside and that insofar is unconscious, or plainly: repressed.

Inner space
> See: Position of the ego outside the drive phantasma ("position outside") and the father imago; the concept of inner space and primary identification; the inner world

Split object
> See: Part object, split object, primal attachment; the reality breast

The structural id

The continued existence of the good-bad split of the object in that part of the psyche that, also after the resolution of the crisis of the depressive position by establishment of the position outside (see there), keeps functioning in the mode of the identity of the ego with the drive phantasma (see: position outside) thus also means the parallel keeping up of two different and mutually incompatible object conceptualizations, namely one, the splitting concept of the object, and two, the concept of time-space identity of the object, with which access to reality is given. This, in my definition, is the reason for which the structural unconscious and therefore the core of the id come into being. This unconscious is thus not, for example, an expression of an assumed continuum of the psychical toward the somatic, but the precipitate of early experiencing at the splitting level, which, with the breakthrough to the time-space identity of the object because of the categorial leap that goes with it, is consciously no longer conceivable.

The structural unconscious and the two parallel worlds of psychical functioning;
primal repression

As with the breakthrough to the position of the ego outside the drive-phantasma (see there) the earlier splitting constitution of the object conceptualization is not compatible with the new time-space identity of the object, this earlier mode of mental functioning and the concomitant way of experiencing that is tied to the identity of the ego with the drive phantasma, is now becoming unconscious. With this process the dimension of the psychogenic unconscious of the mind is being created, in contrast to the so to speak morphological unconsciousness of those areas of the brain which display an essentially unconscious functioning as part of their structural characteristics. To my suggestion this is the primal repression that leads to the <u>structurally</u> unconscious as the core of the id. In so far as the crisis of the conflict of the depressive position (*see there*) is postulated to happen in the second quarter of the first year of life, this would more or less coincide with the moment of birth of the id as an agency of the mental apparatus. It is worth pointing out that this is the same time moment and the same process in which through the position of the ego outside the drive phantasma the birth of the father imago (*see there*)—in any case its structural root, the position of the third—is given.

In this context it is important to note that the early functioning of the psyche which is tied to the identity of the ego with the drive phantasma and, following from it, to early object splitting, is not relinquished with the leap to the position of the ego outside the drive phantasma. The genetically earlier form of perception and experiencing continues to exist, namely in that mode of functioning of the ego in which the latter is not distanced from itself. This area of identity of the ego function, however, is no longer accessible to the self-reflecting ego outside of the drive phantasma, because we are dealing with—with reference, on the one hand, to object splitting, and to the identity of the ego with the drive phantasma on the other—a categorically different way of experiencing, and this is precisely why that area of identity functioning is unconscious in the structural sense.

Conversely, consciousness, the state of being conscious, can be defined as the self-reflexive mode of functioning of the ego outside of the drive phantasma.

We must therefore proceed from the assumption that the ego at all times perceives in two different and mutually incompatible modalities, of which only one is capable of being immediately conscious. It is obvious that these two mutually exclusive modalities or ways of functioning, respectively, of the mind are linked to the distinction between primary and secondary processes, but also to the dichotomies of word and thing presentation, perceptual identity and thought identity.

In any case, I am of the opinion that this view of two forms of functioning of mental life and of the activity of the brain operating permanently simultaneous and in parallel, offers a fruitful approach for the psychoanalytic understanding of a wide field of phenomena, for instance in the domain of the arts, but also with reference to understanding dreams and the dream process.

From this incompatibility of the two modes of functioning of the ego results a further consideration concerning the genetic priority of the agencies. I have deduced the priority in time of the ego before the id, proceeding from the axiom that the dimension of the psychical arises out of the unfolding of the poles of perceiving and that which is perceived, by equating the perceiving agency with the primitive, primal ego.

Before the background of the above consideration, as a consequence of which this primary ego of the identity with the drive phantasma becomes the core of the id and, due to the incompatibility with the new mode of functioning, becomes structurally unconscious, this formulation must be specified: there are two fundamentally divergent modes of functioning of the ego, both existing simultaneously with each other, but the genetically earlier mode is linked to the splitting of the object, and thus does not meet the criteria of correspondence to reality and is ignorant of the ability of self-reflection. This mode is therefore unconscious with relation to the new, henceforward dominant ego constitution, and what is more, constitutes the quality of psychogenic unconsciousness.

The structurally unconscious core of the id is therefore, according to this hypothesis, the early ego of the identity with the drive phantasma. This is also the reason why in the psychoses the classical separation of agencies is being lost, for a psychosis fundamentally consists in the very regression to the identity of the ego with the drive phantasma, which is linked to object splitting, and thus loss of access to reality and of the father imago. Hence, this regressive loss of the secondary-process position of the ego outside the drive phantasma implies the loss of differentiation of the agency of the id from that of the ego, and also, through the collapse of the father imago, the super ego of the structurally neurotic, oedipal plane, is lost.

To conclude, one has to assume that this particular distancing work of the ego, i.e. the taking up of the 'position outside of the drive phantasma', is not operating the whole time or not totally functioning, and that therefore the ego, in parallel, always remains in the functioning mode of the identity with its own experiencing, that is to say, is not in the reflexive distance mode, and insofar functions both consciously and unconsciously at the same time, whereby the unconscious functioning is bound to the splitting constitution.

Subjective object

I consider it important to stress that in my opinion with the new developmental leap of the ego to the position outside the drive phantasma (*see there*) the mental concept of an outside reality, that

325

is to say, of the differentiation between inside and outside, is only ever just being introduced into the psychic realm. Before this point in time the object exists only as a subjective object which has its genetic core in the central nervous system´s representational registration of a temporally contiguous sensory stimulation—without distinguishing whether the source of this stimulation lies outside or inside the body, that is to say, in the outside object or in the self.

Hence all psychoanalytic or descriptive formulations which for the time period before this developmental step proceed from a reaction to an external object—or which deny such a reaction—miss the nature of primary experiencing, in my opinion. Even a descriptive and apparently clear reaction to an external object does not mean just yet that the mental concept of an external real object as distinguished from a subjective internal space, already exists. This distinction only comes about as a consequence of the position of the ego outside the drive phantasma, that is to say, through the suspension of primary object splitting, and in a psychosis it is exactly this distinction which gets lost again.

These difficulties, in the course of psychoanalytic theory formation, have led to the assumption of a primary lack of boundaries between subject and object. This view is not correct in my opinion. There is not a lack of boundaries, but the boundaries that exist by all means, mentally, between the ego and the primary object—that is to say the object imago, the representation of the object—have not yet been brought into an agreement with the reality boundaries. Thus, in the borderline constitution, the pathognomical identity diffusion is a symptom of the beginning return to object splitting and with it to a subjective definition of the object, triggered on the practical-pragmatic plane through the massive use of the mechanism of projective identification which undermines the reality boundary between the ego and the object while in the psychic background the negation of the position outside the drive phantasma—in other words the negation of the position of the third—plays the decisive role.

Sublimation, ego-ideal

Concerning the structural binding of the antagonism of the drives as the principal project of the psyche, one of the most important conclusions refers to the concept of sublimation. It can be understood as the self-renunciation of the ego with regard to the temptation of incestuous corruption of the primal scene (see there), which optimally results from the ego´s dealing with the oedipal conflict (see there) and the meaning of the threat of castration (see there). This sublimational ego has learnt that the threat of castration is not directed against its own interests but rather preserves them, by safeguarding the ego against the only danger threatening it from within, namely the fusional incest. In the sublimation the ego implicitly acknowledges the father imago (see there) as the, so to speak, operative imago of the safety of the ego, as a manifestation of the, by necessity, anti-fusional nature of the ego itself.

The core of the father imago is the self-reflective position of the ego outside the drive phantasma (see there) which implies a split within the ego, contrasting the directly experiencing ego with its self-reflective function. This split renders a fusion (see there) with the primary object (see there) structurally impossible insofar fusion, as a global and total process, is only possible on the basis of a unitary ego, and in this way makes the good-bad split of the object as the early mode of defense against the fusional danger obsolete. This dynamical meaning of the father imago is psychically expressed in the image of the primal scene where the father unites with the mother without getting lost in fusion, because he is the antifusionary principle._

327

The constitution of the father imago as the antifusionary principle is founded, as said, on the self-reflective split of the ego within itself. Seen like this, the father imago defines the nature of the ego as that of a basic non-identity with itself and contains the warning for the ego not to try to be identical with the father, not to try to possess the phallus (*see there*) as the expression and means of his power and potency to ban the fusional danger, as on the phantasmatic plane, this would mean to reverse the self-reflective split within the ego and to confront the ego anew with the unmodulated splitting of the object and the consecutive loss of reality access. This is the essential meaning of the threat of castration (*see there*) which I, for this reason, have designated as the phallic threat of castration, as it is the threat of losing, in the appropriation, the antifusional capacity and potency of the phallus as the phantasmatic condensation and dynamic attribute of the apotropaic power of the father.

When in the process of sublimation these implications and meanings of the primal scene imagination have been worked through and understood by the ego, and the ego has accepted the necessity to give up its wish to intrude into the primal scene and to incestuously corrupt it, the primal scene in its above delineated sense stands out as the phantasmatic, imaginative definition of the security of the ego from the only danger that threatens it from within, i.e. the danger of fusion with the imago, the representation of the object. In this sense, this imago of the primal scene which the ego explicitly stays out of, is the sublimational ego-ideal. This sublimational movement is therefore the solution of the oedipal conflict arising from its very structure itself. In it, the primary traumatisation of the ego from the confrontation with its inherent threat of annihilation as the consequence of its unavoidable fusional desire dissolves. The traumatic nature of the ego which I have described would come to an end in it.

While in the neurotic constellation the Oedipus complex must perish as it is being repressed into the id by the threat of castration in order to, in this way, safeguard the non-identity of ego and phallus and prevent the fusional incest, sublimation offers an alternative here. As the primal scene imago in the case of the sublimational constitution of the ego no longer represents the fusional danger for this ego, but to the contrary shows itself in its true nature as the imago of the safety of the ego, the primal scene must no longer be withdrawn from the realm of the ego and relegated to the id, but can be installed—as the quasi-definitional imago of the ego—in the form of the sublimational ego-ideal, as a 'grade in the ego', in modification of Freud who, within the framework of his structural theory, had addressed the term ego-ideal both in "The Ego and the Id" (1923), and in the "New Introductory Lectures on Psychoanalysis" (1932) as a grade in the superego.

This sublimational ego-ideal in this view represents the completion of the structural development of the psyche, because it defines the antifusional nature of the ego and in this way protects it against the danger arising from within itself. It is the renunciation of the ego with regard to the incestuous demand that makes internalization possible, as the wish for satisfaction through the real object has been given up. To put it differently, the final internalization is not possible as long as the wish for satisfaction has not been given up.

Symbolic equation

As a basic principle it must be noted that the position of the ego outside of the drive phantasma (*see there*), that is to say, the reflective distance of the ego to itself, which eventually gets codified in the father imago (*see there*), is the precondition for the ability of symbol formation as well as language development, insofar as this reflective distance in its turn is the precondition for the indexical designation. It appears to me that under this aspect the process of symbolic equation as described by Hanna Segal (1957, 1978) can be grasped theoretically more precisely: pathological use of projective identification *(see there)* leads to the collapse, to the suspension of the position outside and thus of the father imago, and this is its central intention under the point of view of the death drive *(see there)*. With the collapse of the position outside, the symbolic function also collapses and is replaced by the symbolic equation.

I consider this an important additional assumption, for Hanna Segal's formulations are inherently problematic in that they say nothing about what leads to the equation of the symbol and the symbolised object at the strictly metapsychological level, that is to say at the level of internal structure formation processes concerning the attitude of the ego towards itself and also towards the object imago. Her argumentation is that the psychotic fusional identification of the ego and the object imago leads to a parallel identification of the symbol and the symbolised object, for the simple reason that the symbol is a function of the ego. Identification, with reference to ego and object, is a metapsychologically precise notion, however not with reference to the process taking place between symbol and symbolised object. The argument of parallelity here has the status of a phenomenological description and is no real explanation of the way in which the fusional process between ego and object leads to the falling together of the symbol and that which is symbolised. This explanation is furnished by the concept of the position outside and its collapse in the face of imminent fusion *(see there)*, that is to say, its collapse under the impact of the death drive.

Threat of castration

The classical threat of castration is put in force in as far as the phantasmatic acquisition of the fatherly phallus (*see there*) by the death drive (*see there*) as a means to carry out the incest, leads to the collapse of its efficacy which is seen to consist in the banishment of the danger connected with the fusion (*see there*). For the father imago (*see there*), which stands behind the imago of the phallus, draws its dynamic meaning and effect and thus its existence from the distancing of the ego from itself in the position outside (*see there*), that is to say, from the separation of ego and father imago which would be revoked again in the concretistic appropriation of the phallus. This revocation would therefore be equivalent to the collapse of the father imago, and it is the threat of this event which is behind the threat of castration and which makes out its core, its significance.

When the conflict of the depressive position (*see there*) is resolved by taking the position outside, that is to say, through the 'invention' of the position of the third, and thus, subsequently, of the father, the threat of castration then contains the threat of the return of the conflict of the depressive position. The loss of the father imago brings back the old good-bad split of the object and thus the paranoid attack on the object which is hereby experienced as damaged and jeopardized in its existence. The subject therefore experiences the castration both on himself and on the object. The breakdown of the father imago is the real major catastrophe of mental life.

If the father imago is lost in the castration experience as the result of the transgression of the Oedipal (*see there*) prohibition, the mother imago (*see there*)–and in it the relationship with the whole world of real objects of which the Oedipal mother is the sum-total imago–suffers the loss of reality of the psychotic plane, with the time-space reality of this imago falling apart, regressing.

The fundamental experience is that of the appropriated phallus of the father losing its power. In this way the task of the phallic castration expresses itself, namely to secure the non-identity of the place of the father with the place of the ego and thus to guarantee the functional principle of the position outside.

We must differentiate more clearly, therefore, that the child does not enter the symbolic order with the 'symbolic castration' (Lacan), but before this, with the step of taking up the position outside. This is the crucial step which suspends the primary splitting constitution. Insofar as the ego, with this step, enters into the reflexive distance to itself, this step is correctly described as the entry into the symbolic order. It makes a big difference, however, whether one links this step with an achievement of the ego or with the experience of a prohibition. I remind the reader that the full formulation of the position outside is that of "taking up the position of the ego outside of the drive phantasma".

In my opinion there is only one valid solution to the conflict of the drives, and this is the insight that the threat of castration in reality protects the ego from its annihilation, and, to spin this thought further yet, that the ego itself, in the threat of castration, formulates the principle of its own security and safety insofar as the threat of castration results from the position outside which, as we know, is taken up by the ego itself, and is an achievement of the early ego.

Transitional object, transitional phenomena and transitional space

The gain of access to reality through the position of the ego outside the drive phantasma (*see there*) is the point in development where Winnicott's concepts of the transitional object and transitional space (1953, 1971) come into play. In my view it is the transitional space which enables the child, after access to reality has generally been established, to gradually extend its relationship with the primary object to encompass the whole world of real objects. However, my above argument also implies that, unlike Winnicott, I am not of the opinion that it is the transitional experience which brings about the separation of self and object in the first place. What descriptively looks like this is, as mentioned, the emerging of the child out of the cocoon of the early world of splitting of the object by solving the conflict of the depressive position, which only enables the ego to relate to the world of real objects.

Bibliography

Abraham, K. (1924). A short study of the development of the libido, viewed in the light of mental disorders. In: *Selected Papers. Character-Formation on the Genital Level of Libido-Development.* London: Hogarth Press, 1927.

Bateman, A. W., Fonagy, P. (2006). *Mentalization Based Treatment for Borderline Personality Disorder: A Practical Guide.* Oxford University Press

Bick, E. (1968). The experience of the skin in early object relations. *International Journal of Psychoanalysis,* 49: p. 484–486.

Bick, E. (1986). Further findings on the function of the skin in early object relations: findings from infant observation integrated in child and adult analyses. *British Journal of Psychotherapy: 2:* p. 4.

Bion, W. R. (1959). Attacks on Linking. *International Journal of Psychoanalysis,* 40: p. 308–315.

Bion, W. R. (1962). *Learning from Experience.* London: Heinemann.

Bion, W. R. (1970). *Attention and Interpretation.* London: Heinemann.

Bollas, C. (2000). *Hysteria.* London and New York: Routledge.

Britton, R. (1995). Reality and unreality in phantasy and fiction. In: Person, E.S., Fonagy, P., and Figueira, S. A. (Eds.). On Freud's *'Creative Writers and Day-Dreaming'* (pp. 82–107). New Haven, CT: Yale University Press.

Britton, R. (1999). Getting in on the act: the hysterical solution. *International Journal of Psychoanalysis,* 80: p. 1–14.

Chasseguet-Smirgel, J., (1975). *L'Idéal du Moi. Essai psychanalytique sur la 'maladie d'Idéalité.* Paris: Tchou.

Chasseguet-Smirgel, J. (2003). The question of the father. In: *The Body as Mirror of the World* (2005, 26–41), Free Association Books: London

Damasio, A. (2004). *The Neurobiology of Feeling: Lecture.* Keynote address, IPA Congress New Orleans.

Fairbairn, W. R. D. (1954). Observations on the nature of hysterical states. *British Journal of Medical Psychology, 27*: p. 105–125.

Fairbairn, W. R. D. (1963). Synopsis of an object relations theory of the personality. *International Journal of Psychoanalysis, 44*: pp. 224.

Feldman, M. M. (1989). The Oedipus Complex: Manifestations in the Inner World and the Therapeutic Situation. In: Britton, R., Feldman, M., O'Shaugnessy, E., Segal, H.,Steiner, J. *The Oedipus Complex Today Clinical Implications,* p. 103–128, London: Karnac (1989).

Fonagy, P. (2008). A genuinely developmental theory of sexual enjoyment and its implications for psychoanalytic technique. *Journal of the American Psychoanalytic Association, 56 (1)*: 11–36.

Fonagy, P. (2009). 'Where Id was there shall Ego be'. The Importance of Consciousness in Psychoanalytic Work. *Unpublished conference paper presented at the Robert-Bosch-Hospital, Stuttgart/Germany, on 31.01.2009.*

Fonagy, P., Gergely, G., Target, M., and Jurist, E. (2001). *Affect Regulation and Mentalization.* London: Other Press.

Fonagy, P., Target, M. (1996). Playing with reality: I. Theory of mind and the normal development of psychic reality. *International Journal of Psychoanalysis, 77*: p. 217–233.

Fonagy, P., Target, M. (2000). Playing with reality: III. The persistence of dual psychic reality in borderline patients. *International Journal of Psychoanalysis, 81 (4): 853-873.*

Freud, A. (1952). Mutual Influences in the Development of Ego and Id. *International Journal of Psychoanalysis, 33*: p. 509.

Freud, S. (1905). Three Essays on the Theory of Sexuality. S. E., 7: 125–243. London: Hogarth.

Freud, S. (1909). Some General Remarks on Hysterical Attacks. S. E., 9: 227–234. London: Hogarth.

335

Freud, S. (1914). On Narcissism. S. E., 14: 73-102. London: Hogarth.

Freud, S. (1915). Instincts and their Vicissitudes. S. E., 14: 109-140. London: Hogarth.

Freud, S. (1917). Mourning and Melancholia. S. E., 14: 243–258. London: Hogarth.

Freud, S. (1920). Beyond the Pleasure Principle. S. E., 18: 7–64. London: Hogarth.

Freud, S. (1923b). The Ego and the Id. S. E., 19: 12–68. London: Hogarth.

Freud, S. (1923e). The Infantile Genital Organization (An Interpolation into the Theory of Sexuality). S. E., 19: 141–148. London: Hogarth.

Freud, S. (1924). The Economic Problem of Masochism. S. E., 19: 159–172. London: Hogarth.

Freud, S. (1925). Some Psychical Consequences of the Anatomical Distinction between the Sexes. S. E., 19: 248–260. London: Hogarth.

Freud, S. (1927). Fetishism. S.E., 21: p. 152–158. London: Hogarth.

Freud, S. (1931). Female Sexuality. S.E., 21: p. 225–246. London: Hogarth.

Freud, S. (1932). New Introductory Lectures on Psycho-Analysis and Other Works. S. E., 22: 7–184. London: Hogarth Press and the Institute of Psycho-analysis.

Freud, S. (1938). An Outline of Psycho-Analysis. S. E., 23: 144-208. London: Hogarth.

Frith, U., Baron-Cohen, S. Leslie, A. M. (1985). Does the autistic child have a "theory of mind"? *Cognition, 21(1)*: p. 37–46.

Görg, M. (1997). *Die Beziehungen zwischen dem alten Israel und Ägypten.* Darmstadt: Wissenschaftliche Buchgesellschaft.

Green, A. (1997). Chiasmus. Prospektiv: Die Grenzfälle aus der Sicht der Hysterie; retrospektiv: Die Hysterie aus der Sicht der Grenzfälle. *Psyche 54 (2000), 1191–1221.*

Green, A. (1999). *The Work of the Negative.* London/New York: Free Association Books.

Green, A. (2000). The central phobic position: a new formulation of the free association method. *International Journal of Psychoanalysis 81(3)*: p. 429-451

Grunberger, B. (1983). Narcissus and Anubis. *Psychoanalytic Quarterly, 58*: p. 321.

Grunberger, B. (1988). *Narziß und Anubis. Der Narzißmus jenseits der Triebtheorie.* Verlag Internationale Psychoanalyse. München/Wien.

Herpertz, S. C. (2001). Evidence of abnormal amygdala functioning in borderline personality disorder: a functional MRI study. In: Dietrich, T. M., Wenning, B., Erberich, S.G., Krings T., Thron, A., Sass, H. *Biological Psychiatry 50(4)*: p. 292-298.

Herpertz, S. C. (2006). Darstellung des Projekts "Emotion und Kognition bei Persönlichkeitsstörungen", Homepage Klinik und Poliklinik für Psychiatrie und Psychotherapie, Zentrum für Nervenheilkunde der Universität Rostock (revised 4.1.2006).

Hinshelwood, R. D. (1989). *A Dictionary of Kleinian Thought.* London: Free Association Books (2nd edition), 1991.

Hobson, P. (1986). The autistic child's appraisal of expressions of emotions. *Journal of Child Psychology and Psychiatry, 27*: p. 321-342.

Holt, R. R. (1976). Drive or wish? A reconsideration of the psychoanalytic theory of motivation. In: Gill, M. M., Holzman, P. S. (Eds.) *Psychology versus Metapsychology.*

Psychological Issues Monograph 36: p. 158-197. New York: International Universities Press.

Israël, L. (1976). L'Hysterique, le sexe et le médecin. Paris: Masson.

Jeremias, J. (1965). *Abba. Untersuchungen zur neutestamentlichen Theologie und Zeitgeschichte.* Göttingen: Vandenhoeck und Ruprecht.

Joseph, B. (1987). Projective Identification. In: *Psychic Equilibrium and Psychic Change: Selected Papers of Betty Joseph.* New Library of Psychoanalysis. London and New York: Tavistock and Routledge.

Jung, C.G. (1952). *Antwort auf Hiob.* Zürich: Rascher.

Kanner, L. (1944). Early Infantile Autism. *Journal of Paediatrics, 25.*

Kernberg, O.F. (1990a). Hatred as Pleasure. In: Glick R., Bone S. (eds.) *Pleasure beyond the Pleasure Principle: Developmental and Psychoanalytic Concepts of Affect.* New Haven: Yale University Press, p. 117-188

Kernberg, O.F. (1990b). Sexual excitement and rage: Building blocks of the drives. *Sigmund-Freud-House Bulletin 15: 3-34.*

Kernberg O.F. (1991). Sadomasochism, sexual excitement, and perversion. *J. Am. Psychoanal. Ass. 39: 333-362.*

Kernberg, O. F. (1992). *Aggression in Personality Disorders and Perversions.* New Haven: Yale University Press.

Khan, M. M. R. (1975). Grudge and the hysteric. *International Journal of Psychoanalytic Psychotherapy, Vol 4:* p. 349-357.

Klein, M. (1935). A contribution to the psychogenesis of manic-depressive states. *International Journal of Psychoanalysis, 16:* p. 145-174.

Klein, M. (1940). *Mourning and its relation to manic-depressive states.* The Writings of Melanie Klein, (Vol. 1), 344-69. London: Hogarth, 1975.

Klein, M. (1945). *The Oedipus complex in the light of early anxieties.* The Writings of Melanie Klein (Vol. 1), 370-419. London: Hogarth 1975.

Klein, M. (1946). *Notes on some schizoid mechanisms.* The Writings of Melanie Klein (Vol. 3), 1-24. London: Hogarth, 1975.

Klein, M. (1952). *The Origins of Transference.* The Writings of Melanie Klein (Vol. 3), 48-56. London: Hogarth, 1975.

Klein, M. (1957). *Envy and Gratitude.* The Writings of Melanie Klein (Vol. 3), 176-235. London: Hogarth, 1975.

Klein, M. (1959). *Our Adult World and its Roots in Infancy.* The Writings of Melanie Klein (Vol. 3), 247-263. London: Hogarth, 1975.

Kohon, G. (1999). *No Lost Certainties to be Recovered.* London: Karnac.

Lacan, J. (1975). *Encore. Das Seminar . Buch XX (1972-1973).* Weinheim: Quadriga (1986).

338

Lacan, J. (1991). Le Séminaire Livre XVIII: *L'Envers de la Psychanalyse*. Seuil: Paris.

Lacan, J. (2003). Critical Evaluations in Cultural Theory, Volume 2, Zizek, S. (ed.). London and New York: Routledge.

Lakatos, I. (1970) Falsification and the Methodology of Scientific Research Programs. In: Lakatos, I. and Musgrave, A. (Eds.), *Criticism and the Growth of Knowledge*. Cambridge University Press.

Loch, W. (1985). Anmerkungen zu Pathogenese und Psychodynamik der Hysterie. In: *Jahrbuch der Psychoanalyse 17*: 135-174. Stuttgart: Frommann-Holzboog

Loewald, H. W. (1980). *Papers on Psychoanalysis*. New Haven: Yale University Press.

Marchel, W. (1966). *Dieu-Père dans le Nouveau Testament*. Paris: PUF.

McDougall, J. (1972). Primal scene and sexual perversion. *International Journal of Psychoanalysis 53*: p. 371-384.

McDougall, J. (1978). *Plaidoyer pour une certaine anormalité*. Paris: Gallimard.

Mendel, G. (1968). *La Révolte contre le Père*. Paris: Payot.

Money-Kyrle, R. (1971). The aim of Psychoanalysis. *International Journal of Psychoanalysis 52*: p. 103-106; Reprint: *The Collected Papers of Roger Money-Kyrle*. Pertshire: Clunie Pree (1978), p. 442-449.

Nissen, B. (2010). Plädoyer für eine wissenschaftliche Psychoanalyse. Eine wissenschaftstheoretische Bestimmung. *Psyche 64,7*: S. 602-623.

Rohde-Dachser, C. (2004). Sexualität als inneres Theater. Zur Psychodynamik der Hysterie. *Psyche, 62 (4)*: S. 331-355.

Rosenfeld, H. (1964). On the psychopathology of narcissism: a clinical approach. *International Journal of Psychoanalysis 45*: p. 332-337.

Rosenfeld, H. (1965). *Psychotic States*. London: Hogarth Press.

Rosenfeld, H. (1971). A clinical approach to the psycho-analytical theory of the life and death instincts: an investigation of the aggressive aspects of narcissism. *International Journal of Psychoanalysis 52*: p. 169-178.

Rosenfeld, H. (1983). Primitive object relations. *International Journal of Psychoanalysis, 64*: p. 261–267.

Sandler, J. (1983). Reflections on some relations between psychoanalytic concepts and psychoanalytic practice. *International Journal of Psychoanalysis, 64*: p. 35.

Schmidt, W. H. (1983). *Exodus, Sinai und Mose.* Darmstadt: Wissenschaftliche Buchgesellschaft.

Segal, H. (1957). Notes on symbol formation. *International Journal of Psychoanalysis, 38*: p. 391–397. Republished (1981) in: *The Work of Hanna Segal.* New York: Jason Aronson, pp. 49–65.

Segal, H. (1978). On symbolism. *International Journal of Psychoanalysis, 59*: p. 315–319.

Segal, H. (1995). *Psychoanalysis, Literature and War. Papers 1972–1995,* ed. Steiner, J., London and New York: Routledge.

Segal, H. (2007). *Yesterday, Today and Tomorrow.* London and New York: Routledge.

Sohn, L. (1985). Narcissistic organisation, projective identification and the formation of the identificate. *International Journal of Psychoanalysis, 66*: p. 201–214; reprinted in E. Bott-Spillius: Melanie Klein Today, vol I. London: Routledge 1988.

Steiner, J. (1993). *Psychic Retreats. Pathological Organizations in Psychotic, Neurotic and Borderline Patients.* London and New York: Routledge.

Stern, D. (1985). *The Interpersonal World of the Infant.* New York: Basic Books.

Strenger, C. (1991). *Between Hermeneutics and Science. An Essay on the Epistemology of Psychoanalysis.* Madison: International University Press.

Target, M., Fonagy, P. (1996). Playing with reality: II. The development of psychic reality from a theoretical perspective. *International Journal of Psychoanalysis, 77*: p. 459–479.

Tustin, F. (1972). *Autism and Childhood Psychosis.* London: Hogarth, New York: Jason Aronson.

Tustin, F. (1980). Autistic objects. *International Review of Psychoanalysis*, 7: p. 27–38.

Tustin, F. (1981). *Autistic States in Children*. London and New York: Routledge.

Tustin, F. (1984). Autistic shapes. *International Review of Psychoanalysis*, 11: p. 279–290.

Tustin, F. (1986). *Autistic Barriers in Neurotic Patients*. London: Karnac.

Tustin, F. (1991). Revised understandings of psychogenic autism. *International Journal of Psychoanalysis*, 72: p. 585–591.

Tustin, F. (1994). The perpetuation of an error. *Journal of Child Psychotherapy*, 20 (1):p. 3–23.

Werthmann, H. V. (2006). Psychoanalytische Anmerkungen zum Rotenburger Kannibalismus-Fall. *Psyche* 8: p. 763–775.

Widlöcher, D. (2002). Working at the frontiers: so-called Lacanian practices. *IPA Newsletter 11,2*.

Winnicott, D. W. (1953). Transitional objects and transitional phenomena: a study of the first not-me possession. *International Journal of Psychoanalysis*, 34: p. 89–97.

Winnicott, D. W. (1971). *Playing and Reality*. London: Tavistock.

Wittgenstein, L. (1922). *Tractatus logico-philosophicus*. London: Kegan Paul. New York: Harcourt.

Zagermann, P. (1988). *Eros und Thanatos. Psychoanalytische Untersuchungen zu einer Objektbeziehungstheorie der Triebe*. Mit einem einführenden Aufsatz von Janine Chasseguet-Smirgel. Darmstadt: Wissenschaftliche Buchgesellschaft.

www.ingramcontent.com/pod-product-compliance
Lightning Source LLC
Chambersburg PA
CBHW051711020426
42333CB00014B/933

9 781949 093353